THE POWER TO KNOW.

M000250038

Point-and-Click
Access to the
Power of SAS

The Little SAS® Enterprise Guide® Book

Susan J. Slaughter and *Lora D. Delwiche*

The correct bibliographic citation for this manual is as follows: Slaughter, Susan J. and Lora D. Delwiche. 2017. *The Little SAS® Enterprise Guide® Book*. Cary, NC: SAS Institute Inc.

The Little SAS® Enterprise Guide® Book

Contents

Reference Section 135

About SAS Enterprise Guide

For over four decades, SAS software has been used by programmers, analysts, and scientists to manipulate and analyze data. Today, SAS (pronounced sass) is used around the world in 148 countries and at more than 80,000 sites. SAS users stay with SAS year after year because they know its broad flexibility and depth of functionality will enable them to get the work done.

What SAS Enterprise Guide is SAS Enterprise Guide gives you access to the power of SAS via a point-and-click interface. SAS Enterprise Guide does not itself analyze data. Instead, SAS Enterprise Guide generates SAS programs. Every time you run a task in SAS Enterprise Guide, it writes a SAS program. The List Data task, for example, writes a SAS program for the PRINT procedure. The Summary Tables task writes a SAS program for the TABULATE procedure. There are over 90 such tasks offered within SAS Enterprise Guide. When you click **Run** in SAS Enterprise Guide, it submits the program to SAS. SAS runs the program, and then sends the results (such as reports, graphs, data tables, and SAS logs) back to SAS Enterprise Guide so that you can see them.

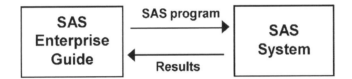

You don't have to be a programmer to use SAS Enterprise Guide, but, if you would like to see the SAS program that SAS Enterprise Guide writes for you, you can do that too. You can also edit the programs written by SAS Enterprise Guide, or open an empty Program window and write a SAS program from scratch using a syntax-sensitive editor similar to the one in Base SAS. Then you can run your SAS program, and view the SAS log and output. So, SAS Enterprise Guide meets the needs of programmers and non-programmers alike.

What software you need To run SAS Enterprise Guide, you need, of course, SAS Enterprise Guide software. SAS Enterprise Guide runs in only the Windows operating environment. Because SAS Enterprise Guide writes programs and submits them to SAS, you also need a machine on which Base SAS is installed. That machine is called a SAS server, and it may be the same machine where SAS Enterprise Guide is installed (in which case, it is called a local server) or it may be a separate machine (called a remote server). SAS runs in many operating environments and on many types of computers. Any computer running SAS can be a SAS server as long as you have access to that machine.

You may have more than one SAS server. For example, you might have SAS installed on both your desktop computer and on a mainframe computer. In that case, you can use SAS Enterprise Guide to run analyses on either computer.

SAS has many different products. To run SAS Enterprise Guide, you need only a few. You must have Base SAS software installed on your SAS server. If you have a remote SAS server, you may need a product called SAS Integration Technologies. If you want to run statistical analyses, then you must also have SAS/STAT software. For running econometric time series analyses, you need SAS/ETS software. For the graphics tasks in SAS Enterprise Guide, you need SAS/GRAPH software. You may or may not need SAS/ACCESS software, depending on your data access needs. (See section 2.1 for more information about using SAS/ACCESS software with SAS Enterprise Guide.)

Getting Help   We have tried to design this book to answer any questions you are likely to have. In addition, SAS Enterprise Guide has extensive built-in help (accessible via the Help menu), and documentation for SAS Enterprise Guide can be found at the SAS Technical Support Web site, **support.sas.com**. This site also provides access to the SAS Support Community for SAS Enterprise Guide—an online forum for users. If you still have questions, you may want to contact SAS Technical Support. With some software companies, very little technical support is available, or the support is available but only for an extra charge—not so with SAS. All licensed SAS sites have access to SAS Technical Support.

There are several ways to contact SAS Technical Support, including via their Web site, **support.sas.com**, or via phone at (919) 677-8008. Before you contact SAS Technical Support you must know your site number and the version of SAS Enterprise Guide that you are running. To find these, start SAS Enterprise Guide and select **Help ▶ About SAS Enterprise Guide**. The About SAS Enterprise Guide window will open, displaying both the version of software and your site number.

About This Book

This book is divided into two distinct but complementary sections: a tutorials section and a reference section. Each tutorial is designed to give you a quick introduction to a general subject. The reference section, on the other hand, gives you focused information on specific topics.

Tutorials section   If you are new to SAS Enterprise Guide, you'll probably want to start with the tutorials. Each of the four tutorials leads you step-by-step through a complete project, from starting SAS Enterprise Guide to documenting what you've done before you exit. The tutorials are self-contained so you can do them in any order. People who know nothing about SAS or SAS Enterprise Guide should be able to complete a tutorial in 30 to 45 minutes.

Reference section   Once you feel comfortable with SAS Enterprise Guide, you'll be ready to use the reference section. This is where you'll turn when you need a quick refresher on how to join data tables, or a detailed explanation of filtering data in a query. With 8 chapters and 67 topics, the reference section covers more information than the tutorials, but each topic is covered in just two pages so you can read it in a few minutes.

The data for this book   The data used for the examples in this book revolve around a theme: the Fire and Ice Tours company, a fictional company offering tours to volcanoes around the world. Using a small number of data sets over and over saves you from having to learn new data for every example. The data sets are small enough that you can type them in if you want to run the examples, but to make it even easier, the data are also available for downloading via the Internet. Appendix A contains both the data and instructions on how to download the data files.

Acknowledgments

How do you describe something that is dynamic and graphical with mere printed words and static screen shots? That's the fundamental challenge we have faced in writing this book. We have struggled at every point: finding the best and most useful features, discovering all those little points of confusion that are likely to trip up users of the software, and wrestling with sentences in an effort to express ideas clearly within the confines of a two-page format. Now that we are nearing the completion of this project, we offer this quote to describe our feelings:

"Zounds! I was never so bethump'd with words."

William Shakespeare, King John

Fortunately, we've had plenty of help with those words. Among the many people we'd like to thank are our technical reviewers: Marie Dexter, Rich Papel, Casey Smith, and Jennifer Tamburro; our technical publishing specialist: Denise T. Jones; our designer, Robert Harris; our marketing specialist: Cindy Puryear; our copy editor: John West; and Julie Platt , Editor-in-Chief. All these people worked hard to ensure that this book is accurate and appealing. Special thanks go to Stacey Hamilton, our developmental editor.

And, as always, we thank our families for everything.

TUTORIALS SECTION

A

"**D**imidium facti qui coepit habet."

"What's well begun is half done."

HORACE

From *Epistolae*, I. 2. 40, 20 BC. As quoted in *The Cyclopedia of Practical Quotations: English, Latin, and Modern Foreign Languages* by Jehiel Keeler Hoyt, 1896.

Getting Started with SAS Enterprise Guide

This first tutorial will give you a basic understanding of how SAS Enterprise Guide works and how quickly tasks can be accomplished. The following topics will be covered:

- Starting SAS Enterprise Guide

- A quick tour of SAS Enterprise Guide windows

- Data types

- Entering data into the Data Grid

- Using SAS Enterprise Guide tasks

- Making changes to tasks

The data for this tutorial come from Fire and Ice Tours, a fictional company that arranges tours of volcanoes around the world. For each tour, the company keeps track of the name of the volcano, the city from which the tour departs, the number of days of the tour, and the price. Because the tours can require some physical exertion, the company gives each tour a difficulty rating: easy, moderate, or challenging.

Starting SAS Enterprise Guide

Start SAS Enterprise Guide by either double-clicking the **SAS Enterprise Guide** icon on your desktop, or selecting **SAS Enterprise Guide** from the Windows **Start** menu. Starting SAS Enterprise Guide brings up the SAS Enterprise Guide window in the background, with the Welcome window in the foreground. The Welcome window allows you to choose between opening an existing project or starting a new project. Click **New Project**.

Desktop

✓ Double-click SAS Enterprise Guide icon

SAS Enterprise Guide Projects

SAS Enterprise Guide organizes all your work into projects. You can work on only one project at a time, and each project is stored in a single file. A project will contain all the reports that you produce, plus shortcuts to all the data files that you use.

Welcome Window

✓ Click New Project

Welcome to SAS Enterprise Guide   ✕

Select one of these options to get started:

Open a project
📂 More projects ...

New
🗊 New Project
🗋 New SAS Program
🗊 New Data

Assistance
📕 Tutorial: Getting Started with SAS Enterprise Guide

☐ Don't show this window again

SAS Enterprise Guide window When you first start SAS Enterprise Guide, your screen should look something like the following. There are several parts to the SAS Enterprise Guide window: some are visible, while others may be hidden or temporarily closed.

Resetting SAS Enterprise Guide Options

There are many options in SAS Enterprise Guide that affect how it works. For example, you can turn off the Welcome window, or change the default format and appearance of results. If someone has already used SAS Enterprise Guide on your computer, they may have made some changes to the initial settings. To reset all options to their original settings, select **Tools ▶ Options** from the menu bar. Then click **Reset All**.

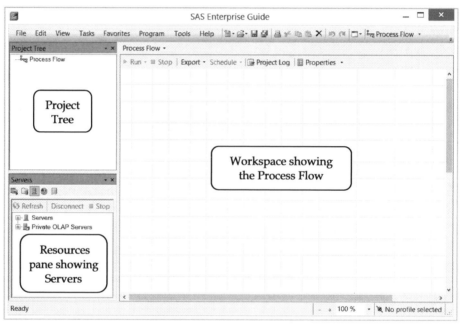

Basic elements of SAS Enterprise Guide

Project Tree: This window displays your project in a hierarchical tree diagram.

Workspace: This is a container for the Process Flow, results from tasks that you run, Data Grids, SAS code, SAS logs, and Notes.

Process Flow: This window displays a graphical representation of your project.

Resources pane: This pane shows either the Servers, Tasks, SAS Folders, Prompt Manager, or Data Exploration History windows. The Servers window displays all the SAS servers that you can access during your SAS Enterprise Guide session. A SAS server is any computer on which SAS software is installed. The Tasks window displays all available tasks. The SAS Folders contain links to your stored processes, information maps, and projects. The Prompt Manager displays all available prompts. The Data Exploration History provides links to any data exploration done in the project. To switch between the windows, click their icons at the top of the pane: 🗍 for Servers, 🗍 for Tasks, 🗍 for SAS Folders, 🗍 for the Prompt Manager, or 🗍 for Data Exploration History.

Task Status (not shown): When you are running a task, messages about the progress of the task appear in the Task Status window. To open the Task Status window, select **View ▶ Task Status** from the menu bar.

Entering data There are many ways to get data into SAS Enterprise Guide, and SAS Enterprise Guide can use data from a variety of sources including SAS data sets, Microsoft Excel files, and plain text files. For this example, you are simply going to type the data directly into SAS Enterprise Guide. To bring up the Data Grid so you can enter the data, select **File ▶ New ▶ Data** from the menu bar.

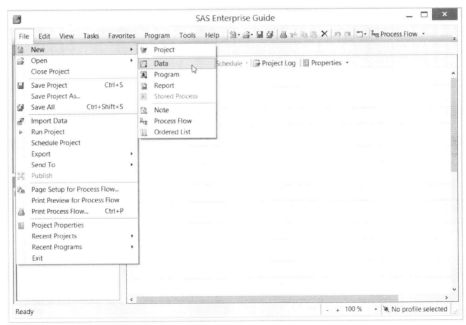

This opens the New Data wizard. In the first window of the wizard, SAS Enterprise Guide asks what you want to name the data table and where you want to save the data. The name for the data table is initially set to Data.

SAS Data Sets or SAS Data Tables?

A SAS data set and a SAS data table are the same thing. The two terms are used interchangeably, and you will see both terms used in this book.

Data Table Member Names

You can give your data tables almost any names you want, but the names must be 32 characters or fewer in length and not start with a period or a space. While it is possible to have special characters (including spaces) in your names, you may want to stick with just letters, numerals, and underscores. These characters are all that are allowed under the default naming rules for SAS programs. In addition, names must start with a letter or underscore. Using these rules will make it easier if you ever want to refer to your data in SAS programs that you or someone else writes.

Give the new data table the name Tours by typing **Tours** in the **Name** box. To see all the SAS libraries (storage locations) available to you, click the plus signs next to the words Local and then Libraries. For this example, save the data in the SASUSER library. Click **SASUSER** to select the SASUSER library. The SAS Enterprise Guide administrator at your site may have set up the SASUSER library so that you cannot save files there. If this is the case for you, choose an alternate library that is available to you (but do not choose WORK since that is a temporary storage location).

New Data
Wizard

✓ In Name box
   type **Tours**
✓ Click + next
   to Local
✓ Click + next
   to Libraries
✓ Click
   SASUSER
✓ Click Next

Click **Next** to open the second window of the New Data wizard.

Libraries

SAS Enterprise Guide and SAS organize SAS data tables into libraries. Libraries are locations, or folders, where data tables are stored. Instead of referring to the folders by their full path, SAS Enterprise Guide gives the folders short nicknames, called librefs. The WORK library points to a temporary storage location that is automatically erased when you exit SAS Enterprise Guide. The SASUSER library is a permanent storage location. If the EGTASK library is defined for your site, then data tables produced by tasks will be stored in the EGTASK library. If the EGTASK library is not defined, then data tables produced by tasks will be stored in the SASUSER library. Libraries can be created using the Assign Project Library wizard available from the Tools menu.

The second window of the New Data wizard is where you assign names and properties to the columns in your data table. As a starting point, the New Data wizard sets up six columns with one-letter names from A to F. All these initial columns have the same properties.

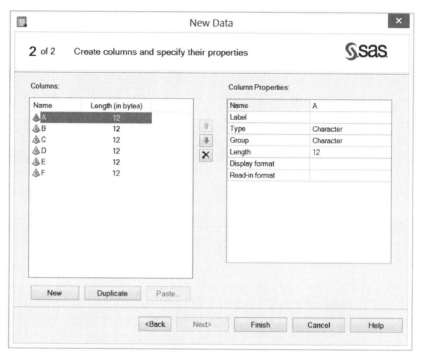

Column Names

You can give your columns almost any names you want, but the names must be 32 characters or fewer in length. While it is possible to have special characters (including spaces) in your names, you may want to stick with just letters, numerals, and underscores. These characters are all that are allowed under the default naming rules for SAS programs. In addition, names must start with a letter or underscore. Using these rules will make it easier if you ever want to refer to your data in SAS programs that you or someone else writes.

In the Column Properties box, you can assign each column a name, label, type, group, length, display format, and read-in format. The first column will contain the names of the volcanoes, so type **Volcano** in the box next to **Name**.

New Data
Wizard

✓ In Name
box, type
Volcano

✓ Press Enter

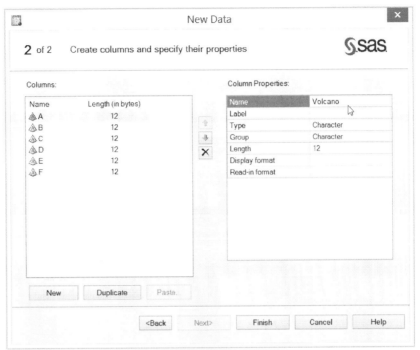

When you press **Enter**, the name you typed in the Name box will replace the name, in this case A, in the Columns box on the left. Because the names of the volcanoes contain characters, as opposed to numbers, leave the **Type** and **Group** properties as **Character**, and because none of the volcano names are longer than 12 characters, leave the **Length** set to **12**.

> ### Lengths of Character Columns
>
> The New Data wizard in SAS Enterprise Guide gives character columns a length of 12. If your character data are longer than 12 characters, you need to change the length of the column to be at least as long as the longest data value. If all your data values are shorter than 12 characters, you can shorten the length for the column. Using shorter lengths for character data decreases the storage space needed for the data table.

Now click the column named **B** in the **Columns** box on the left. This column will contain the name of the departure city for the tour, so type the word **Departs** next to **Name** in the **Column Properties** box on the right. Leave the other settings as they are.

New Data
Wizard

✓ Click Column
  B

✓ In Name box,
  type
  Departs

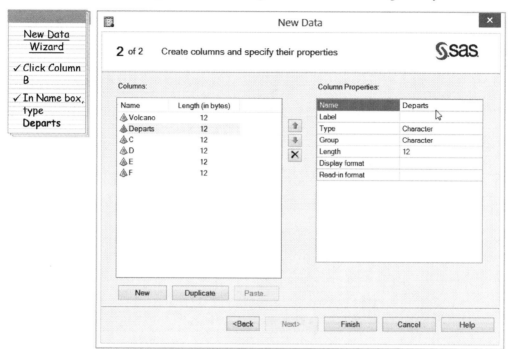

The third column contains the number of days the tour lasts. Give it the name **Days**, and because the values in this column are numbers, use the pull-down list to select **Numeric** for the **Type** property.

New Data
Wizard

✓ Click Column C

✓ In Name box, type **Days**

✓ From Type list, select Numeric

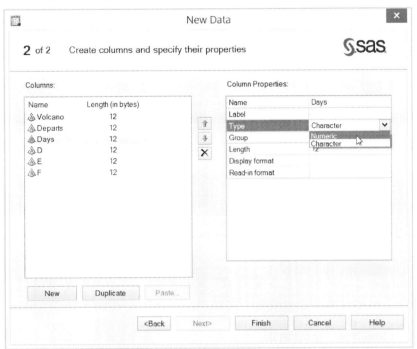

Notice that when you set the column type to numeric, the icon next to the column name changes from the red pyramid ⚠ (character) to the blue ball ⓛ (numeric). The length of **8** is the default for all numeric columns and means that the numbers will be stored with maximum precision. Generally, there is no need to change the length of numeric columns.

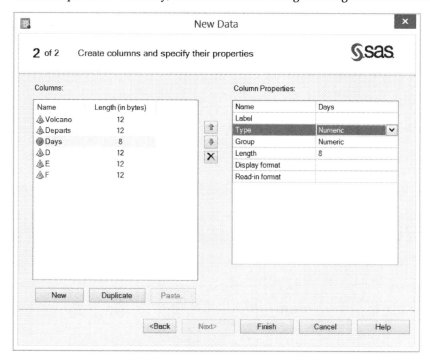

Character versus Numeric

How do you decide if a column should be character or numeric? If the values for the column have letters or special characters in them, then the column must be character. If the column contains only numerals, then it could be either character or numeric. Generally, if it does not make sense to add or subtract the values, then the column should be character.

Name the fourth column **Price** and give it the type **Numeric**. When you choose the numeric type, you have several options for **Group**: numeric, date, time, and currency. Because Price will contain currency values, select the group **Currency**.

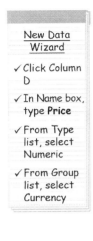

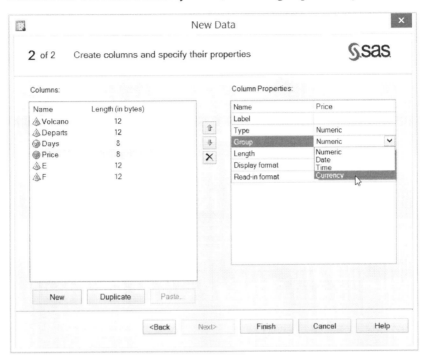

Numeric Groups

By choosing a group for your numeric column, what you are doing is assigning a format to your column. A format is a way of displaying the values in the column. If you choose currency, then when you type a number like 1200, SAS Enterprise Guide will automatically display the number as $1,200. SAS Enterprise Guide has made it easy for you to assign some of the frequently used formats to your columns.

Notice that when you do this, the icon changes from the blue ball to the currency icon 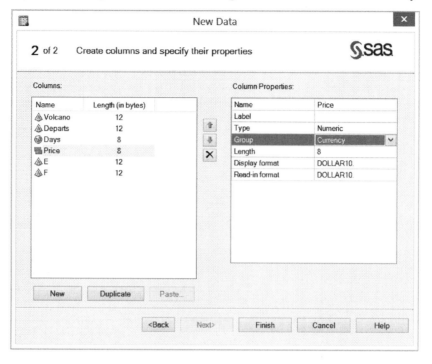 .

The final column will contain the difficulty ratings of each tour. The most challenging tours have values of **c**, the moderately challenging tours have values of **m**, while the easiest tours have values of **e**. Give the column the name **Difficulty** and because the values for the column are single characters, change the length to **1**. You could leave the column as length 12, but then the column would take more storeage space than it really needs.

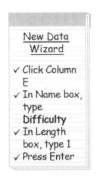

New Data
Wizard

✓ Click Column E
✓ In Name box, type **Difficulty**
✓ In Length box, type **1**
✓ Press Enter

Now the properties for all the columns have been set. However, there is one extra column: column F. Delete the unnecessary column by clicking it in the **Columns** box and then clicking the delete button  to the right of the **Columns** box.

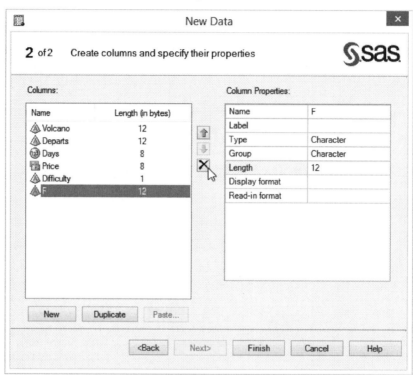

Now all the columns have been given names and properties, and there are no extra columns.

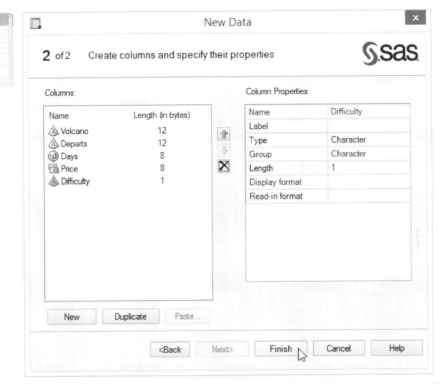

Click **Finish** to create the new data table. The Tours data table appears in a Data Grid in the workspace with all the columns that you just defined. There is also an icon for the Tours data table in the Project Tree under the words Process Flow.

Notice that the numeric columns, Days and Price, have periods in the data cells. This is because in SAS Enterprise Guide missing numeric values are represented by a single period, whereas missing character values are represented by blanks. Because no data have been entered into the Data Grid, all the values are missing.

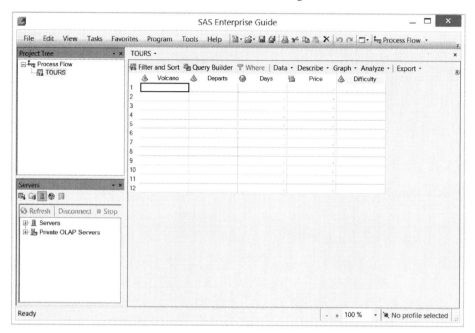

You can now start entering the data into the Data Grid. To enter data into the Data Grid, simply click a cell and start typing the data. Click the first cell in the **Volcano** column and type the volcano name **Etna**.

Tours Data Grid

✓ In Volcano column, click first cell

✓ Type **Etna**

	Volcano	Departs	Days	Price	Difficulty
1	Etna				
2					
3					
4					
5					
6					
7					
8					
9					
10					
11					
12					

TOURS ▾

Filter and Sort   Query Builder   Where   Data ▾   Describe ▾   Graph ▾   Analyze ▾   Expo

To move over to the next column, press the **Tab** key. To move down to the cell below, press the **Enter** key. You can also use the arrow keys to move around in the Data Grid, or you can simply click the cell where you want to type. Enter all the data for the volcano tours so that your Data Grid looks like the following. Notice that when you enter the data for the Price column, you do not need to enter the dollar signs and commas. Simply enter the numerals that make up the number, and then when you move on to another cell, SAS Enterprise Guide will give your number the proper formatting.

Tours Data Grid

✓ Enter data into columns

TOURS ▾

Filter and Sort   Query Builder   Where   Data ▾   Describe ▾   Graph ▾   Analyze ▾   Expo

	Volcano	Departs	Days	Price	Difficulty
1	Etna	Catania	7	$1,610	m
2	Fuji	Tokyo	2	$335	c
3	Kenya	Nairobi	6	$1,245	m
4	Kilauea	Hilo	1	$85	e
5	Kilmanjaro	Nairobi	9	$1,965	c
6	Krakatau	Jakarta	7	$1,345	e
7	Poas	San Jose	1	$97	e
8	Reventador	Quito	4	$875	m
9	St. Helens	Portland	2	$250	e
10	Vesuvius	Rome	6	$1,495	e
11					
12					

If you need to go back and make any changes, just click the cell and type the new data value.

By default, SAS Enterprise Guide provides 12 rows for data entry. If you have more than 12 rows of data, then you can press the **Enter** key from any cell in the last row and SAS Enterprise Guide will automatically generate a new blank row for you. Because there are only 10 tours in this data file, you will need to delete the two extra blank rows. If you don't delete the blank rows, then all the values for those rows will be missing, and these missing values will appear in any report or analysis that you perform. Highlight both blank rows by clicking row 11 and dragging the cursor to row 12. Then right-click one of the rows and select **Delete rows**.

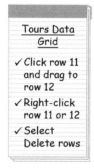

Tours Data Grid

✓ Click row 11 and drag to row 12

✓ Right-click row 11 or 12

✓ Select Delete rows

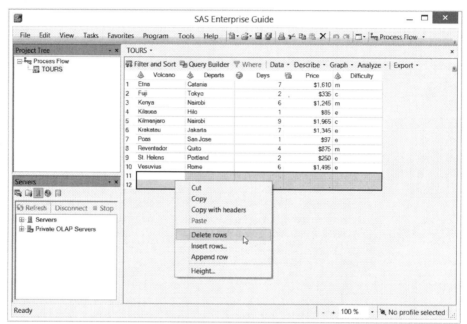

Confirm that you want to delete the rows by clicking **Yes** in the pop-up dialog box.

Delete Rows?

✓ Click Yes

Now the Data Grid is completely filled without any extra rows or columns.

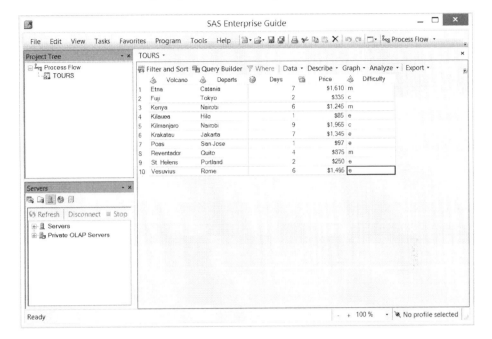

Creating a frequency report To create a simple frequency report that will show the number of easy, moderate, and challenging tours, use the One-Way Frequencies task. Select **Describe ▶ One-Way Frequencies** from the workspace toolbar located just above the data.

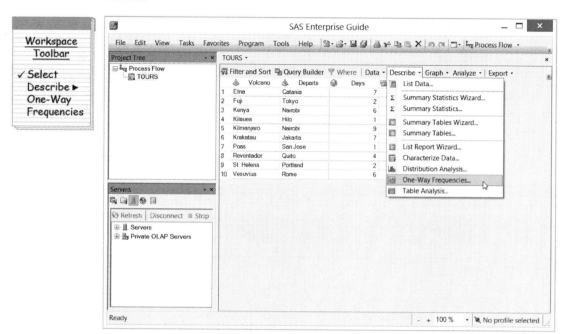

Opening Tasks and Wizards

You can open tasks by selecting them from the workspace toolbar of a Data Grid, the **Tasks** item on the menu bar, or the Task List window. Use whichever method feels more comfortable for you. In the tutorials, we describe how to open tasks using the workspace toolbar.

Some tasks have wizards in addition to the regular task window. A wizard guides you through the task one window at a time and gives access to some of the features of the task. Not all tasks have wizards, but if a task does have a wizard, it will be listed next to the task in the pull-down list.

Because the data have just been entered into the Data Grid, the following dialog box appears.

Data must be protected before you can perform any task on your data. Protecting the data ensures that the data cannot be accidentally changed. If your data are not protected, SAS Enterprise Guide will prompt you. Click **Yes**.

This opens the One-Way Frequencies task window, which has six pages: Data, Statistics, Plots, Results, Titles, and Properties. When you first open the task, the Data page will be displayed. All six pages for the task are listed in the selection pane on the left, with the displayed page highlighted.

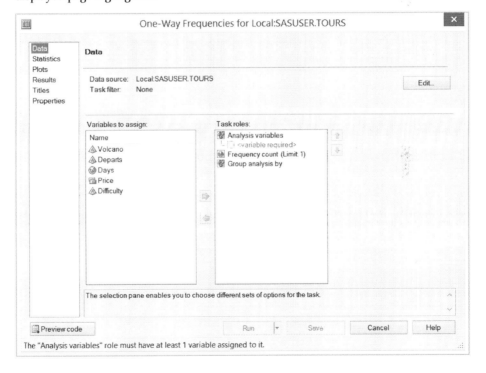

For most tasks that you perform in SAS Enterprise Guide, you will need to assign variables to roles. To produce a report with the number of tours in each category of the variable Difficulty, click the variable **Difficulty** and drag it to the **Analysis variables** role.

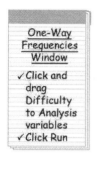

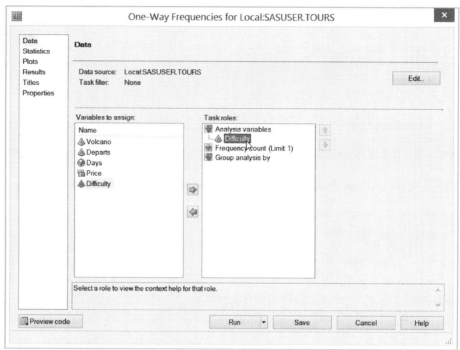

Click **Run** to run the task and produce your report.

Columns or Variables?

A column and a variable are the same thing. The two terms are used interchangeably, and you will see both terms used in SAS Enterprise Guide. For example, the One-Way Frequencies task uses the term "variable," while the Scatter Plot task uses the term "column." Just remember, a variable is a column, and a column is a variable.

The results from the task appear in the workspace on the Results tab. Along with the Results tab, the task has also generated an Input Data tab, a Code tab, and a Log tab. The Input Data tab contains the data used in the task. The Code tab shows the SAS code generated by the task, and the Log tab shows the code along with any messages SAS produced while running the task. The results show that two tours are challenging, five are easy, and three are moderate.

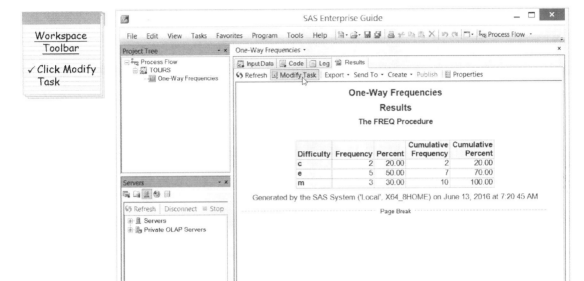

To make changes to the task and modify the results, click **Modify Task** on the workspace toolbar to reopen the task. This reopens the One-Way Frequencies task.

> ### Workspace Toolbar
>
> The workspace toolbar gives you quick access to many features you might want when viewing a particular item in the workspace. For example, the **Modify Task** button appears on the toolbar when you are viewing the results, log, or code for a task.

Notice that when you reopen the task, all the choices you made are still there. For this example, we are going to remove the cumulative statistics from the table, so click **Statistics** in the selection pane on the left to open the Statistics page.

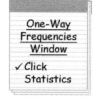

One-Way
Frequencies
Window

✓ Click
Statistics

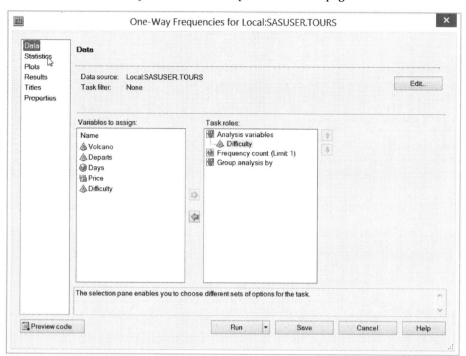

There are many options in the Statistics page. In the area labeled **Frequency table options**, you can choose which frequencies and percentages will appear in the table. By default, frequencies, percentages, cumulative frequencies, and cumulative percentages will appear in the table. To exclude the cumulative statistics, check **Frequencies and percentages**.

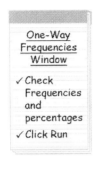

One-Way
Frequencies
Window

✓ Check
Frequencies
and
percentages

✓ Click Run

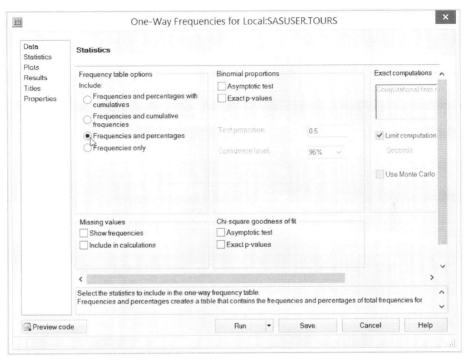

Rerun the task by clicking the **Run** button at the bottom of the window. When you do this, SAS Enterprise Guide gives you a choice. You can either replace the results that you generated the last time you ran the task, or you can create new results.

Replace
results?

✓ Click Yes

In this case, there is no reason to keep the old results, so click **Yes**.

Here are the results that will appear in the workspace showing just the frequencies and percentages without the cumulative statistics.

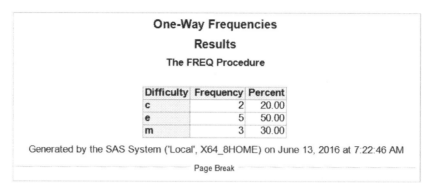

Here are the results:

One-Way Frequencies

Results

The FREQ Procedure

Difficulty	Frequency	Percent
c	2	20.00
e	5	50.00
m	3	30.00

Generated by the SAS System ('Local', X64_8HOME) on June 13, 2016 at 7:22:46 AM

Page Break

Creating a scatter plot   To generate a scatter plot of the data, you will need to use a different task. First reopen the Tours data table to display the data. Right-click the **TOURS** data table icon in the Project Tree and select **Open TOURS**.

Project Tree

✓ Right-click TOURS icon

✓ Select Open TOURS

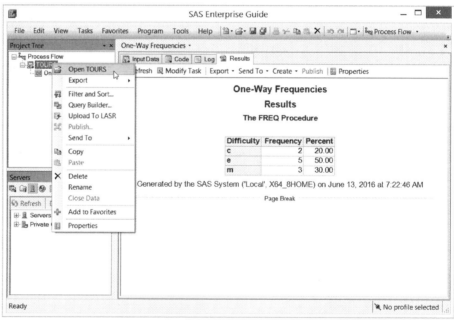

With the Tours data table open in the workspace, the workspace toolbar now shows menu items that apply to data. Select **Graph ▶ Scatter Plot.**

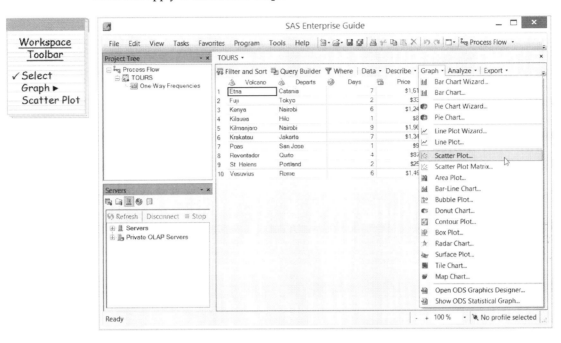

Opening Data Tables in the Workspace

There are several ways to display data tables in the workspace. You can right-click the data table icon in the Project Tree or Process Flow and select Open. You can double-click the data table icon in the Project Tree or Process Flow. Or, if you have run a task using the data, you can click the **Input Data** tab in the workspace to view the input data for the task.

This opens the Scatter Plot window. Before assigning roles to columns, you need to choose the type of scatter plot to produce. A simple two-dimensional scatter plot is appropriate for this report, so click **2D Scatter Plot**.

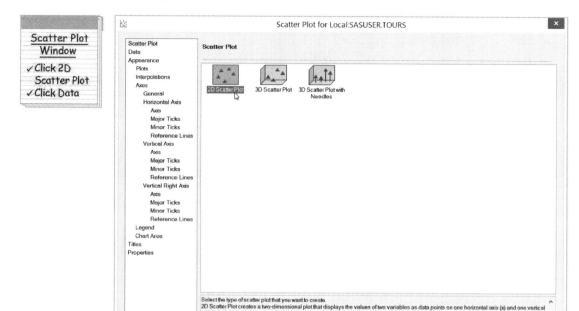

Next, click **Data** in the selection pane on the left to assign columns to roles.

For this plot, the column Days should be on the horizontal axis, and the column Price should be on the vertical axis. So, click **Days** and drag it to the **Horizontal** task role, and click **Price** and drag it to the **Vertical** task role.

Scatter Plot
Window

✓ Click and
   drag Days to
   Horizontal
   role
✓ Click and
   drag Price to
   Vertical
   role
✓ Click Run

The Scatter Plot task has many groups of options, but to produce a simple plot, there is no need to change anything else. Click **Run**.

Here are the results of the Scatter Plot task that appear in the workspace.

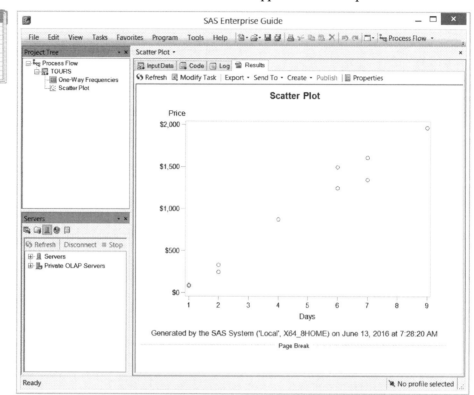

Now click **Process Flow** on the menu bar and take a look at the Process Flow.

Displaying the Process Flow

There are several ways to display the Process Flow in the workspace. You can select it from the Process Flow drop-down list on the menu bar, double-click its name in the Project Tree, select it from the **View** menu, select it from the drop-down list located above the workspace but below the main toolbar, or press **F4**.

Both the Project Tree and the Process Flow show the various parts of your project and how they are related. In the Process Flow, you can see that there are two arrows coming from the Tours data table. There is an arrow for the One-Way Frequencies task and one for the Scatter Plot task. Each task produces a report. The Process Flow makes it easy to see how the different parts of the project are related.

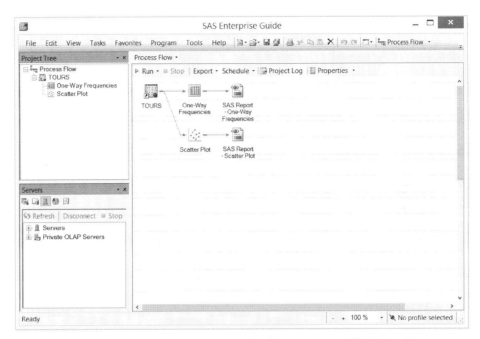

An alternate view of your project can be found in the Project Tree. The Project Tree displays the same elements as the Process Flow, except they are arranged in a hierarchical tree diagram. The Project Tree is always visible, but since the Process Flow is in the workspace, it sometimes gets hidden by other items.

Project Tree

✓ Click
Process Flow

Adding a note to the project A nice feature of SAS Enterprise Guide is that you can add notes to your projects to document them. To add a note to the project, click the words **Process Flow** in the Project Tree so that the note will be associated with the entire process flow instead of a particular item. Then select **File ▶ New ▶ Note** from the menu bar.

Menu Bar

✓ Select
File ▶ New
▶ Note

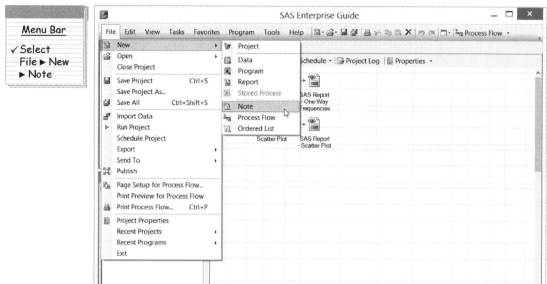

Enter a brief description of the project in the Note text box that appears in the workspace.

Note

✓Type
descriptive
text

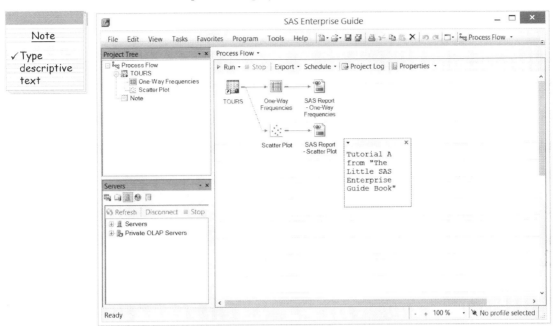

You can collapse the note into an icon by clicking the x in the upper right corner of the text box, or you can enlarge the text box by clicking the down-arrow in the upper left corner and selecting **Open** from the pop-up menu. You can also drag the note to another location in the Process Flow.

Saving the project SAS Enterprise Guide will always ask if you want to save any changes before allowing you to exit. Of course, you can save your work at any time before exiting. All the tasks created in your project, along with the results and any notes, are saved in the project. The data files are saved outside the project file—only the shortcuts to the data files are saved in the project. To save the project, select **File ▶ Save Project As** from the menu bar.

Menu Bar

✓ Select
File ▶ Save
Project As

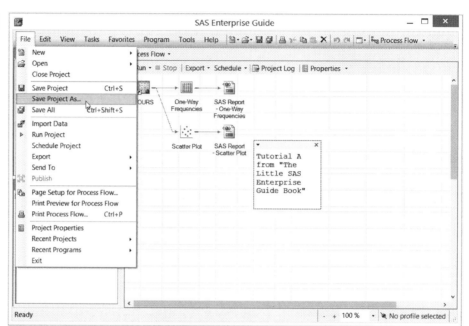

Navigate to the location where you want to save the project. Give the project the filename **TutorialA** and click **Save**.

Now you can exit SAS Enterprise Guide and all your work and data will be saved. From the menu bar, select **File ▶ Exit** to exit SAS Enterprise Guide and complete the first tutorial.

B "The obvious is that which is never seen until someone expresses it simply."

KAHLIL GIBRAN

From *Sand and Foam: A Book of Aphorisms*, 1926.

B ▶ Creating Reports

In this tutorial, you will create a basic report using the List Data task. Then using several of the options in the List Data task, you will make modifications to the report. Also, you will learn ways of formatting data that apply to most tasks. Here are the topics covered in this tutorial:

- Creating list reports

- Titles, footnotes, and labels

- Display formats

- User-defined formats

- Styles

- Result types

Before beginning this tutorial This tutorial uses the Tours data table, which contains information about the volcano tours offered by the Fire and Ice Tours company. The Tours data table is created as part of Tutorial A. If you did not complete Tutorial A, see Appendix A for the data and instructions for downloading the Tours data table.

Starting SAS Enterprise Guide Start SAS Enterprise Guide by either double-clicking the **SAS Enterprise Guide** icon on your desktop, or selecting **SAS Enterprise Guide** from the Windows **Start** menu. Starting SAS Enterprise Guide brings up the SAS Enterprise Guide window in the background, with the Welcome window in the foreground. The Welcome window allows you to choose between opening an existing project or starting a new project. Click **New Project**.

Desktop

✓ Double-click
SAS
Enterprise
Guide icon

Welcome
Window

✓ Click New
Project

Opening the Tours data table Open the Tours data table created in Tutorial A by selecting **File ▶ Open ▶ Data** from the menu bar.

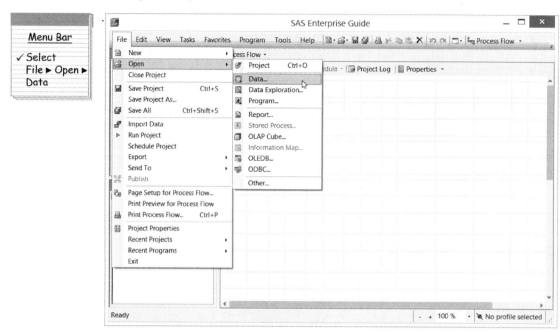

This opens the Open Data window. In the panel on the left, you can choose to open files from several locations. The Tours data table from Tutorial A was stored in the SASUSER library. The easiest way to access SAS libraries in the Open Data window is through the servers view, so click **Servers** in the selection pane on the left. The servers view shows which servers are available to you, including Local.

Open Data
Window

✓ Click
Servers

✓ Click Local

✓ Click Open

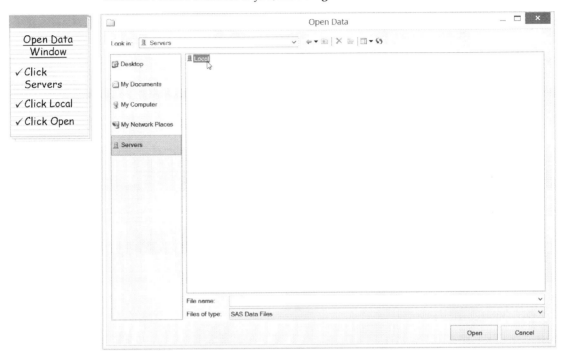

Then click **Local** to select it (if your SASUSER library is not on your local computer, then choose the appropriate server), and click **Open**.

Click **Libraries**, then click **Open** to display all the SAS libraries that are defined for your computer.

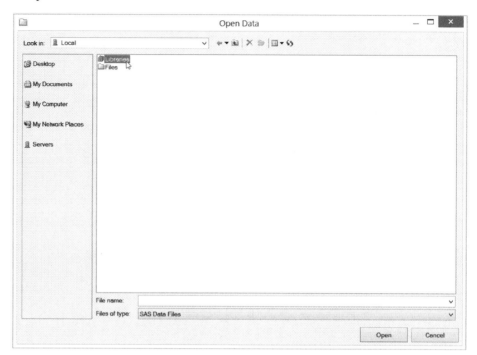

There are six libraries defined in this example: MAPS, MAPSGFK, MAPSSAS, SASHELP, SASUSER, and WORK. You may have additional libraries defined.

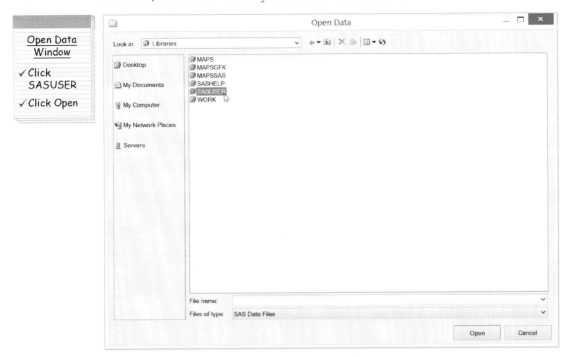

Open Data Window

✓ Click SASUSER

✓ Click Open

Click **SASUSER,** then click **Open** to view the data tables in the SASUSER library.

Select the **Tours** data table and click **Open**. You may have additional data tables in your SASUSER library.

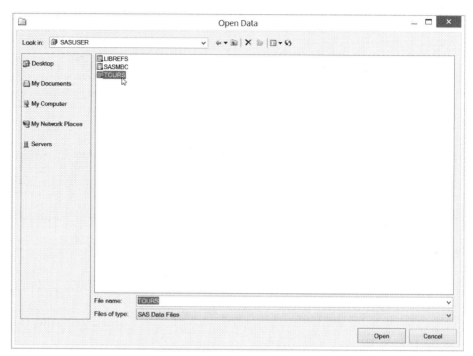

After you open the Tours data table, your screen should look like the following:

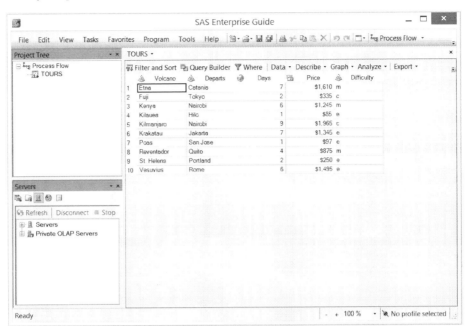

Creating a simple report To produce a price list of all the tours offered by the Fire and Ice Tours company, use the List Data task. Select **Describe ▶ List Data** from the workspace toolbar above the data.

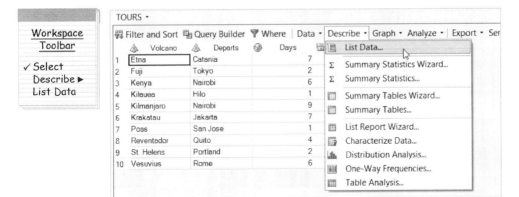

This opens the List Data window. Before doing anything else, you need to assign variables to task roles. For a price list, all the variables in the data table should be listed, so assign all the variables to the **List variables** role. You can drag each variable separately, or you can highlight all the variables, and then drag the group to the List variables role. The order of the variables under List variables will be the order that the variables will appear in the report. To change the order, click and drag the variables up or down the list, or highlight the variable and use the up or down arrow buttons next to the **Task roles** box.

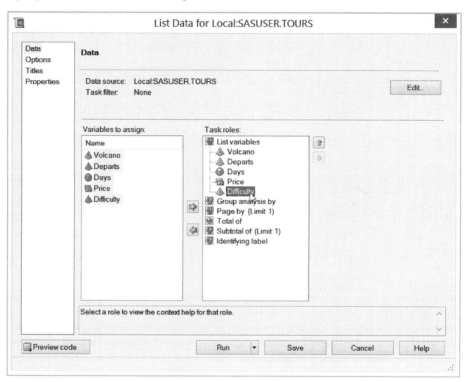

When you have all the variables under List variables in the proper order, click **Run**.

This produces a list of all the data in the Tours data table with some simple formatting. The result appears in the workspace, and, by default, the result will be in SAS Report format.

Report Listing

Row number	Volcano	Departs	Days	Price	Difficulty
1	Etna	Catania	7	$1,610	m
2	Fuji	Tokyo	2	$335	c
3	Kenya	Nairobi	6	$1,245	m
4	Kilauea	Hilo	1	$85	e
5	Kilmanjaro	Nairobi	9	$1,965	c
6	Krakatau	Jakarta	7	$1,345	e
7	Poas	San Jose	1	$97	e
8	Reventador	Quito	4	$875	m
9	St. Helens	Portland	2	$250	e
10	Vesuvius	Rome	6	$1,495	e

Generated by the SAS System ('Local', X64_8HOME) on June 14, 2016 at 5:30:50 AM

Page Break

What is SAS Report Format?

SAS Report is the default format for results generated by SAS Enterprise Guide. Like HTML, SAS Report format can be viewed in a web browser but it prints and copies more seamlessly than HTML. In addition, multiple results in SAS Report format can be combined into a single report using the report builder. To open the report builder, choose **File ▶ New ▶ Report** from the menu bar. Results in SAS Report format can also easily be exported to other formats like HTML and PDF.

Changing titles and footnotes The report contains all the information needed for the price list, but it could use some improvements. There are many parts of this simple listing that can be changed to meet specific needs. The first change to be made is to edit the title and footnote for the report. To change the titles and footnotes, reopen the List Data task by clicking **Modify Task** on the workspace toolbar for the results.

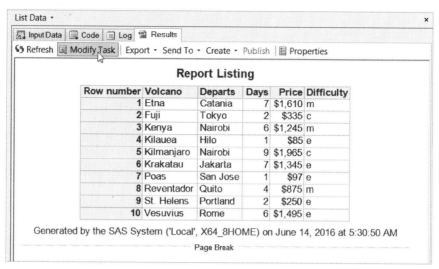

Report Listing

Row number	Volcano	Departs	Days	Price	Difficulty
1	Etna	Catania	7	$1,610	m
2	Fuji	Tokyo	2	$335	c
3	Kenya	Nairobi	6	$1,245	m
4	Kilauea	Hilo	1	$85	e
5	Kilmanjaro	Nairobi	9	$1,965	c
6	Krakatau	Jakarta	7	$1,345	e
7	Poas	San Jose	1	$97	e
8	Reventador	Quito	4	$875	m
9	St. Helens	Portland	2	$250	e
10	Vesuvius	Rome	6	$1,495	e

Generated by the SAS System ('Local', X64_8HOME) on June 14, 2016 at 5:30:50 AM

Page Break

Reopening Tasks

To reopen a task you can either click **Modify Task** on the workspace toolbar for the task result, or you can right-click the task icon in either the Process Flow or the Project Tree and select **Modify *task-name*** from the pop-up window.

Click **Titles** in the selection pane on the left of the List Data window. You can make changes to both the titles and the footnotes in this window. When you click **Report Titles** in the box labeled **Section**, the current title is displayed in the text box on the right side of the window. SAS Enterprise Guide has default text that it will use for your report for both titles and footnotes. To change the title for your report, uncheck the box to the left of **Use default text**. Now you can edit the default text that SAS Enterprise Guide supplied. Delete the default text and replace it with **Fire and Ice Tours** on one line, followed by **Price List** on the second line. This produces a two-line title with both lines centered at the top of the report.

To make changes to the footnote, click **Footnote** in the box labeled **Section**.

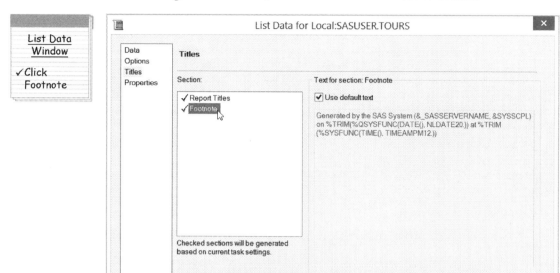

List Data
Window

✓ Click
Footnote

Why Does the Default Footnote Text Look So Odd?

If you take a close look at the default text for the footnote, you will notice that it does not look much like the footnote that appears at the bottom of your reports. The default text contains calls to SAS macros (starting with %) and macro variables (starting with &). These calls generate the actual text for the footnote, and the text that is generated depends on the date and time the report was produced, and the name and type of SAS server that generated the report. You can change the default footnote for all tasks by selecting **Tools ▶ Options** from the menu bar and selecting the **Tasks General** page. Enter the desired text in the **Default footnote text for task output** box. Then all tasks run after this change will have the new footnote text, even if you open a new project.

Change the footnote the same way you changed the title. Uncheck **Use default text**. Then because no footnote is necessary for this report, simply delete the text that SAS Enterprise Guide supplied.

List Data
Window

✓ Uncheck Use
default text

✓ Delete text

✓ Click Run

List Data for Local:SASUSER.TOURS

Data
Options
Titles
Properties

Titles

Section:

✓ Report Titles
✓ Footnote

Checked sections will be generated
based on current task settings.

Text for section: Footnote

☐ Use default text

Displays the text that is associated with the selected section in the Section area. You can edit this text.

Preview code   Run ▾   Save   Cancel   Help

Replace
Results?

✓ Click Yes

Click **Run** to produce a revised report with a new title and no footnote. When SAS Enterprise Guide asks if you want to replace the previous results, click **Yes**.

The following report will appear in the workspace. Note the new title and the lack of a footnote.

Row number	Volcano	Departs	Days	Price	Difficulty
	Fire and Ice Tours				
	Price List				
1	Etna	Catania	7	$1,610	m
2	Fuji	Tokyo	2	$335	c
3	Kenya	Nairobi	6	$1,245	m
4	Kilauea	Hilo	1	$85	e
5	Kilmanjaro	Nairobi	9	$1,965	c
6	Krakatau	Jakarta	7	$1,345	e
7	Poas	San Jose	1	$97	e
8	Reventador	Quito	4	$875	m
9	St. Helens	Portland	2	$250	e
10	Vesuvius	Rome	6	$1,495	e

Page Break

Workspace
Toolbar

✓Click Modify
Task

List Data
Window

✓ Click Options

✓ Type **Tour**
in Column
heading box

Changing column labels and formatting values To make more changes to the report, open the List Data task window again by clicking **Modify Task** on the workspace toolbar for the results. Click **Options** in the selection pane on the left. By default, SAS Enterprise Guide will show the row number in the report and give it the label Row number. You can choose not to show the row numbers by unchecking **Print the row number**. For this report, keep the row numbers, but replace the label for the column heading with the word **Tour**.

Now click **Data** in the selection pane on the left. Each variable in the task has properties associated with it and you can make changes to the properties. Right-click the variable **Price** and select **Properties** from the pop-up menu.

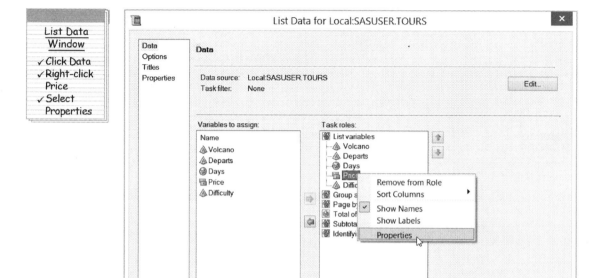

This opens the Properties window for the variable Price.

There are six properties listed in the Properties window, two of which you can change: the Label and the Format. Changes that you make in this window will affect only the results of the List Data task. The changes are not stored with the data. The Label is text that can be used for labeling the variable in the report. If the variable does not have a label, then SAS Enterprise Guide will use the variable's name as a label. Give the variable Price the label "Price USD" by typing **Price USD** in the box next to the word **Label**.

Properties
Window

✓ Type **Price USD**

✓ Click Change

The current format for Price is the DOLLAR10. format. Click **Change** to change the format for Price. This opens the Formats window.

Formats determine how values for the variable will be displayed. The format DOLLAR10. that was assigned to Price displays values with dollar signs and commas. The number at the end of the format name determines how many positions to allow for the value, including any commas, decimal places, and dollar signs. If decimal places are to be displayed, then the number of decimals follows the period at the end of the format name. Because there is no number after the period in the DOLLAR10. format, no decimal places will be displayed. Change the number of decimal places displayed for Price to **2** in the box next to **Decimal places**. Notice that when you do this, an example of how values will be displayed using this format appears at the bottom of the Formats window.

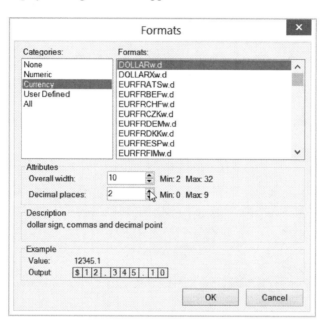

Click **OK** to close the Formats window.

Now Price has a label and will be formatted with the DOLLAR10.2 format.

Properties
Window

✓ Click OK

Price Properties   ✕

General

Price

Label:	Price USD
Type:	Currency
Length:	8
Format:	DOLLAR10.2	Change...
Informat:	DOLLAR10.
Sorted:	No

OK   Cancel

List Data
Window

✓ Click Run

Click **OK** to close the Properties window, and then click **Run** in the List Data window.

Select **Yes** when SAS Enterprise Guide asks if you want to replace the previous results.

Replace
Results?

✓ Click Yes

The following report will appear in the workspace. Notice the new column headings for the row number and the Price variable, and that the values for Price are now displayed in dollars and cents.

Fire and Ice Tours
Price List

Tour	Volcano	Departs	Days	Price USD	Difficulty
1	Etna	Catania	7	$1,610.00	m
2	Fuji	Tokyo	2	$335.00	c
3	Kenya	Nairobi	6	$1,245.00	m
4	Kilauea	Hilo	1	$85.00	e
5	Kilmanjaro	Nairobi	9	$1,965.00	c
6	Krakatau	Jakarta	7	$1,345.00	e
7	Poas	San Jose	1	$97.00	e
8	Reventador	Quito	4	$875.00	m
9	St. Helens	Portland	2	$250.00	e
10	Vesuvius	Rome	6	$1,495.00	e

Page Break

Defining your own formats   Many different formats come with SAS Enterprise Guide, but sooner or later you will have a particular need for which there is no format defined. Fortunately, SAS Enterprise Guide provides a way for you to create your own formats. This type of format is called a user-defined format. For example, the variable **Difficulty** has coded values of c, e, and m. These single-letter values are too cryptic for a price list; it would be better to spell out the values: Challenging, Easy, and Moderate. To create a user-defined format, select **Tasks ▶ Data ▶ Create Format** from the menu bar to open the Create Format window.

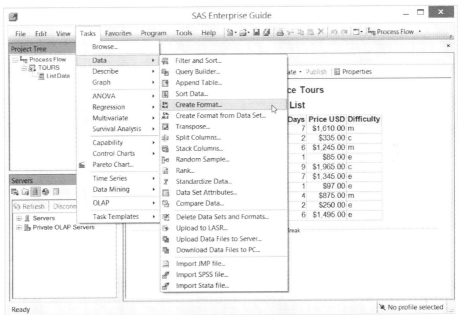

Location for Storing Formats

Formats can be temporary or permanent. If they are temporary, they are stored in the WORK library and are automatically deleted when you exit SAS Enterprise Guide. If you have a temporary format in your project that you want to use, then you will need to rerun the Create Format task every time you open that project. You can save a format permanently by choosing a library other than WORK. Then the format will not only be available for the project in which it was created, it will also be available for other projects. If you have access to more than one SAS server, store the format on the same server that is used for the task. To see which server is used for a task, place the cursor over the task icon in the Process Flow and the server name will be displayed in the pop-up window. The server is also displayed in the Properties window for the task.

Give the format a name by typing **Diff** in the box under **Format name**. Because this format will be used for a character variable, leave the **Format type** as **Character**.

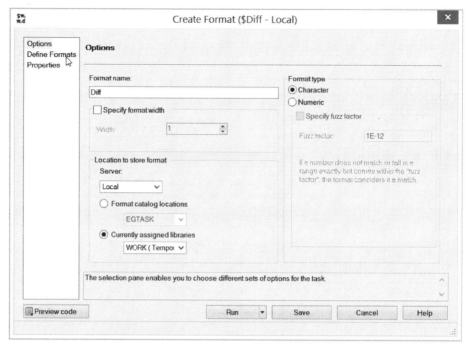

Click **Define formats** in the selection pane on the left to set values and ranges for the format.

Format Names

Character format names must be 31 characters or fewer in length, while numeric format names must be 32 characters or fewer. For both format types, names must contain only letters, numerals, or underscores, and cannot start or end with a numeral.

Defining a format is a two-part process. First, click **New** next to Label to start defining values.

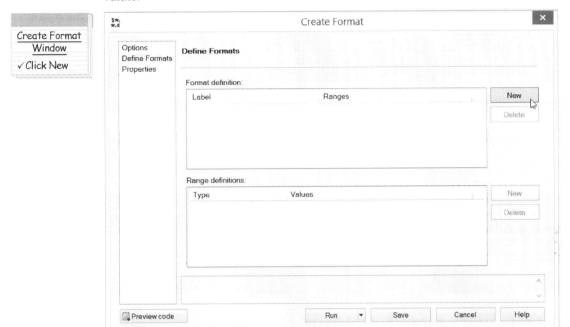

Type **Easy** in the box under the word **Label** in the Format definition portion of the window. Second, in the box under **Values**, type the lowercase letter **e**, which is the value to be associated with the label Easy. When you enter text values, it is important that the case of the text matches the case of the actual value. Character formats are case sensitive. As you type the value, it will appear in the Ranges box at the top of the window, beside the label Easy.

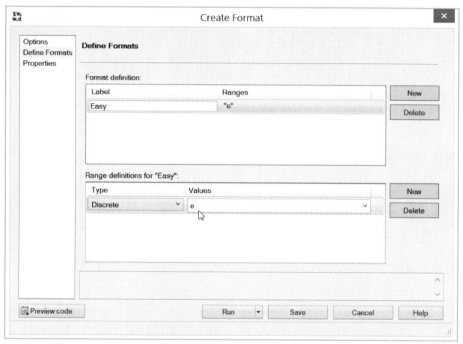

Multiple Ranges for a Label

You can enter more than one range for a label by clicking **New** in the Range definition portion of the window before adding another new label. For example, you might want the months SEP, OCT, and NOV to all be given the label Fall (or Spring if you are in the southern hemisphere). If you have a consecutive range of values that should all have the same label, then select **Range** from the **Type** drop-down list. For example, you might want the values 13 to 19 to all have the label Teenager. If your format is character and you use the Range type, then all values that fall alphabetically between the end points of the range will be included.

Now add labels for the other two values, m and c. In the Format definition portion of the window, click **New** and type **Moderate** in the box under the word **Label.** In the Range definitions portion of the window, type the letter **m** in the box under **Values**. Next, in the Format definition portion of the window, click **New** and type **Challenging** in the box under **Label.** In the Range definitions portion of the window, type the letter **c** in the box under **Values**.

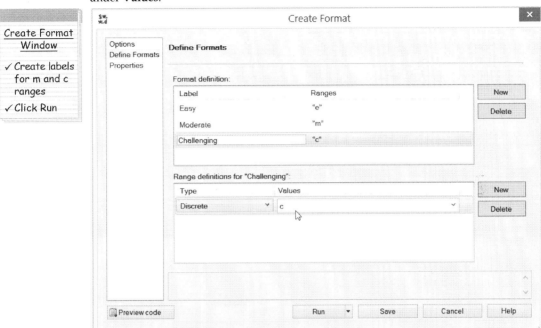

When you have all the labels and ranges defined, click **Run**.

Since there is no output from the Create Format task, after running, the SAS log is displayed in the workspace. Click **Process Flow** on the menu bar to view the Process Flow. An icon for the Create Format task appears in the Project Tree and the Process Flow. Notice that the Create Format task is not connected to anything in the Process Flow, and nothing in the report changed.

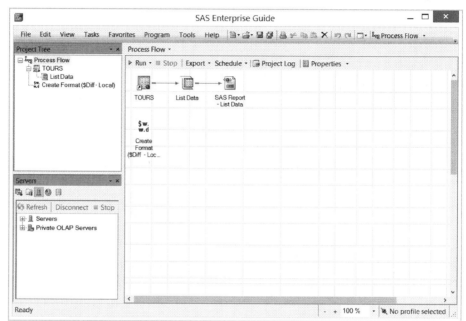

You created the format, but the format has not been associated with any variables yet. To associate the new format with the Difficulty variable, reopen the List Data window by right-clicking the **List Data** icon in the Project Tree or Process Flow and selecting **Modify List Data**. Then right-click the **Difficulty** variable and select **Properties**.

Project Tree

✓ Right-click List Data icon

✓ Select Modify List Data

List Data Window

✓ Right-click Difficulty

✓ Select Properties

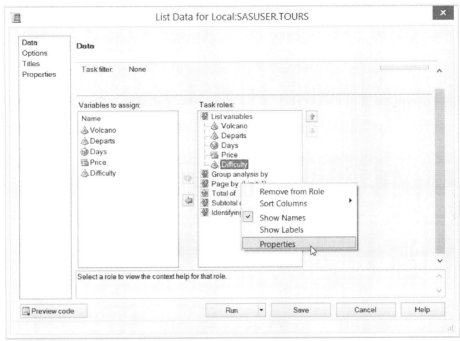

This opens the Properties window for the variable Difficulty.

Properties Window

✓ Click Change

Click **Change** to open the Formats window.

From the **Categories** list, select **User Defined**. Any formats defined in the current SAS Enterprise Guide session or any formats that have been saved in a permanent location appear in the list of formats. The format $DIFF. should be in your list and you may or may not have additional formats. The $ in the format name indicates that the format is for character values. Click the **$DIFF.** format.

Click **OK** to close the Formats window, and then click **OK** again in the Properties window to return to the List Data window. Click **Run** in the List Data window, and click **Yes** to replace the previous results.

The following report will appear in the workspace, showing the formatted values for the Difficulty variable.

Fire and Ice Tours
Price List

Tour	Volcano	Departs	Days	Price USD	Difficulty
1	Etna	Catania	7	$1,610.00	Moderate
2	Fuji	Tokyo	2	$335.00	Challenging
3	Kenya	Nairobi	6	$1,245.00	Moderate
4	Kilauea	Hilo	1	$85.00	Easy
5	Kilmanjaro	Nairobi	9	$1,965.00	Challenging
6	Krakatau	Jakarta	7	$1,345.00	Easy
7	Poas	San Jose	1	$97.00	Easy
8	Reventador	Quito	4	$875.00	Moderate
9	St. Helens	Portland	2	$250.00	Easy
10	Vesuvius	Rome	6	$1,495.00	Easy

Page Break

Click **Process Flow** on the menu bar to view the Process Flow. Notice that even though the List Data task uses the format created in the Create Format task, no link appears between the two task icons in the Process Flow.

Menu Bar

✓ Click
Process Flow

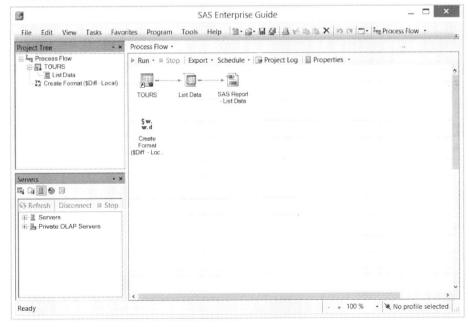

Adding manual links You can add a link to show that the Create Format task is needed for the List Data task. Click the Create Format icon in the Process Flow to select it, then position the cursor to the side of the Create Format icon so that the cursor changes to crosshairs ╋ . Click and drag the cursor over to the List Data task icon.

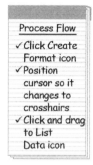

Process Flow

✓ Click Create
   Format icon
✓ Position
   cursor so it
   changes to
   crosshairs
✓ Click and drag
   to List
   Data icon

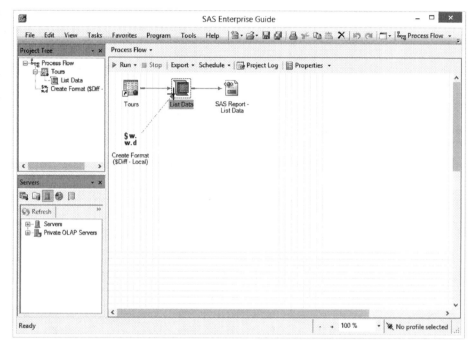

When you release the mouse button, a link will be created between the two icons. If you look closely, you will see that the manually added link uses a dashed line, but the automatic links use solid lines. Now whenever you rerun this project, the Create Format task will run before the List Data task.

Selecting a style for the report Every report that you produce in SAS Enterprise Guide has a style associated with it (except for results produced in text format which have no style). All the reports that you have produced so far have been in SAS Report format, and the default style for SAS Report format is HtmlBlue. The style of the report includes the color scheme, fonts, and the size and style of the font. You do not have to use the default style for your reports. SAS Enterprise Guide comes with many different styles for you to choose from, and if you can't find one that suits your needs, you can create your own.

To change the style for results, first double-click the List Data icon in the Process Flow to show the results of the task. Then click **Properties** on the workspace toolbar for the results.

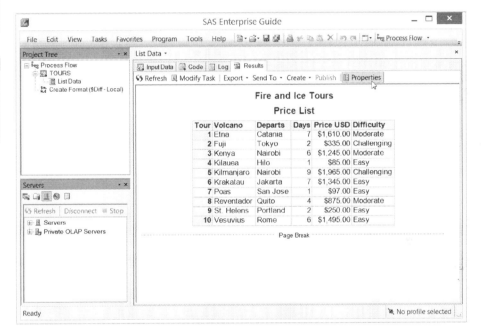

Changing the Default Style

If you find a style that you want to use for all your SAS Enterprise Guide projects, you can set it to be the default. Select **Tools ▶ Options** from the menu bar. In the selection pane on the left, select a result format: SAS Report, HTML, RTF, PDF, Excel or PowerPoint. Then select the style from the **Style** drop-down list.

This opens the Properties window for the SAS Report results created from the List Data task. Select the **BarrettsBlue** style from the drop-down **Style** menu.

Properties for SAS Report Window

✓ Select BarrettsBlue from Style drop-down menu

✓ Click OK

Click **OK**. Your report should look like the following, except that yours will be in shades of blue.

Fire and Ice Tours

Price List

Tour	Volcano	Departs	Days	Price USD	Difficulty
1	Etna	Catania	7	$1,610.00	Moderate
2	Fuji	Tokyo	2	$335.00	Challenging
3	Kenya	Nairobi	6	$1,245.00	Moderate
4	Kilauea	Hilo	1	$85.00	Easy
5	Kilmanjaro	Nairobi	9	$1,965.00	Challenging
6	Krakatau	Jakarta	7	$1,345.00	Easy
7	Poas	San Jose	1	$97.00	Easy
8	Reventador	Quito	4	$875.00	Moderate
9	St. Helens	Portland	2	$250.00	Easy
10	Vesuvius	Rome	6	$1,495.00	Easy

Page Break

Workspace
Toolbar

✓Click Modify
Task

List Data
Window

✓Click
Properties

✓Click Edit

Changing the output format for the report So far all the results we have produced have been in the SAS Report format. But you can also produce results in HTML, RTF, PDF, Excel, PowerPoint, or text format. Reopen the List Data task by clicking **Modify Task** on the workspace toolbar for the List Data result. Then click **Properties** in the selection pane on the left.

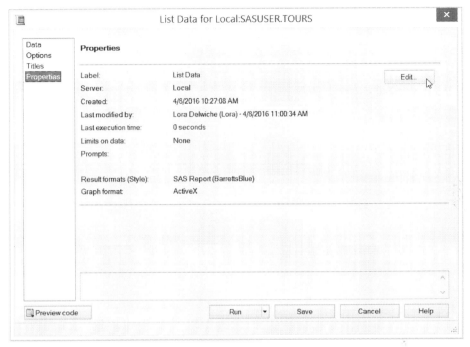

Click **Edit** to make changes to the properties of the task.

This opens the Properties window for the List Data task. Click **Results** in the selection pane on the left. On the Results page you can choose from several different result formats, as well as choose alternate styles for the task result. Uncheck the box next to SAS Report to turn off the SAS Report result format, then check PDF.

Properties for List Data Window

✓ Click Results

✓ Uncheck SAS Report

✓ Check PDF

✓ Click OK

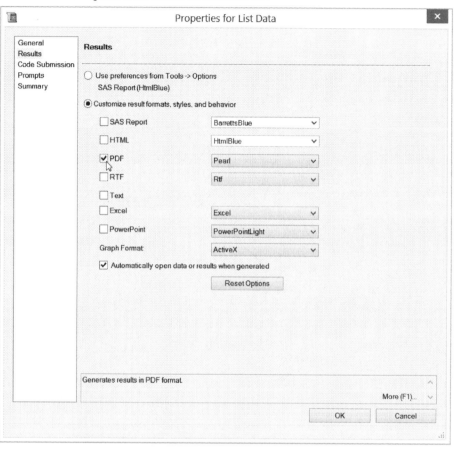

Click **OK** to close the Properties window, click **Run** in the List Data window, and click **Yes** to replace the previous results.

List Data Window

✓ Click Run

Replace Results?

✓ Click Yes

Choosing Default or Custom Result Formats and Styles

To use the default format and style, check **Use preferences from Tools -> Options** in the Results page of the Properties window for the task. To customize the format and style for the result of the task, check **Customize result formats, styles, and behavior**. Because we already changed the style for this task, the results are customized. Normally, if no changes were made to the task formats or styles, **Use preferences from Tools -> Options** will be checked.

PDF results will open in an external viewer. If the results do not automatically open, click **View** on the **Results** tab of the workspace to view the PDF results.

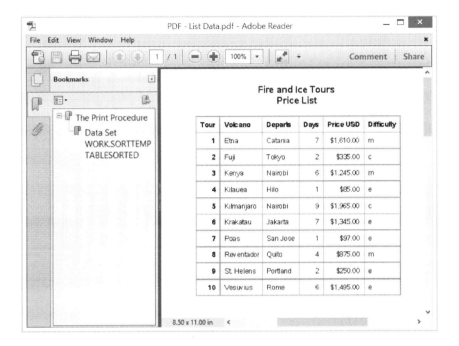

Completing the tutorial To complete the tutorial, add a note to the project with a project description. Double-click **Process Flow** in the Project Tree, and then select **File ▶ New ▶ Note** from the menu bar. Enter a brief description of the project in the Note window that appears in the workspace.

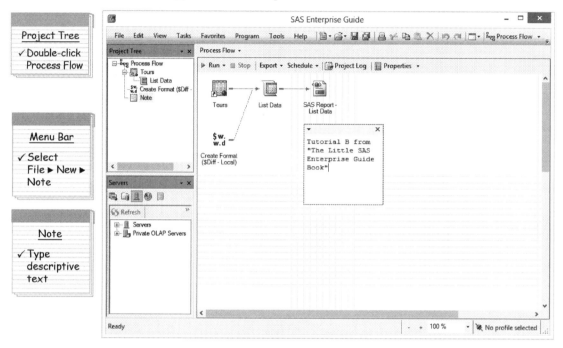

Now save the project and exit SAS Enterprise Guide. Select **File ▶ Save Project As** from the menu bar. Navigate to the location where you want to save the project, give the project the name **TutorialB**, and click **Save**. Select **File ▶ Exit** from the menu bar to close SAS Enterprise Guide.

C " The power of imagination makes us infinite. "

JOHN MUIR

From *John of the Mountains: The Unpublished Journals of John Muir*, 1938.

Working with Data in the Query Builder

Often the data tables you have are not exactly what you want. You may need to compute a new column based on existing columns, or you may need just part of the data table for your analysis. Using SAS Enterprise Guide, there are many ways in which you can manipulate your data. This tutorial covers the following topics in the Query Builder:

- Selecting columns

- Using the Expression Editor to create new columns

- Filtering rows

- Sorting data

Before beginning this tutorial This tutorial uses the Volcanoes SAS data table, which contains information about volcanoes around the world. The data and instructions for downloading the file can be found in Appendix A.

Starting SAS Enterprise Guide Start SAS Enterprise Guide by either double-clicking the **SAS Enterprise Guide** icon on your desktop, or selecting **SAS Enterprise Guide** from the Windows **Start** menu. Starting SAS Enterprise Guide brings up the SAS Enterprise Guide window in the background, with the Welcome window in the foreground. The Welcome window allows you to choose between opening an existing project or starting a new project. Click **New Project**.

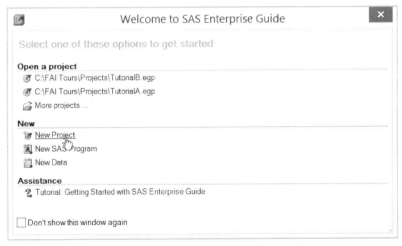

This opens an empty SAS Enterprise Guide window.

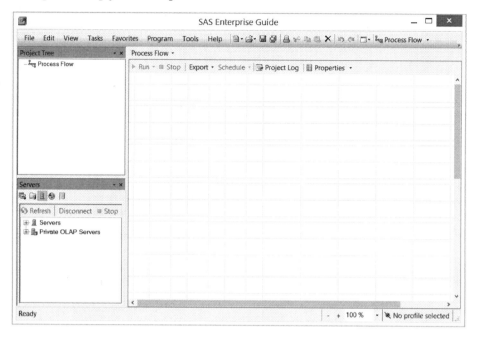

Opening the Volcanoes SAS data table   Open the Volcanoes SAS data table by selecting **File ▶ Open ▶ Data** from the menu bar. Because the Volcanoes data table is not stored in a defined SAS library, click **My Computer** in the selection pane on the left.

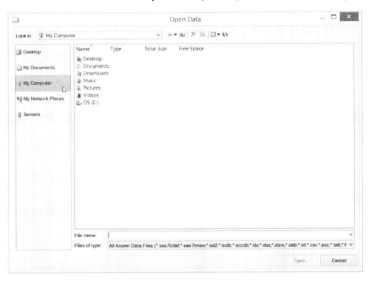

Navigate to the location where you stored the Volcanoes file and click its name to select it.

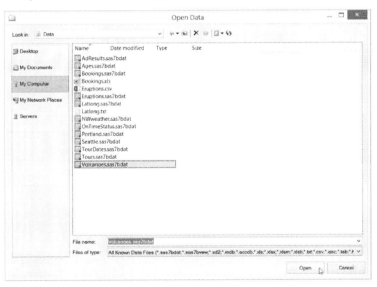

Click **Open**.

After you open the Volcanoes SAS data table, your screen should look like the following:

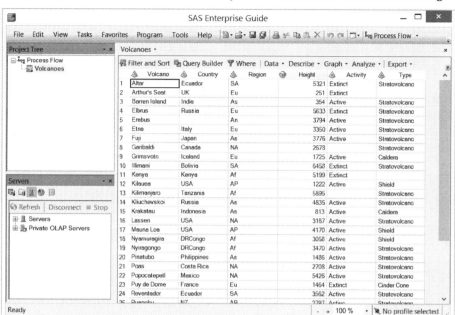

Opening the Query Builder The Query Builder is a powerful tool for data manipulation. In the Query Builder, you can filter and sort data, create new columns, and join tables. To open the Query Builder, click **Query Builder** on the workspace toolbar for the Volcanoes data table.

Workspace Toolbar

✓Click Query Builder

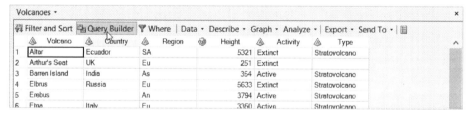

The Query Builder window has three tabs for different tasks: Select Data, Filter Data, and Sort Data. In addition, there are several buttons including Add Tables, Delete, Join Tables, Computed Columns, and Prompt Manager. So, you can see that there is a lot going on in the Query Builder. The name of the active data table appears in the list on the left, along with all the columns in the data table. The Query Builder opens with the Select Data tab on top and no columns selected.

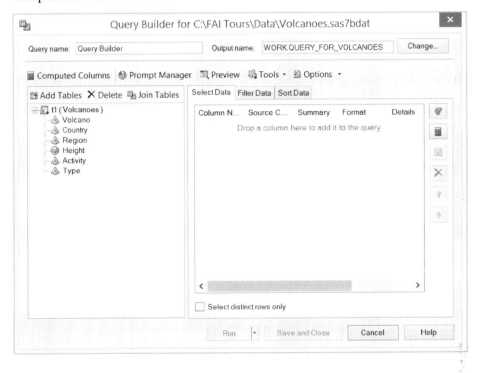

Naming Queries

If you have several queries in your project, it is a good idea to give the queries names so you can tell them apart in the Process Flow and Project Tree. Name the query by replacing the default name in the **Query name** box located in the top left corner of the Query Builder window. You can also rename items in your project by right-clicking the icon for the item in the Process Flow or Project Tree and selecting **Rename** from the pop-up menu.

Selecting columns To select columns for your query, click a column name in the box on the left and drag it over to the box on the right on the Select Data tab. For this query, select all the columns except Type. You can select them individually, or you can select the whole group at once by clicking Volcano, and then holding down the shift key and clicking Activity. Drag the selected columns to the Select Data tab.

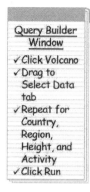

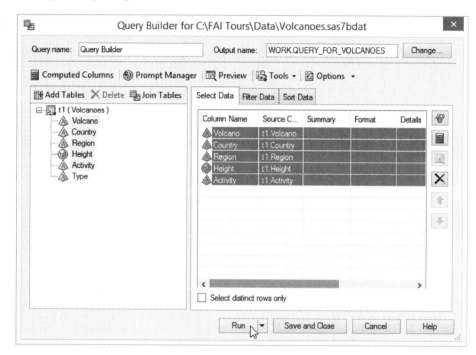

Click **Run** to see the results of this simple query.

Alternate Methods for Selecting Columns

In addition to clicking and dragging a column, you can double-click a column name to select it. After you double-click it, the column name will appear on the Select Data tab. To select all columns from a data table, click and drag the table name to the Select Data tab.

When you run the query, SAS Enterprise Guide will create a SAS data table by default. The new data table is given a name starting with Query, and is stored in a default location. The data table is displayed in the workspace. Notice that all the columns from the Volcanoes data table appear in the result except the Type column.

Workspace Toolbar

✓ Click Modify Task

Query Builder ▾

| 🔲 Input Data | 🔲 Code | 🔲 Log | 🔲 Output Data |

↺ | 🔲 Modify Task | 🔲 Filter and Sort | 🔲 Query Builder | ▼ Where | Data ▾ | Describe ▾ | Gra|

	Volcano	Country	Region	Height	Activity
1	Altar	Ecuador	SA	5321	Extinct
2	Arthur's Seat	UK	Eu	251	Extinct
3	Barren Island	India	As	354	Active
4	Elbrus	Russia	Eu	5633	Extinct
5	Erebus		An	3794	Active
6	Etna	Italy	Eu	3350	Active
7	Fuji	Japan	As	3776	Active
8	Garibaldi	Canada	NA	2678	
9	Grimsvotn	Iceland	Eu	1725	Active
10	Ulimani	Bolivia	SA	6458	Extinct

To make changes to the query, click **Modify Task** on the workspace toolbar for the query results.

Specifying the Format, Name, and Location for the Results of a Query

In this example, you are creating a SAS data table as a result of the query. If you want, you can create a report instead. Also, you may want to specify a meaningful name for your results, or store the results in a different location. To change the name and/or storage location for the resulting data table, click the Change button located in the upper right corner of the Query Builder window next to the Output Name. To change the result type of the query from data table to report, select **Options for this query** from the Options drop-down menu in the Query Builder window. On the Results page of the Query Options window that opens (not shown), check **Override the corresponding default settings in Tools -> Options**. Then check **Report**.

Creating a new column Sometimes you want to create a new column based on values in an existing column. For example, the Height column in the Volcanoes data table contains the height of each volcano in meters. You can create a new column that uses the values in the Height column to compute a new column containing the height in feet.

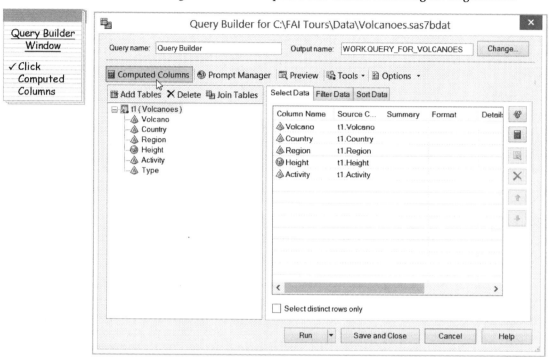

To create a new column that contains the height in feet, click **Computed Columns**. This opens the Computed Columns window where you can create new columns as well as edit, delete, or rename existing computed columns.

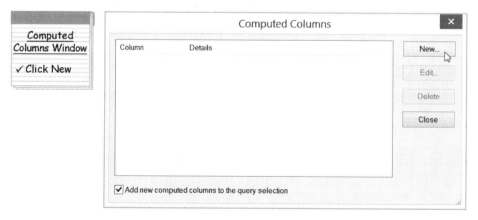

To create a new computed column, click **New**.

This opens the New Computed Column wizard. There are four types of computed columns to choose from: Summarized column, Recoded column, Advanced expression, and From an existing computed column (if there are any). Click **Advanced Expression**.

New Computed
Column Wizard
✓ Click
  Advanced
  expression
✓ Click Next

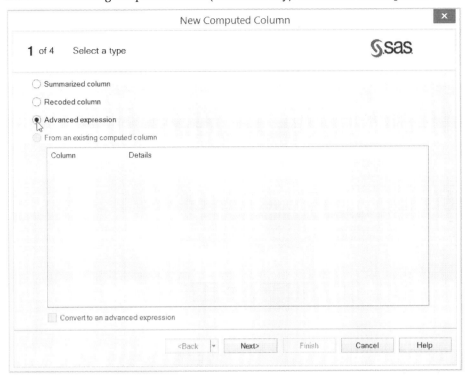

Click **Next**.

What Is a Summarized Column?

Use the Summarized column option when you want to compute a summary statistic such as mean, minimum, sum, or count for a column. By default, the chosen statistic is produced for the summarized column for each combination of all other selected columns in the query. To specify which columns to use to group statistics, use the Summary Groups area of the Query Builder window located on the Select Data tab.

What Is a Recoded Column?

If you create a new column by building an expression, then all values in the new column will be generated using that expression. But what if you want to take an existing column and change only some of the values, or treat a group of values differently from others? For example, the Activity column has some missing values. You could recode those missing values as "Unknown." Or, say you want to group the volcanoes according to height: short, medium, and tall. To do these types of operations, you would choose **Recoded column**.

The next window is where you build your expression. The empty box at the top of the window is where the expression is displayed. If you know the expression you want to use, you can type it directly in the box. But, if you are unsure exactly what the expression should look like, you can get some help from SAS Enterprise Guide. Under the box are several mathematical symbols that you can add to the expression. Below the symbols are folders for Functions and Tables and a node for Selected Columns. Expand the Selected Columns node by clicking the + symbol located to the left of the Selected Columns icon.

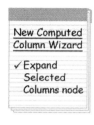

New Computed
Column Wizard

✓ Expand
   Selected
   Columns node

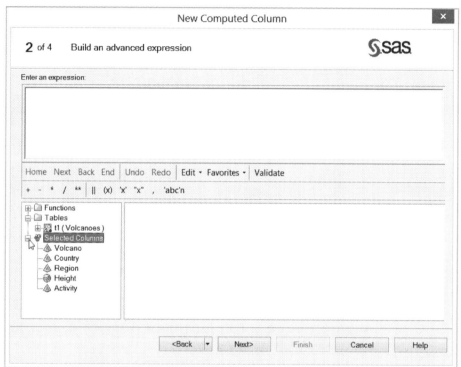

What Are Functions?

If you find you can't build the expression you want using the simple mathematical operators, then chances are SAS Enterprise Guide has a function that can help. Functions take a value, perform an operation on the value, and return a related value. For example, the ABS function takes a number and returns the absolute value of that number. There are hundreds of functions available to you in several categories including: arithmetic, character, mathematical, date, and time.

To calculate the volcano's height in feet, you need to multiply the Height column by 3.25. Double-click **Height** in the Selected Columns list. When you do this, the full name of the Height column is inserted into the expression text box at the top of the window. The full name, t1.Height, includes the source for the column, which is table one (Volcanoes).

New Computed Column Wizard

✓ Double-click Height

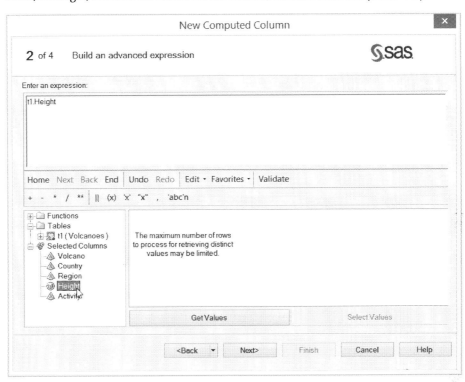

Table Aliases in Queries

When you bring a data table into a query, SAS Enterprise Guide gives the table an alias. The first table will have the alias t1, the second t2, and so forth. In some places the Query Builder uses these aliases instead of the table name. For example, when showing the full name for a column, the Query Builder will use the table alias followed by a period and then the column name. You can change the alias in the Table Properties window for the table in the Query Builder. Right-click the table name in the Query Builder and select **Properties** to open this window.

Now, under the box labeled **Enter an expression,** click the multiplication button .
Notice that the asterisk is inserted after the column name in the expression.

To complete the expression, type the number **3.25** in the expression text box after the asterisk.

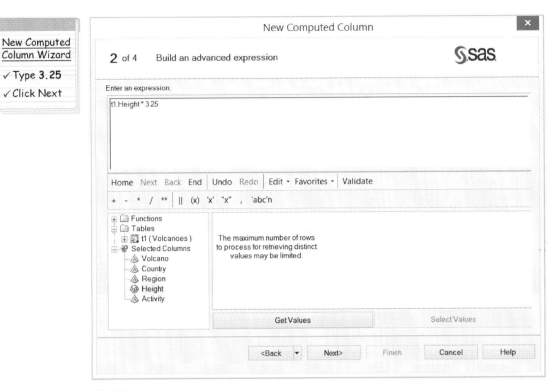

Click **Next**.

Notice that the column has been given the name Calculation. You could leave the name as is, but it is better to give the column a meaningful name. In the Column Name text box enter **HeightInFeet**.

Click **Next**.

The final window of the New Computed Column wizard simply gives a summary of the new computed column.

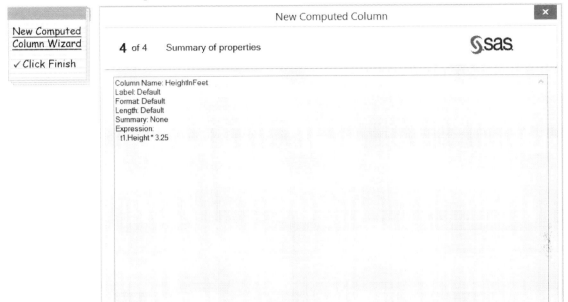

New Computed
Column Wizard

✓ Click Finish

Click **Finish** to return to the Computed Columns window.

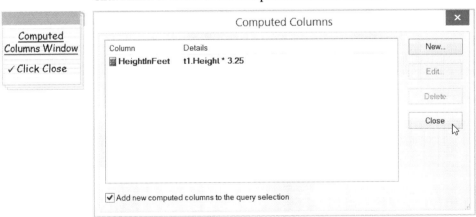

Computed
Columns Window

✓ Click Close

Click **Close**.

Notice that the new column, HeightInFeet, appears in the list of columns on the Select Data tab as well as under Computed Columns in the list on the left.

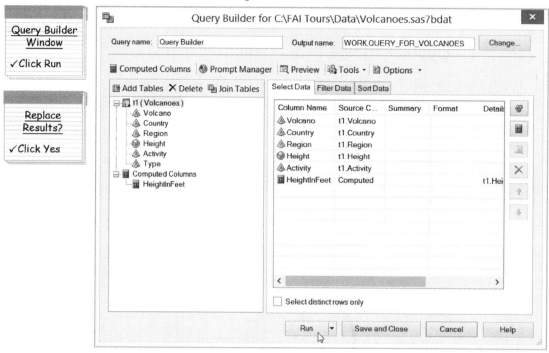

Click **Run** to view the result of the query with the newly computed column. When SAS Enterprise Guide asks if you want to replace the previous results, click **Yes**.

The values for HeightInFeet are correct, but they could use some formatting. It is not necessary to show fractions of feet, and it would be nice to have commas in the numbers to make them easier to read.

Workspace
Toolbar

✓ Click Modify
Task

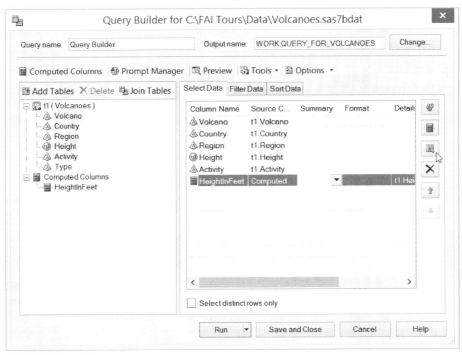

Click **Modify Task** on the workspace toolbar to reopen the Query Builder.

To change the display format of the HeightInFeet column, open the Properties window for the column. Click **HeightInFeet** in the list of column names on the Select Data tab.

Query Builder
Window

✓ Click
HeightInFeet

✓ Click
Properties
icon

Then click the Properties icon located on the right side of the Query Builder window.

The HeightInFeet column currently has no format associated with it.

Properties for HeightInFeet

Column Name: HeightInFeet

Label:

Format: Change...

Summary: None   Length (in bytes):

Expression: t1.Height * 3.25

Edit...

Source Column: Computed

OK   Cancel   Help

Click **Change**. This opens a window where you can select a format for the column. Select the **COMMAw.d** format from the **Numeric** group. The default width of 6 is fine for this column because the heights of all the volcanoes are at most 6 digits including the comma. Make sure that the number of decimal places is set to **0**.

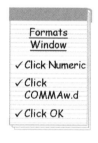

Formats
Window

✓Click Numeric

✓Click
  COMMAw.d

✓Click OK

Formats

Categories: Formats:
None   B8601DXw.d
Numeric   B8601LXw.d
Date   B8601TXw.d
Time   BESTDOTXw.d
Date/Time   BESTDw.d
Currency   BESTw.d
User Defined   BESTXw.d
All   BINARYw.d
                           COMMAw.d
                           COMMAXw.d

Attributes
Overall width: 6   Min: 1 Max: 32
Decimal places: 0   Min: 0 Max: 5

Description
commas in numbers

Example
Value: 12345.1
Output: 1 2 . 3 4 5

OK   Cancel

Click **OK** to return to the Properties window.

Now the format for the column, COMMA6., appears in the Format area of the Properties window.

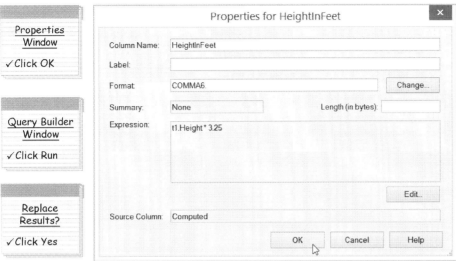

Properties Window

✓ Click OK

Query Builder Window

✓ Click Run

Replace Results?

✓ Click Yes

Click **OK**, then click **Run** in the Query Builder window to see the result of setting the format for the HeightInFeet column. When SAS Enterprise Guide asks if you want to replace the previous results, click **Yes**.

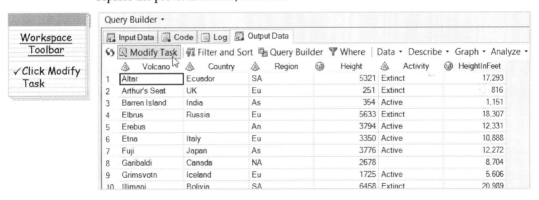

Workspace Toolbar

✓ Click Modify Task

To make more changes to the query, click **Modify Task** on the workspace toolbar.

Ordering and removing columns Now that you have the HeightInFeet column, you no longer need the Height column. To remove it from the query, first select it by clicking **Height** in the list of columns on the Select Data tab.

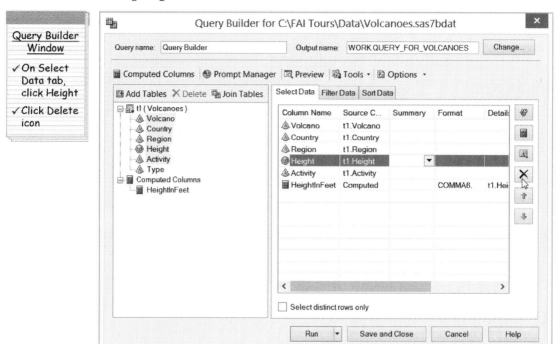

Query Builder
Window

✓ On Select
Data tab,
click Height

✓ Click Delete
icon

Then click the Delete icon ❌ located on the right side of the Query Builder window. It is important to note that deleting the column from the query result does not delete the column from the original data table.

In the results, the columns will be listed in the order that they appear in the Query Builder. You can change the order on the Select Data tab. Click the new column

HeightInFeet and then click the up-arrow icon  located on the right side of the Query Builder window until the column is listed just above the column Activity.

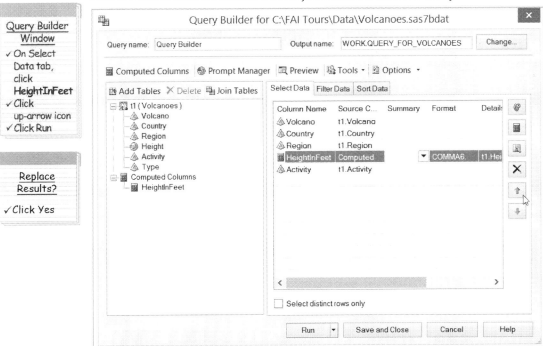

Click **Run** to view the result of the query. When SAS Enterprise Guide asks if you want to replace the previous results, click **Yes**. Notice that HeightInFeet now appears before Activity and the Height column is no longer in the result.

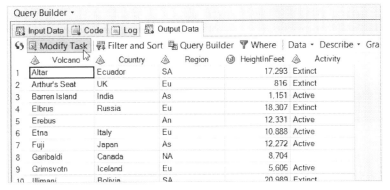

To make more changes to the query, click **Modify Task** on the workspace toolbar.

Filtering data   To filter or create subsets of your data, use the Filter Data tab of the Query Builder. Click the **Filter Data** tab to bring it forward. To create a filter, drag the column that you want to use as the basis of your filter over to the Filter Data tab. For this example, use the HeightInFeet column to select only the volcanoes with heights over 12,000 feet.

Query Builder
Window

✓ Click Filter
   Data tab

✓ Drag
   HeightInFeet

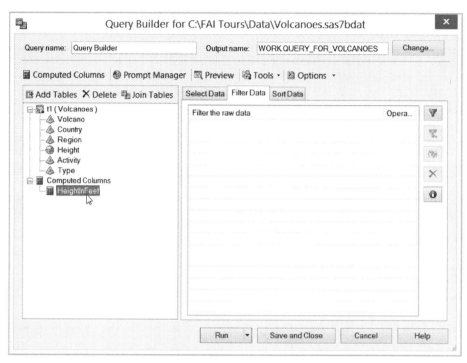

Click the **HeightInFeet** column on the left side of the window and drag it over to the **Filter Data** tab.

> **Other Ways to Filter Data**
>
> In addition to the Filter Data tab in the Query Builder, you can filter data using the Filter and Sort task accessible by clicking **Filter and Sort** on the workspace toolbar for Data Grids, or by selecting **Tasks ▶ Data ▶ Filter and Sort** from the menu bar. You can also filter data used for tasks by clicking the **Edit** button located near the top of the Data page for tasks. This opens the Edit Data and Filter window where you can define your filter.

As soon as you release the mouse button, the New Filter wizard will open. The column for the filter is automatically set to HeightInFeet, and the Operator is initially set to Equal to.

Because you want all volcanoes with a height over 12,000 feet, you need to select a different operator. Click the down-arrow to the right of **Operator** to display the drop-down list of operators. Select the **Greater than** operator. Next, type the value **12000** in the box labeled **Value**. When you enter numeric values, do not enter any commas or dollar signs.

New Filter
Wizard

✓ From
Operator
list, select
Greater than

✓ In Value box,
type **12000**

✓ Click Next

Click **Next** to display a summary of the filter.

Click **Finish**.

Now the Filter Data tab shows the filter you created.

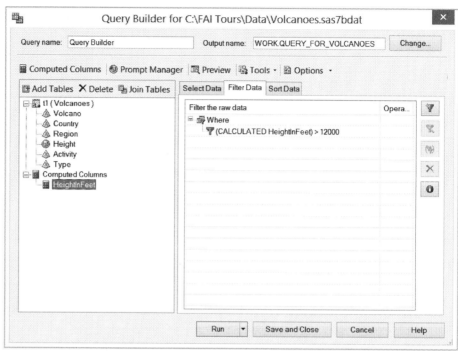

Click **Run** in the Query Builder window. When SAS Enterprise Guide asks if you want to replace the previous results, click **Yes**.

Now you can see that all the volcanoes in the results are over 12,000 feet.

	Volcano	Country	Region	HeightInFeet	Activity
1	Altar	Ecuador	SA	17,293	Extinct
2	Elbrus	Russia	Eu	18,307	Extinct
3	Erebus		An	12,331	Active
4	Fuji	Japan	As	12,272	Active
5	Illimani	Bolivia	SA	20,989	Extinct
6	Kenya	Kenya	Af	16,897	Extinct
7	Kilimanjaro	Tanzania	Af	19,159	
8	Kliuchevskoi	Russia	As	15,714	Active
9	Mauna Loa	USA	AP	13,553	Active
10	Popocatepetl	Mexico	NA	17,635	Active
11	Sabancaya	Peru	SA	19,422	Active

You can create more complicated filters by adding more conditions to your filter. Click **Modify Task** on the workspace toolbar to reopen the Query Builder.

Click the **Filter Data** tab in the Query Builder window. Add the Activity column to the filter to create a data table having only volcanoes that are over 12,000 feet and are active.

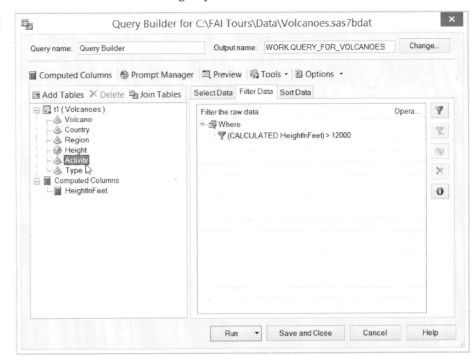

Click the column **Activity** and drag it over to the **Filter Data** tab.

When you release the mouse button, the New Filter wizard will open. This time, there is no need to change the operator because you want all volcanoes where the column Activity equals Active. At this point, you could type the value **Active** (paying attention to the casing of the letters) in the **Value** box to complete the filter. However, SAS Enterprise Guide gives you the option of choosing from a list of values for the column. Choosing the value from a list has the advantage that you can't accidentally misspell the value or use lowercase where it should be uppercase. But use caution if your data tables are very large, as it may take a long time to generate the list of values.

New Filter
Wizard

✓ Click
down-arrow
next to
Value box

Click the down-arrow next to the **Value** box to open a new window where you can view the values for the Activity column.

Values Tab

✓ Click Get
Values

Click **Get Values** to load all possible values for Activity.

The Activity column has three values: Active, Extinct, and a null or missing value. Click **Active** in the list of values.

The window will close, and the value will appear in the Value box of the New Filter window. Because these are character values, make sure that the **Enclose values in quotes** box located at the bottom of the window is checked.

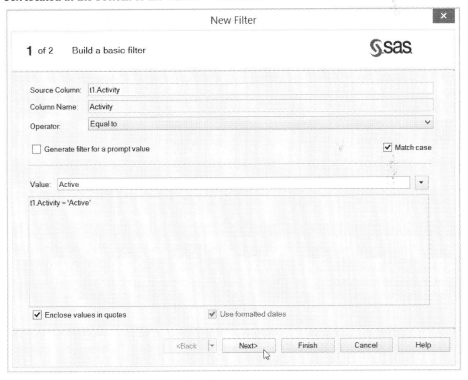

Click **Next** to display a summary of the filter.

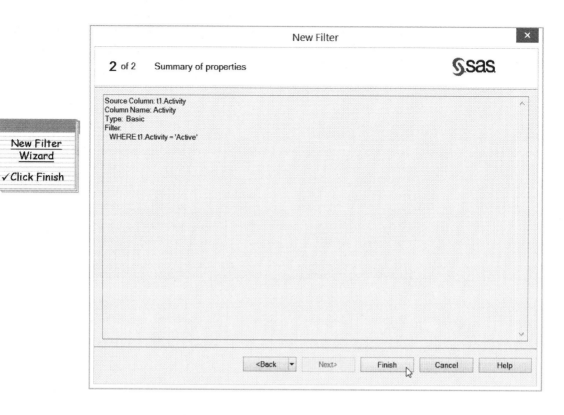

Click **Finish**.

Notice that a new condition has been added to the filter on the Filter Data tab.

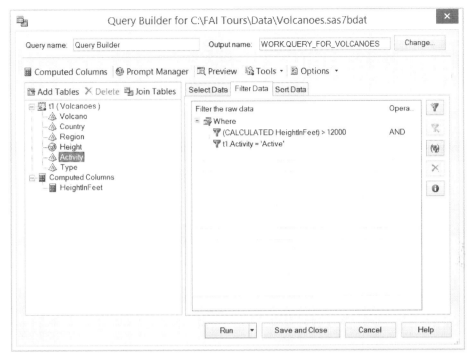

If you wanted to change either filter condition, you could simply double-click the condition to reopen the Edit Filter window, or highlight the filter on the Filter Data tab and click the Edit Filter icon located on the right side of the window.

Click **Run** in the Query Builder window. When SAS Enterprise Guide asks if you want to replace the previous results, click **Yes**.

Query Builder
Window

✓ Click Run

Replace
Results?

✓ Click Yes

AND or OR?

In this example, you want all rows that meet two conditions: volcanoes over 12,000 feet and Active. Because the volcano must pass both conditions, you use the AND operator (the default). But suppose you are not such a thrill seeker, and you would rather just look at volcanoes that are either extinct or less than 8,000 feet. The volcano has to meet only one of the conditions to be included. For this type of filter, use the OR operator. To change the operator from AND to OR, click the AND operator on the Filter Data tab of the Query Builder and choose OR from the drop-down list.

Notice that all the volcanoes listed are over 12,000 feet and are active.

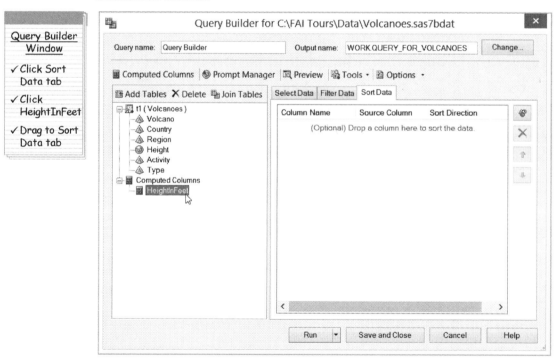

To make more changes to the query, click **Modify Task** on the workspace toolbar.

Sorting the data rows

Sorting the data rows There is one last change to make to this query. The data came sorted alphabetically by the name of the volcano. For this list, it would be better to sort the volcanoes by height, showing the tallest volcano at the top of the list. To sort the data, click the **Sort Data** tab.

Click and drag the **HeightInFeet** column over to the **Sort Data** tab.

Initially, the sort direction for the column is set to Ascending. To change the sort direction so that the tallest volcano will be first, click **Ascending** and select **Descending** from the drop-down list.

Sort Data Tab

✓ In Sort Direction box, click Ascending

✓ Select Descending

Query Builder Window

✓ Click Run

Replace Results?

✓ Click Yes

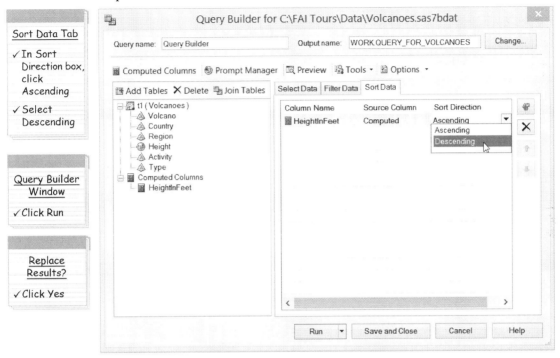

Click **Run** in the Query Builder window. When SAS Enterprise Guide asks if you want to replace the previous results, click **Yes**. Notice how the volcanoes are now sorted according to height, with the tallest volcano listed first.

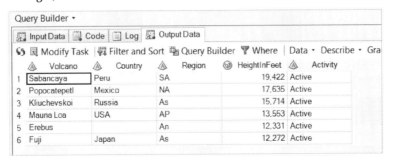

	Volcano	Country	Region	HeightInFeet	Activity
1	Sabancaya	Peru	SA	19,422	Active
2	Popocatepetl	Mexico	NA	17,635	Active
3	Kliuchevskoi	Russia	As	15,714	Active
4	Mauna Loa	USA	AP	13,553	Active
5	Erebus		An	12,331	Active
6	Fuji	Japan	As	12,272	Active

Completing the tutorial To complete the tutorial, add a note documenting the project. Double-click the words **Process Flow** in the Project Tree, and then select **File ▶ New ▶ Note** from the menu bar. Type comments about the project into the Note window in the workspace.

Project Tree
✓ Double-click Process Flow

Menu Bar
✓ Select File ▶ New ▶ Note

Note
✓ Type descriptive text

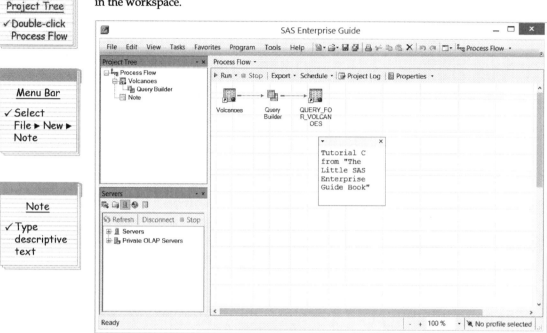

Now save the project and exit SAS Enterprise Guide. Select **File ▶ Save Project as** from the menu bar. Navigate to the location where you want to save the project, give the project the name **TutorialC**, and click **Save**. Then select **File ▶ Exit** from the menu bar to close SAS Enterprise Guide. Because the results of the query may be saved in the temporary WORK library by default, you may see the following window when exiting SAS Enterprise Guide. In this case, there is no need to save the results of the query in a permanent location since you can easily rerun the query the next time you open the project.

Menu Bar
✓ Save project
✓ Exit

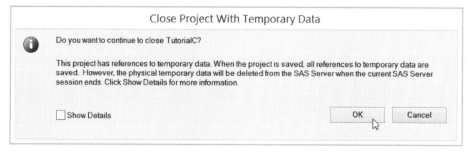

Click **OK**.

Close Project Window
✓ Click OK

D "One must travel, to learn."

MARK TWAIN

From *The Innocents Abroad: or, The New Pilgrim's Progress*, 1869.

D Joining Two Data Tables Together

Often the data you need for a particular analysis are in more than one table. To perform the analysis, you need to join tables together. In this tutorial, you will be joining together two data tables, and then manipulating the data after the join. Here are the topics covered in this tutorial:

- Joining tables together

- Filtering data after the join

- Selecting which data rows to keep

Before beginning this tutorial This tutorial uses the Volcanoes SAS data table, which contains information about volcanoes around the world. This tutorial also uses the Tours data table, which contains information about the volcano tours offered by the Fire and Ice Tours company. The data and instructions for downloading the data tables can be found in Appendix A.

The Fire and Ice Tours company wants to produce a list of tours for all volcanoes in Asia and Europe. The problem is that the Tours data table does not contain information about the region of the volcano. The region of the volcano is contained in the Volcanoes file. So, for the company to produce the desired list, the Volcanoes data and the Tours data must be joined together.

Starting SAS Enterprise Guide Start SAS Enterprise Guide by either double-clicking the **SAS Enterprise Guide** icon on your desktop, or selecting **SAS Enterprise Guide** from the Windows **Start** menu. Starting SAS Enterprise Guide brings up the SAS Enterprise Guide window in the background, with the Welcome window in the foreground. The Welcome window allows you to choose between opening an existing project or starting a new project. Click **New Project**.

Welcome to SAS Enterprise Guide

Select one of these options to get started:

Open a project
- C:\FAI Tours\Projects\TutorialC.egp
- C:\FAI Tours\Projects\TutorialB.egp
- C:\FAI Tours\Projects\TutorialA.egp
- More projects ...

New
- New Project
- New SAS Program
- New Data

Assistance
- Tutorial: Getting Started with SAS Enterprise Guide

Don't show this window again

This opens an empty SAS Enterprise Guide window.

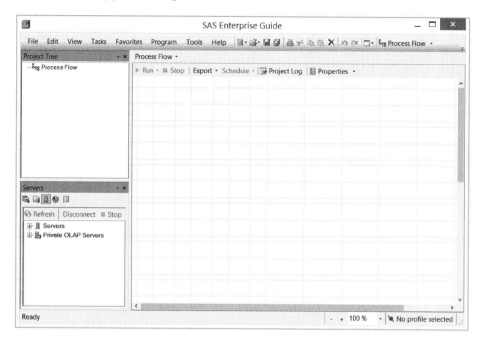

Menu Bar

✓ Select File ▶
  Open ▶ Data
✓ Click
  My Computer
✓ Open
  Volcanoes
  and Tours

Opening the two data files to be joined Open the Volcanoes and Tours data tables by selecting **File ▶ Open ▶ Data** from the menu bar, clicking **My Computer**, and navigating to the location where you saved the data for this book. You can select both tables at once by clicking one table, holding the control (CTRL) key down and then clicking the other table. Click **Open**. (If you created the Tours data table in Tutorial A and saved it in the SASUSER library, you may prefer to open your version instead by selecting **File ▶ Open ▶ Data** from the menu bar, clicking **Servers**, and navigating to the SASUSER library.)

After opening both files, you should see both the Volcanoes and the Tours data tables listed in the Project Tree.

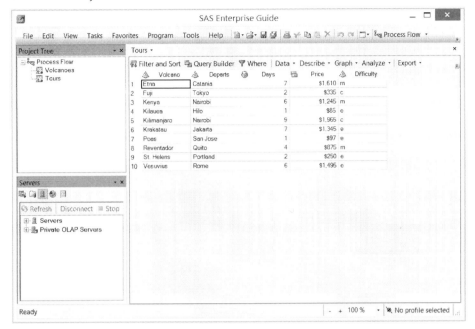

Here is what the Tours data table looks like. The Tours data contain information about the tour: the name of the volcano, the city where the tour departs, the number of days the tour lasts, the price, and a difficulty rating for the tour. The region of the volcano is not part of the Tours data table, so it would not be possible, using this data table alone, to produce a list of volcano tours in Asia and Europe.

	Volcano	Departs	Days	Price	Difficulty
1	Etna	Catania	7	$1,610	m
2	Fuji	Tokyo	2	$335	c
3	Kenya	Nairobi	6	$1,245	m
4	Kilauea	Hilo	1	$85	e
5	Kilimanjaro	Nairobi	9	$1,965	c
6	Krakatau	Jakarta	7	$1,345	e
7	Poas	San Jose	1	$97	e
8	Reventador	Quito	4	$875	m
9	St. Helens	Portland	2	$250	e
10	Vesuvius	Rome	6	$1,495	e

Here is a partial listing of the Volcanoes data table. This table includes the country and region of the volcano, as well as the height, activity, and type of volcano. While the two data tables contain different information, they do have one column in common, the name of the volcano. To join data tables together in a meaningful way, the tables must have at least one column that appears in both data tables. The common column does not have to have the same name in both data tables, but it must contain the same information and have the same possible values.

	Volcano	Country	Region	Height	Activity	Type
1	Altar	Ecuador	SA	5321	Extinct	Stratovolcano
2	Arthur's Seat	UK	Eu	251	Extinct	
3	Barren Island	India	As	354	Active	Stratovolcano
4	Elbrus	Russia	Eu	5633	Extinct	Stratovolcano
5	Erebus		An	3794	Active	Stratovolcano
6	Etna	Italy	Eu	3350	Active	Stratovolcano
7	Fuji	Japan	As	3776	Active	Stratovolcano
8	Garibaldi	Canada	NA	2678		Stratovolcano
9	Grimsvotn	Iceland	Eu	1725	Active	Caldera
10	Illimani	Bolivia	SA	6458	Extinct	Stratovolcano
11	Kenya	Kenya	Af	5199	Extinct	
12	Kilauea	USA	AP	1222	Active	Shield

Joining tables   You join tables using the Query Builder. In the Query Builder, in addition to joining tables, you can filter and sort data, and create new columns. To open both tables simultaneously in the Query Builder, click Volcanoes in the Project Tree, then hold the control (CTRL) key down and click Tours. Then right-click either Volcanoes or Tours, and select **Query Builder** from the pop-up menu. (If you are using a version of SAS Enterprise Guide earlier than 7.1, then you cannot open both tables simultaneously in the Query Builder. Instead open one table in the Query Builder, then click **Add Tables** in the Query Builder to open the second table.)

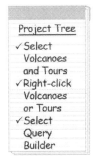

Project Tree
- ✓ Select Volcanoes and Tours
- ✓ Right-click Volcanoes or Tours
- ✓ Select Query Builder

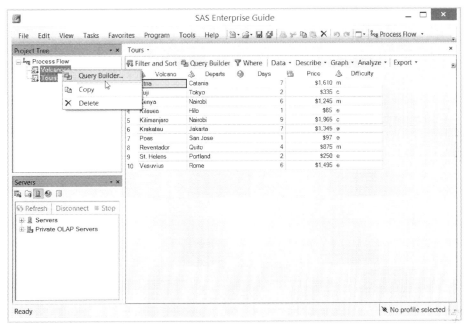

The Query Builder window has three tabs: Select Data, Filter Data, and Sort Data. In addition, in the box on the left side of the Query Builder, you can choose: Add Tables, Delete, and Join Tables. The data table names appear in the list on the left, along with all the columns in the data tables.

When you have multiple data tables in a query, SAS Enterprise Guide checks to see if the data tables have a column in common. Common columns must have the same name and be the same type (numeric or character). If there is a common column, SAS Enterprise Guide will automatically use that column for the join. Because the Volcanoes data table and the Tours data table both have a character column named Volcano, SAS Enterprise Guide will use it to find matching rows.

Query Builder
Window

✓ Click Join
Tables

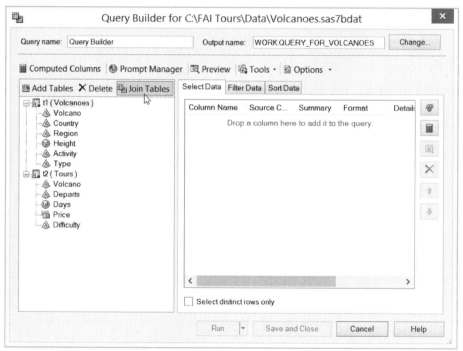

It's not obvious from the Query Builder window that SAS Enterprise Guide has found common columns for the join. To see what the join looks like, click **Join Tables** to open the Tables and Joins window.

What If the Common Columns Have Different Names?

No problem! When you try to join the two tables, SAS Enterprise Guide will let you know that it cannot determine how to join them and that you will need to do it manually. Click **OK**, and the Tables and Joins window will open automatically. Click the first table, then right-click the common column, select **Join With** from the pop-up menu, and select the column from the second table. Next, choose a join type from the Join Properties window, and click **OK**. SAS Enterprise Guide will draw a line between the two columns, and the columns will be linked.

In the Tables and Joins window, both tables are visible along with the columns in the tables. Notice the line drawn between the Volcano column in the Volcanoes table and the Volcano column in the Tours table. This shows how the tables will be joined. Also, there is a diagram on the line, and a message at the bottom of the window that shows the type of join. In this case, only rows with identical values of the common variable (Volcano) in both tables will be included in the resulting table. This type of join is called an inner join.

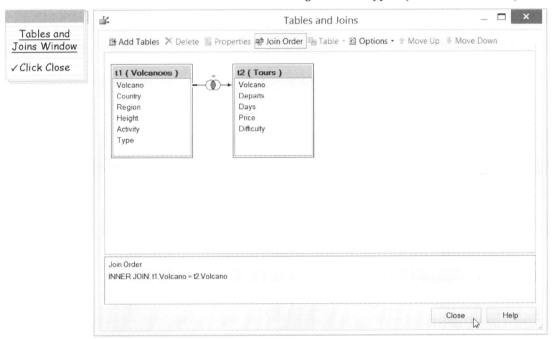

Click **Close** to close the Tables and Joins window and return to the Query Builder.

> ### Tables with More Than One Common Column
>
> It is possible to join data tables that have more than one common column. For example, you may have year and month columns in both data tables, and you want to match the tables based on the values of both columns. SAS Enterprise Guide does not handle this type of join automatically, but it is easy to do it yourself. SAS Enterprise Guide will link the first pair of columns for you. To link the second pair, open the Tables and Joins window by clicking **Join Tables** in the Query Builder window. Create another link by clicking the first table, then right-clicking the column name, choosing **Join With** in the pop-up menu, and selecting the column from the second table.

Before you can run the query, you must select the columns you want in the result. To select columns, click the column in the box on the left and drag it over to the Select Data tab. For this query, select the **Volcano**, **Country**, **Region**, **Height**, and **Activity** columns from the Volcanoes table. Then select the **Departs**, **Days**, and **Price** columns from the Tours table.

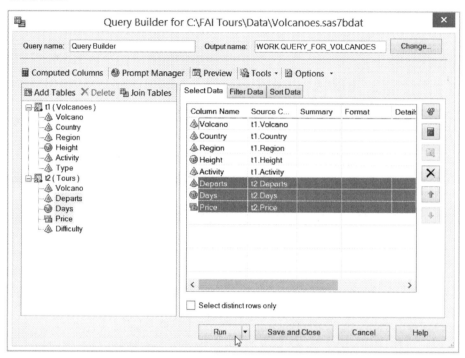

Click **Run** in the Query Builder window to run the query.

What If One Table Has Repeated Values of the Common Column?

In this example, each table has only one entry for each volcano, so there is a one-to-one match between the tables. But suppose the Tours table had two tours for one volcano. Then the values for the columns in the Volcanoes data table will be repeated for these two tours for the same volcano.

The data table created by the query will display in the workspace. Notice that the volcanoes from the Volcanoes data table have been matched with the corresponding row from the Tours data table and that only the rows that appear in both data tables are part of the result. This is the default type of join for SAS Enterprise Guide. Because all the volcanoes in the Tours data table also appear in the Volcanoes data table, all the tours are represented here. However, some volcanoes do not have matching tours, and so they are not included in the result.

Query Builder ▾

Input Data (2) Code Log Output Data

Modify Task Filter and Sort Query Builder Where Data ▾ Describe ▾ Graph ▾ An

	Volcano	Country	Region	Height	Activity	Departs	Days	Price
1	Etna	Italy	Eu	3350	Active	Catania	7	$1,610
2	Fuji	Japan	As	3776	Active	Tokyo	2	$335
3	Kenya	Kenya	Af	5199	Extinct	Nairobi	6	$1,245
4	Kilauea	USA	AP	1222	Active	Hilo	1	$85
5	Kilimanjaro	Tanzania	Af	5895		Nairobi	9	$1,965
6	Krakatau	Indonesia	As	813	Active	Jakarta	7	$1,345
7	Poas	Costa Rica	NA	2708	Active	San Jose	1	$97
8	Reventador	Ecuador	SA	3562	Active	Quito	4	$875
9	St. Helens	USA	NA	2549	Active	Portland	2	$250
10	Vesuvius	Italy	Eu	1281	Active	Rome	6	$1,495

Click the **Process Flow** button on the menu bar to view the Process Flow for the project. It is not obvious from the Project Tree that the query uses both the Tours and the Volcanoes tables, but in the Process Flow it is easy to see that both tables contribute to the query. By default, results of queries are given an arbitrary name starting with the word QUERY and are stored in a default location.

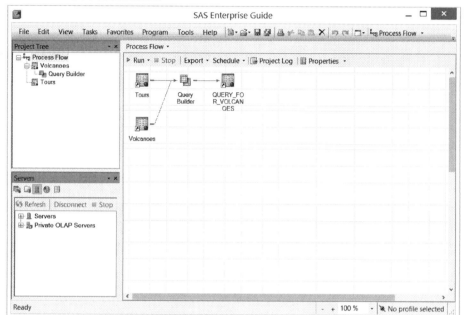

Filtering the data   Now that the Tours data table and the Volcanoes data table have been joined together, it is possible to create a data table of tours for volcanoes in Asia and Europe. To do this, you create a filter as part of the same query that you used to join the data tables.

Right-click the Query Builder icon in the Project Tree or Process Flow and select **Modify Query Builder** to reopen the query. The Query Builder window opens with the Select Data tab on top. Click **Filter Data** to open the Filter Data tab. The Region column in the Volcanoes data table gives the general location of the volcano: North America, South America, Europe, Asia, Australia Pacific, Africa, or Antarctica.

Project Tree

✓ Right-click
  Query
  Builder icon

✓ Select
  Modify
  Query
  Builder

Query Builder
Window

✓ Click Filter
  Data tab

✓ Drag Region

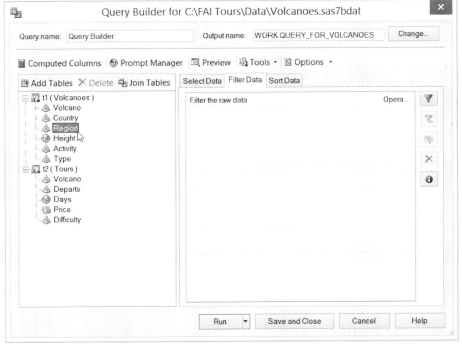

To create a filter based on the Region column, click **Region** in the list on the left, and drag it to the **Filter Data** tab.

This automatically opens the New Filter wizard with Region from the Volcanoes data table (table 1) listed as the Column. Initially, the operator is set to Equal to. For this example, we want all volcanoes in both Asia and Europe, so click the down-arrow next to **Operator** and select **In a list**.

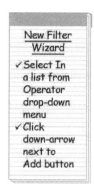

New Filter Wizard
✓ Select In a list from Operator drop-down menu
✓ Click down-arrow next to Add button

Values Box
✓ Click Get Values

Next, click the down-arrow to the right of the **Add** button to open a window where you can display all possible values for Region. Click **Get Values**.

Values Box
✓ Select As and Eu
✓ Click OK

The values for Region are coded, and the codes for Asia and Europe are As and Eu. Select both regions by clicking **As**, then holding the control (CTRL) key down and clicking **Eu**. Click **OK**.

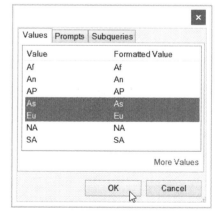

The selected values, As and Eu, will appear in the box next to Values in the New Filter wizard. Because these are character values, make sure that the **Enclose values in quotes** box located at the bottom of the window is checked.

New Filter
Wizard

✓ Click Next

Click **Next.**

> ### What if the column has a large number of unique values?
>
> Using the Get Values feature when building a filter really only makes sense if the column has a relatively small number of unique values and the data table is not too large. By default, SAS Enterprise Guide will look for unique values in the first 100,000 data rows, and will display only 250 values at one time. This increases the efficiency of the query, but may not catch all unique values in the data. For columns with large numbers of unique values, it is better to simply type the desired values in the **Values** box in the New Filter window.

The final window of the New Filter wizard shows a summary of the filter you just created.

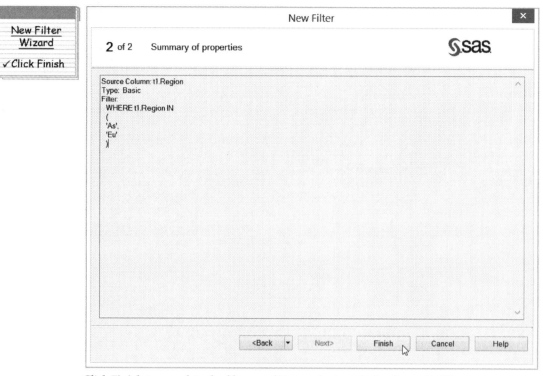

Click **Finish** to complete the filter condition and return to the Query Builder.

Now the filter appears on the Filter Data tab of the Query Builder window.

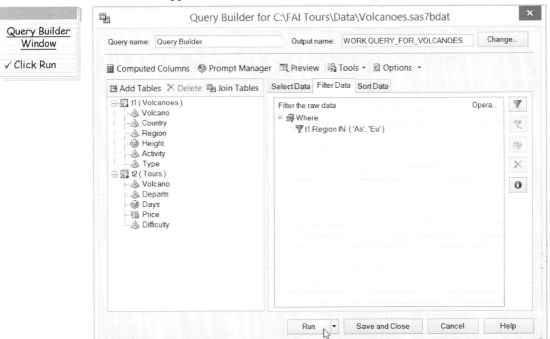

Click **Run** to see the results of this change to the query.

When SAS Enterprise Guide asks if you would like to replace the results from the previous run, click **Yes**.

Look at the resulting data table and note that only the tours of volcanoes in Asia and Europe appear in the data table.

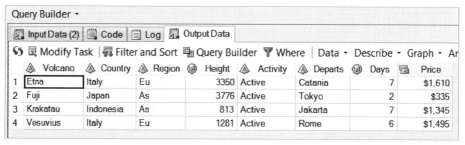

Selecting which rows to keep Suppose the Fire and Ice Tours company wants to expand the number of tours that it offers in Asia and Europe. The company wants to include in the list all the volcanoes in Asia and Europe, not just volcanoes that currently have tours. In SAS Enterprise Guide, the default action of a join is to include only the rows that appear in both tables. To change this default action, you need to change the type of join.

To reopen the query, right-click the Query Builder icon in the Project Tree or Process Flow and select **Modify Query Builder** or simply click **Modify Task** on the workspace toolbar for the query result.

Workspace
Toolbar

✓ Click Modify
Task

Query Builder
Window

✓ Click Join
Tables

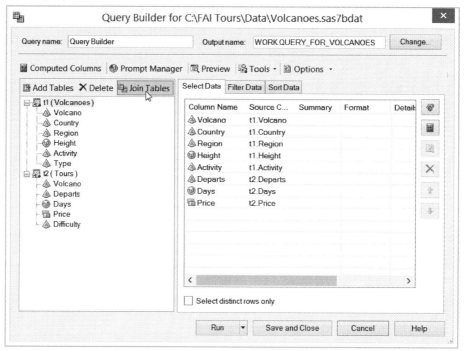

Click **Join Tables** to open the Tables and Joins window.

In the Tables and Joins window, notice the diagram  with the equal sign (=) above it on the line connecting the two tables. Right-click this join indicator and select **Properties** from the pop-up list.

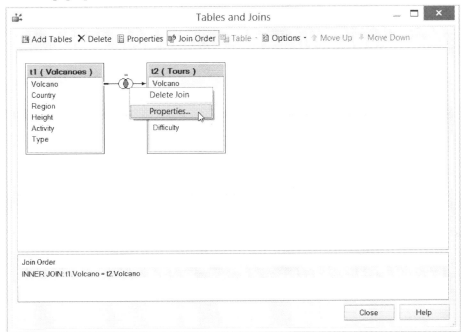

Tables and
Joins Window

✓ Right-click
join indicator

✓ Select
Properties

This opens the Join Properties window. There are several types of joins listed under Join type. Each type of join has its own diagram using overlapping circles. This diagram is called a join indicator or a Venn diagram. For the **Matching rows only given a condition (Inner Join)** type of join, only the intersection of the two circles is filled with black.

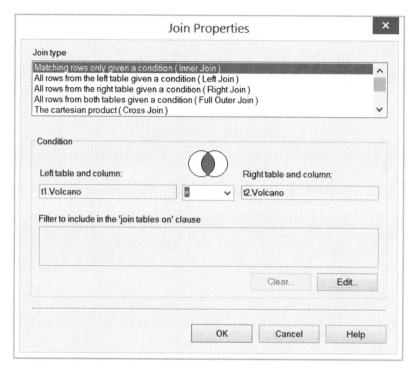

For this join, you want all the rows from each data table, even if there is no match. So, select **All rows from both tables given a condition (Full Outer Join)**.

Notice that the join symbol has changed so that now both circles are completely filled with black. Click **OK**.

Right and Left Joins

If you want all rows from one table and only the matching rows from the other, then you would choose either a Right or Left join. Which one you choose depends on the order in which the tables appear in the Tables and Joins window. This order is determined by the order of the data tables in the Project Tree or Process Flow when you first open the data tables in the Query Builder.

The join indicator in the Tables and Joins window has changed to reflect the type of join you just selected.

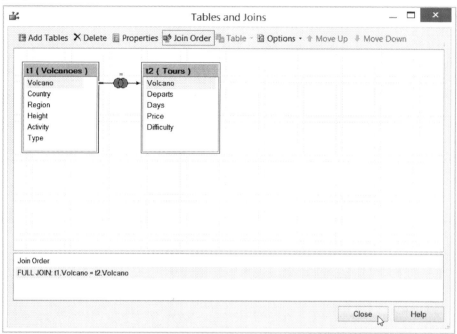

Click **Close** to return to the Query Builder window.

In the Query Builder window, click **Run** to see the results.

Click **Yes** when SAS Enterprise Guide asks if you would like to replace the previous results.

Look at the resulting data table in the workspace. Now the data include all the volcanoes in Asia and Europe, even if they don't have tours. Notice that all the columns from the Tours data table (Departs, Days, and Price) have missing values for the volcanoes for which there are no tours. Because all the volcanoes in the Tours data table also appear in the Volcanoes data table, all the columns from the Volcanoes data table have values.

Query Builder ▾

Input Data (2) | Code | Log | Output Data

↺ Modify Task | Filter and Sort | Query Builder | Where | Data ▾ | Describe ▾ | Graph ▾ | Ar

	Volcano	Country	Region	Height	Activity	Departs	Days	Price
1	Arthur's Seat	UK	Eu	251	Extinct			
2	Barren Island	India	As	354	Active			
3	Elbrus	Russia	Eu	5633	Extinct			
4	Etna	Italy	Eu	3350	Active	Catania	7	$1,610
5	Fuji	Japan	As	3776	Active	Tokyo	2	$335
6	Grimsvotn	Iceland	Eu	1725	Active			
7	Kliuchevskoi	Russia	As	4835	Active			
8	Krakatau	Indonesia	As	813	Active	Jakarta	7	$1,345
9	Pinatubo	Philippines	As	1486	Active			
10	Puy de Dome	France	Eu	1464	Extinct			
11	Santorini	Greece	Eu	367	Active			
12	Vesuvius	Italy	Eu	1281	Active	Rome	6	$1,495

Completing the tutorial To complete the tutorial, add a note describing the project. Double-click the words **Process Flow** in the Project Tree. Then select **File ▶ New ▶ Note** from the menu bar. Enter a brief description of the project in the Note window in the workspace.

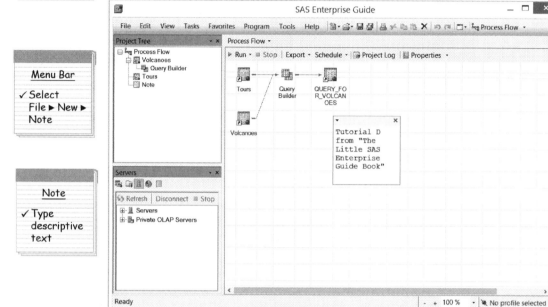

Now save the project and exit SAS Enterprise Guide. Select **File ▶ Save Project As** from the menu bar. Navigate to the location where you want to save the project, give the project the name **TutorialD**, and click **Save**. Then select **File ▶ Exit** from the menu bar to close SAS Enterprise Guide. Because the results of the query may be saved in the temporary WORK library by default, you may see the following window when exiting SAS Enterprise Guide. In this case, there is no need to save the results of the query in a permanent location since you can easily rerun the query the next time you open the project.

Click **OK**.

REFERENCE SECTION

1

"Every tradition begins as an innovation, and every innovation is built on the traditions before it."

JOE CRAVEN

From Joe Craven, award-winning multi-instrumentalist, musical archaeologist, and educator, www.joecraven.com. Reprinted by permission of the author.

CHAPTER 1

SAS Enterprise Guide Basics

1.1   SAS Enterprise Guide Windows

SAS Enterprise Guide has many windows. You can customize the appearance of SAS Enterprise Guide—closing some windows, opening others, and resizing them all—until it looks just the way you want. Then SAS Enterprise Guide will remember those settings so the next time you open it, everything will be just where you left it.

Here is SAS Enterprise Guide with its windows in their default positions.

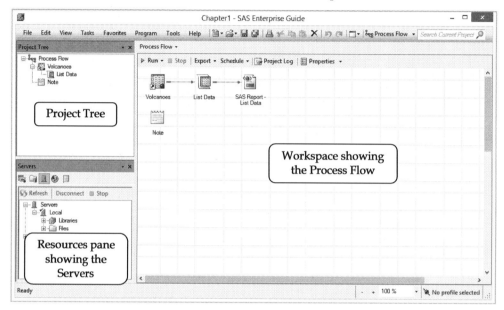

Some windows are open by default while some are closed or hidden behind other windows. You can open or unhide the major windows using the **View** menu.

Docked windows Some of the windows in SAS Enterprise Guide are docked. Most of the docked windows can appear on the left or right side of the SAS Enterprise Guide window. To change a window from one side to the other, click the down-arrow in the upper-right corner of the window and select **Dock Left** or **Dock Right** from the pop-up menu. From this menu, you can also select **Auto Hide**. If you hide a window, it will be reduced to a tab along the side. To view a hidden window, position your cursor over the window's tab. When you move the cursor out of the window, it will be reduced to a tab again. To unhide a window, click its tab or select it from the **View** menu. These windows are docked:

 Project Tree The Project Tree window displays the items in a project in a hierarchical tree diagram. This window is open by default.

 Servers The Servers window lists all available SAS servers, and the files and SAS data libraries on those servers. A SAS server is any computer on which SAS software is installed. The computer on which you run SAS Enterprise Guide may or may not be a SAS server. This window appears in the Resources pane, and is open by default.

Tasks   The Tasks window lists all available tasks. You can open a task by double-clicking its name in this window. This window appears in the Resources pane, and is closed by default. To open this window, click its icon in the Resources pane.

 SAS Folders   The SAS Folders window lists any SAS folders that have been defined on the SAS server. This window appears in the Resources pane, and is closed by default. To open this window, click its icon in the Resources pane.

 Data Exploration History   The Data Exploration History window displays a list of SAS data tables you have viewed in the Data Explorer. This window appears in the Resources pane, and is closed by default. To open this window, click its icon in the Resources pane.

 Prompt Manager   The Prompt Manager window lists any prompts defined for the current project. This window appears in the Resources pane, and is closed by default. To open this window, click its icon in the Resources pane.

 Task Status   The Task Status window displays notes about tasks that are currently running. This window is different from other docked windows because it is docked to the bottom, and you cannot move it or reduce it to a tab. This window is closed by default. To open the Task Status window, select it from the **View** menu.

Workspace   The workspace is not itself a window, but it is very important. This is where the Process Flow window and other items appear including data, results, programs, logs, and notes. The workspace is always there and cannot be closed. However, you can open and close individual items inside the workspace.

Process Flow   The Process Flow window displays the items in a project and their relationship using a schematic diagram. You can create as many process flows as you want inside a single project. There are several ways to open a process flow. You can select it from the **View** menu, double-click its name in the Project Tree, select it from the drop-down list at the top of the workspace, select the Process Flow drop-down list on the menu bar, or press **F4**.

Menus and tools   The menus and tools across the top of SAS Enterprise Guide (also called the menu bar) are always the same. However, the menus and tools inside the workspace (also called the workspace toolbar) change. For example, the options above a Process Flow are different from the options above a data table. You can also right-click many objects to open a pop-up menu for that object. So you can see that there are often several ways to do the same thing. This book cannot list all the ways to do every action, but with a little exploration you can find them.

Restoring windows   Once you have rearranged your windows, you may decide you want them back where they started. To restore them to their original locations, select **Tools ▶ Options** from the menu bar. Then in the General page of the Options window, click **Restore Window Layout**.

1.2 Projects

In SAS Enterprise Guide, all the work you do is organized into projects. A project is a collection of related data, tasks, results, programs, and notes. Projects help you by keeping track of everything, even if your data are scattered in many directories or on more than one computer. That way, when you come back to an old project six months or a year later, you won't be left wondering which data tables you used or what reports you ran.

You can have as many projects as you like, and you can use a data table over and over again in different projects, so there is a lot of flexibility. In a single SAS Enterprise Guide session, you can open only one project at a time. However, you can open more than one SAS Enterprise Guide session, each displaying a different project. Also, keep in mind that if you share a project with someone else, that person must have access to your data files and any other items you reference.

To create a new project, select **File ▶ New ▶ Project** from the menu bar. To open an existing project, select **File ▶ Open ▶ Project** and navigate to your project.

Project Tree and Process Flow The Project Tree window displays projects in a hierarchical tree diagram, while the Process Flow window displays projects using a schematic diagram. In either window, the items in your project are represented by icons, and connected to show the relationship between items. Here are examples of a Project Tree and a Process Flow showing the same project. This project contains several types of items: data, tasks, results, a program, and a note.

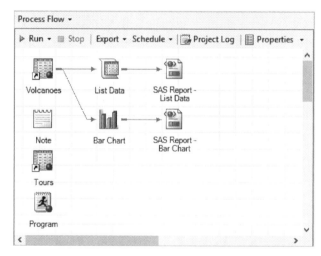

 Data Data files in a project may be SAS data tables, raw data files, or files from other databases or applications, such as Microsoft Excel spreadsheets. Projects contain shortcuts to data files, not the actual data. If you delete a project, your data files will still exist. This icon represents a SAS data table.

 Tasks Tasks are specific analyses or reports that you run, such as List Data or Bar Chart. Every time you run a task, SAS Enterprise Guide adds an icon representing that task. This icon represents the Bar Chart task.

Results Results are the reports or graphs produced by tasks you run. Results are represented by icons labeled with the type of output (SAS Report, HTML, PDF, RTF, text, PowerPoint, or Excel) and the name of the task. This icon represents output in SAS Report format.

 Notes Notes are optional text files you can use to document your work, or record comments or instructions for later use.

 Programs Programs are files that contain SAS code. You can open existing programs in SAS Enterprise Guide, or you can write new programs.

Showing properties and opening items You can display the properties for any item by right-clicking its icon in the Project Tree or Process Flow and selecting **Properties** from the pop-up menu. You can open any item by double-clicking its icon, or by right-clicking its icon and selecting **Open** from the pop-up menu.

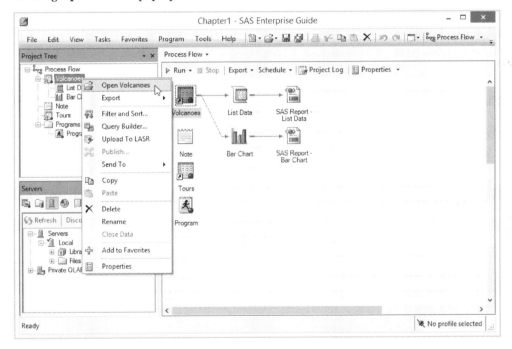

Renaming and deleting items You can rename most items by right-clicking the item and selecting **Rename** from the pop-up menu. You can delete an item from a project by right-clicking and selecting **Delete**. Note that if you delete data from a project, only the shortcut is deleted, not the actual data file.

Saving a project To save a project, select **File ▸ Save** *project-name* or **File ▸ Save** *project-name* **As** from the menu bar. Each project is saved as a single file and has a file extension of .egp. You can save data, programs, and results in separate files by right-clicking the icon for that item and selecting **Export** from the pop-up menu.

1.3 Maximizing and Splitting the Workspace

The workspace is a busy place. In addition to the process flow diagram, it is home to your data, results, program, log, and notes. By default, you can see only one of these items at a time, but you can see two if you split the workspace.

Maximizing the workspace If
your screen is small, you may want to
make the workspace as large as possible
before you split it. To do this, select **View
▶ Maximize Workspace** from the menu
bar. When you maximize the workspace,
the Project Tree and Resources pane
become tabs pinned to the edge. You can
temporarily expand those windows by
moving the cursor over a tab. When you
move the cursor away, the window will
be reduced to a tab again. To return the workspace to its
normal size, select **View ▶ Maximize Workspace** again.

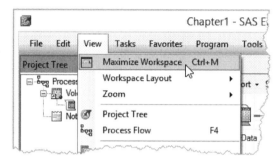

Splitting the workspace You can split the workspace into two pieces. To do this, click the

Workspace Layout icon ⬚ on the menu bar, and select either **Stacked** or **Side By Side** from the pull-down list. You can also do this by selecting **View ▶ Workspace Layout** from the menu bar.

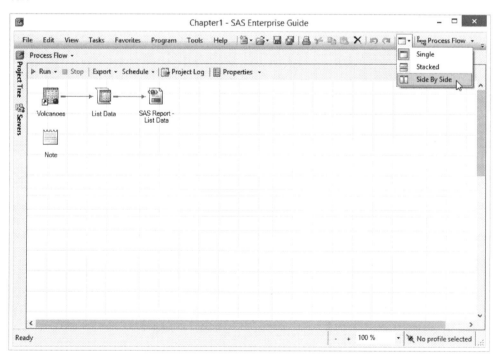

You can click the down-arrow at the top of the workspace to view a pull-down list of recently viewed items in your project. To display an item, select it from the list. In this example, the workspace has been split side by side. The left side shows a Process Flow window while the right shows a Data Grid.

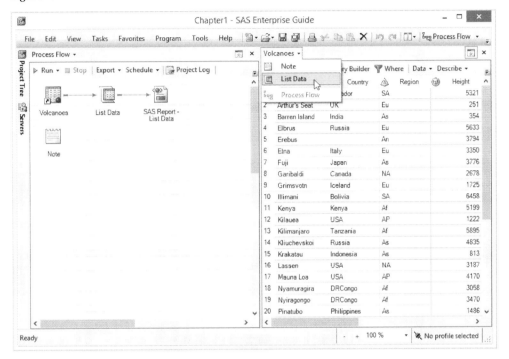

To unsplit the workspace, click the Workspace Layout icon again, and select **Single** from the pull-down list. You can also click one of the Xs in the upper-right corners to close that section of the workspace.

1.4 ▶ Managing Process Flows

SAS Enterprise Guide projects can contain an unlimited number of process flows. So, if you have a complex project, you may want to divide it into several process flows.

Adding new process flows To add a new process flow to a project, select **File ▶ New ▶ Process Flow** from the menu bar, or right-click the current process flow and select **New ▶ Process Flow** from the pop-up menu. No matter how many process flows you create, the Project Tree will show all of them in a single tree diagram.

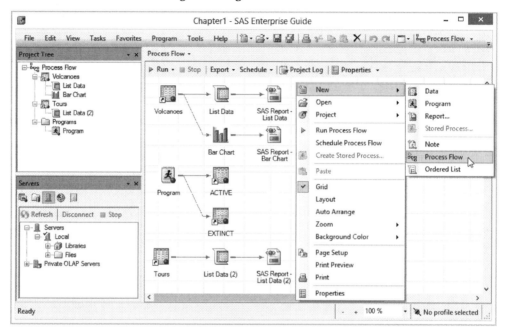

To view a process flow, double-click its name in the Project Tree, select it from the ▶▶▶ Process Flow ▾ drop-down list on the menu bar, or click the down-arrow above the workspace to open a pull-down list of recently viewed items.

Customizing process flows When you right-click a process flow, the pop-up menu displays options for customizing the appearance of that process flow. Options include Grid, Layout, Auto Arrange, Zoom, and Background Color.

Renaming and deleting process flows
When you add a new process flow, it is named Process Flow (*n*). To give a process flow a more descriptive name, right-click its name in the Project Tree and select **Rename** from the pop-up menu. To delete a process flow, right-click its name in the Project Tree and select **Delete** from the pop-up menu.

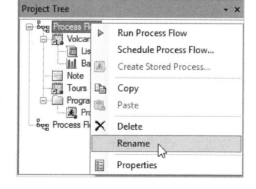

Moving and copying items To move items from one process flow to another, hold down the control key (CTRL), and click all the items you want to move. Then right-click, and select **Move to ▶** *process-flow-name* from the pop-up menu. In this example, three items are being moved to a process flow named TourReports.

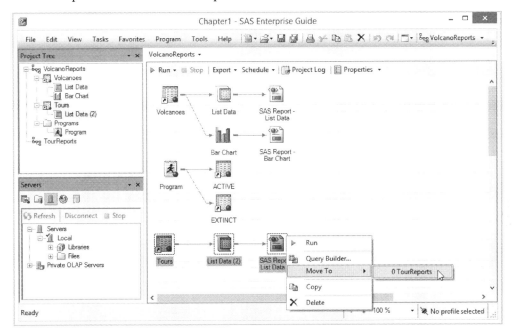

Copying items is similar to moving items except that you must also paste the items. Select the items to be copied using control-click. Then right-click the items and select **Copy** from the pop-up menu, and right-click the target process flow and select **Paste**.

Printing process flows You can print a copy of your process flow. To control the page size and orientation, click the process flow and select **File ▶ Page setup for Process Flow** from the menu bar. To preview a printout, select **File ▶ Print preview for Process Flow**. To print the process flow, select **File ▶ Print Process Flow**. Here is the Print preview window for the new process flow named TourReports.

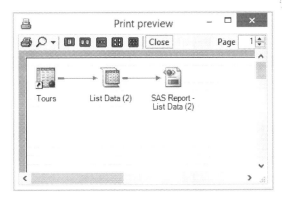

1.5 ▸ Running Projects and Process Flows

Projects have a lot of different parts. When you use a project, you may want to run the entire project, or one process flow, or a branch of a process flow, or even just one item. You can run any part of your project, but the way you do that depends on which part you want to run.

Running a project   To run a complete project, select **File ▸ Run** *project-name* from the menu bar, or click **Run** on the workspace toolbar above a Process Flow and select **Run Project** from the pull-down menu.

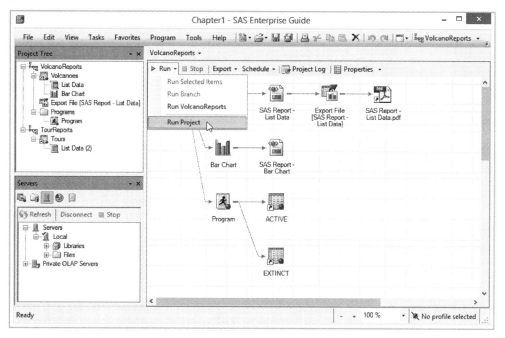

If you have more than one process flow in your project, then they will run in the order in which they appear in the Project Tree. To change that order, click the name of a process flow in the Project Tree and drag it to the place where you want it to be.

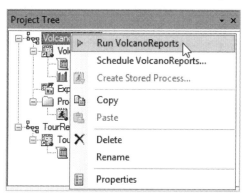

Running a process flow   To run a particular process flow, right-click the name of the process flow in the Project Tree and select **Run** *process-flow-name* from the pop-up menu, or click **Run** on the workspace toolbar above that Process Flow and select **Run** *process-flow-name* from the pull-down menu. The branches in the process flow will run from top left to bottom right. In this example, a process flow named VolcanoReports is being run from the Project Tree.

Running part of a process flow

To run one branch of a process flow or an individual item, right-click the icon for that item or branch, and select **Run** or **Run Branch from** *item-name* from the pop-up menu. You can also click that icon (to make it active) and then click **Run** on the workspace toolbar and select **Run** *item-name* or **Run Branch**

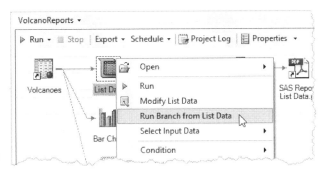

from *item-name* from the pull-down menu. In this example, a branch starting with a List Data task is being run from the process flow.

Creating an Autoexec process flow

Sometimes you have items in a project that must run first. For example, you might have an Assign Library or Create Format task that must run before anything else in your project. Dragging these items to the top left corner of your process flow will make them run first if you run the entire process flow, but that doesn't help if you run some other part of your process flow. For situations like this, you can create a special process flow called an Autoexec process flow. When SAS Enterprise Guide sees a process flow with the name Autoexec, it knows to run it whenever you open that project. To create an Autoexec process flow, simply add a new process flow as described in the preceding section, and give it the name Autoexec. Then, by default, every time you open that project, a box will open asking if you want to run the Autoexec process flow.

You can tell SAS Enterprise Guide to run the Autoexec process flow automatically without prompting you. To do that, select **Tools ▶ Options** from the menu bar to open the Options window. In the General page, check **Automatically run "Autoexec" process flow when project opens,** and click **OK.**

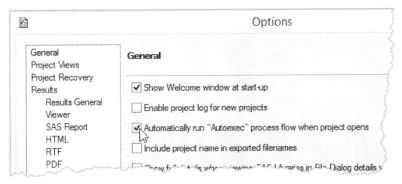

1.6 Linking Items in Process Flows

When you run a process flow, items are executed from top left to bottom right, following the branches created by links between items. If you want to change the order in which items run, you can click and drag icons to a new place in the process flow, or you can add links. For example, if you create a format that is used by a report, you might want to add a link to make sure that the task creating the format runs before the task creating the report. Adding links is also a good way to show relationships that may not be clear. Note that adding links does not change which data tables are used or how tasks are run. It only changes the order and shows relationships.

This process flow contains a program that uses the Volcanoes data table. By default, the data table and program icons are not connected. Adding a link would make the relationships between items more clear.

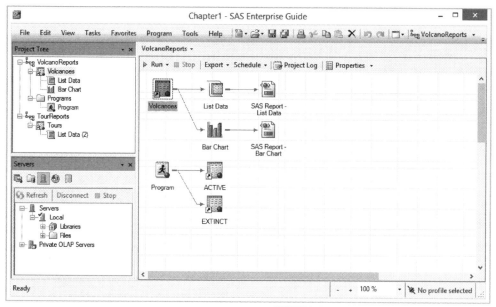

Adding links To add a link, hover your cursor to one side of the first item. When the cursor changes from a cross with four arrows ⊕ to crosshairs ┼, then you can click and drag the cursor to the second item to link them. You can also right-click the initial item and select **Link item-name to** from the pop-up menu. In this window, a link is being added from the Volcanoes data table to the Program icon.

Now the Volcanoes data icon has been linked to the program icon. If you look closely, you will see that the new link uses a dashed line instead of a solid line.

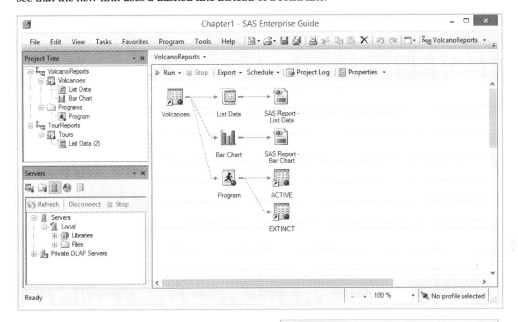

Deleting links To delete a link that you previously added, right-click the dashed line of the link and select **Delete** from the pop-up menu. A Delete Items window will open asking you to confirm whether you want to delete the link.

1.7 SAS Data Tables

SAS Enterprise Guide can read and write many kinds of data files (see Chapter 2 for more on this topic), but for most purposes, you will want to have your data in a special form called a SAS data table. When you open a SAS data table, it is displayed in the workspace in a Data Grid. The following Data Grid shows the Tours data table that was created in Tutorial A. A new tour has been added for the volcano Lassen.

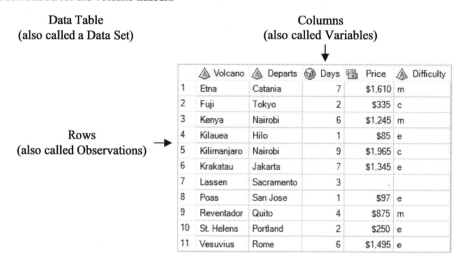

Data Table
(also called a Data Set)

Columns
(also called Variables)

Rows
(also called Observations)

Terminology In SAS Enterprise Guide, rows are also called observations, columns are also called variables, and data tables are also called data sets. SAS Enterprise Guide uses all these terms. Some tasks use the term columns and others refer to variables, depending on the context.

Data types and data groups In SAS Enterprise Guide, there are two basic types of data: numeric and character. Numeric data are divided into four data groups: numeric, currency, time, and date. For each of these, SAS Enterprise Guide has special tools including functions for manipulating that type of data, and formats for displaying that type of data. SAS Enterprise Guide uses a different icon to identify each kind of data.

 Character data may contain numerals, letters, or special characters (such as $ and !) and can be up to 32,767 characters long. Character data are represented by a red pyramid with the letter A on it.

 Currency data are numeric values for money and are represented by a picture of banknotes.

 Date data are numeric values equal to the number of days since January 1, 1960. The table below lists four dates, and their corresponding SAS date and formatted values:

Date	SAS date value	MMDDYY10. formatted value
January 1, 1959	-365	01/01/1959
January 1, 1960	0	01/01/1960
January 1, 1961	366	01/01/1961
January 1, 2020	21915	01/01/2020

You will rarely see unformatted SAS date values in SAS Enterprise Guide. However, because dates are numeric, you can use them in arithmetic expressions to find, for example, the number of days between two dates. Datetime values are included in this data group, and are the number of seconds since January 1, 1960. Date data are represented by a picture of a calendar.

 Time data are numeric values equal to the number of seconds since midnight. Time data are represented by a picture of a clock.

 Other numeric data, that are not dates, times, or currency, are simply called numeric. They may contain only numerals, decimal places (.), plus signs (+), minus signs (-), and E for scientific notation. Numeric data are represented by a blue ball with the numbers 1, 2, and 3 on it.

Numeric versus character If the values of a column contain letters or special characters, they must be character data. However, if the values contain only numerals, then they may be either numeric or character. You should base your decision on how you will use the data. Sometimes data that consist solely of numerals make more sense as character data than as numeric. Zip codes, for example, are made up of numerals, but it just doesn't make sense to add or subtract zip codes. Such values work better as character data.

Names By default, the names of data tables and columns in SAS Enterprise Guide may be up to 32 characters in length, and can contain any character, including blanks. Table names cannot start with a blank or period.

Moving data between SAS Enterprise Guide and Base SAS Any data created in SAS Enterprise Guide can be used in Base SAS, but the default rules for names are different. Base SAS uses the VALIDMEMNAME=COMPATIBLE SAS system option for tables and VALIDVARNAME=V7 for columns. SAS Enterprise Guide uses VALIDMEMNAME=EXTEND for tables, and VALIDVARNAME=ANY for columns. For the sake of compatibility, you may want to follow these rules: choose names that are 32 characters or fewer in length, start with a letter or underscore, and contain only letters, numerals, and underscores.

To tell SAS Enterprise Guide to use the same rules for names as Base SAS, select **Tools ▶ Options** from the menu bar to open the Options window, and select **Data General** in the selection pane on the left. In the section labeled **Naming Options**, click the down-arrow for **Valid variable names**, and select **Basic variable names (V7)**. Then click the down-arrow for **Valid member names**, and select **Basic member names (COMPATIBLE)**.

Missing data Sometimes, despite your best efforts, your data may be incomplete. The data values in a particular column may be missing for some rows. In those cases, missing character data are represented by blanks, and missing numeric data are represented by a single period (.). In the preceding Data Grid, the value of Price is missing for the tour of Lassen, and its place is marked by a period. The value of Difficulty is missing for the same tour and is left blank.

Documentation stored in SAS data tables In addition to your actual data, SAS data tables contain information about the data table, such as its name, the date that you created it, and the version of SAS that you used to create it. SAS also stores information about each column in the data table, including its name, type, and length. This information is called the descriptor portion of the data table, and it makes SAS data tables self-documenting. This information is what you see in the Properties windows for data tables and columns. These Properties windows are described in more detail in the next two sections.

1.8 Viewing Properties of Data Tables and Columns

The Properties window for a data table displays general information about the data table, such as the date the table was created, along with information about each column in the table. You cannot make any changes in this window, but it is a handy way to find out more about your data.

Opening the Properties window To display information about a data table, first open it in a Data Grid by double-clicking the data icon in the Project Tree or Process Flow. Then click the Properties icon ▦ on the workspace toolbar to open the table Properties window. In this example, the Properties window is being opened for the Volcanoes data table.

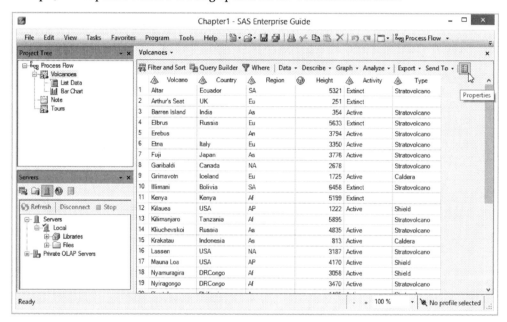

You can also right-click a data icon in the Project Tree or Process Flow, and select Properties from the pop-up menu.

General page When the table Properties window opens, it displays the General page. The General page lists basic information about the table: its name, when it was created and last modified, and whether it is a SAS data table or some other type of file.

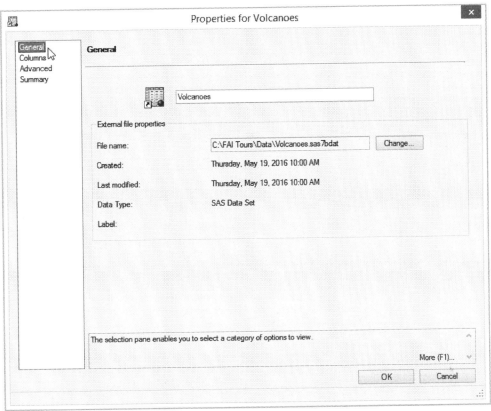

Columns page If you click **Columns** in the selection pane on the left, the Columns page will open. Here, SAS Enterprise Guide displays information about each column: its name, type, length, format, informat, and label. You cannot change the properties of columns in the Properties window for a data table. To make changes, use the Properties window for an individual column as described in the next section.

Properties for Volcanoes

Columns

General
Columns
Advanced
Summary

Name	Type	Length	Format	Informat	Label
Volcano	Character	13			
Country	Character	13			
Region	Character	8			
Height	Numeric	8			
Activity	Character	10			
Type	Character	15			

1.9 ▸ Changing Properties of Columns

The column Properties window displays properties for an individual column. You can use this window inside a task to change labels and display formats, but those changes will apply only to the results of that task rather than to the original data table. However, if you open the column Properties window inside a Data Grid, then any changes you make will be saved with the data table.

Setting the update mode   The Data Grid opens in read-only mode. In this mode you cannot edit the data, and you cannot change column properties. To switch to update mode, select **Edit ▸ Protect Data** from the menu bar. This toggles the data table from read-only to update mode. To return to read-only mode, select **Edit ▸ Protect Data** again.

Opening the Properties window   To open the column Properties window, right-click the header of a column and select **Properties** from the pop-up menu. In this Data Grid, Properties is being selected for the column Height.

General page   The Properties window has several pages. If there is no selection pane on the left, then the data table is in read-only mode and you need to switch to update mode.

The General page displays basic information for the column: its name, label, type, group, and length. You can change any of these properties. In this example, the column name has been changed to **HeightMeters**, and the label to **Height in Meters**. This column is **numeric** and has a length of **8**.

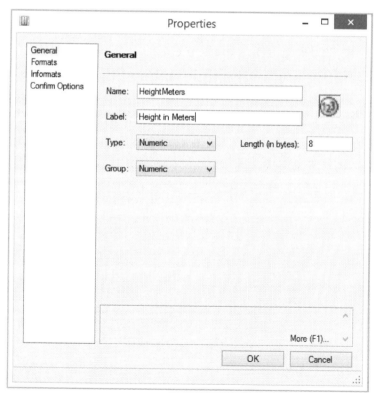

Formats page Click **Formats** in the selection pane on the left to open the Formats page. Formats (also called display formats) tell SAS Enterprise Guide how data should look in Data Grids or reports. There are different formats for character, numeric, date, time, and currency data. In this example, the format **COMMA***w.d* with a width of **6** and no decimal places (COMMA6.0) has been selected. See the next section for a table of commonly used formats. To apply your changes, click **OK**.

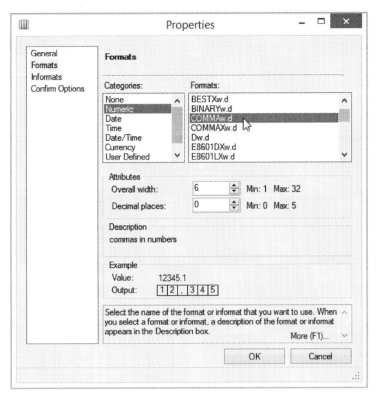

Informats page If you click **Informats** in the selection pane on the left, the Informats page will open (not shown). Informats (also called input formats or read-in formats) tell SAS how to interpret input data. In SAS Enterprise Guide, you can use informats when you import certain types of data files, and when you write SAS programs. However, informats are not used when you type data values into a Data Grid. Instead, the Data Grid uses the data type and data group that you specify to determine how to interpret any data values you enter. So, informats are rarely used in SAS Enterprise Guide.

	Volcano	Country	Region	HeightMeters	Activity	Type
1	Altar	Ecuador	SA	5,321	Extinct	Stratovolcano
2	Arthur's Seat	UK	Eu	251	Extinct	
3	Barren Island	India	As	354	Active	Stratovolcano
4	Elbrus	Russia	Eu	5,633	Extinct	Stratovolcano
5	Erebus		An	3,794	Active	Stratovolcano
6	Etna	Italy	Eu	3,350	Active	Stratovolcano

Results Here is the Data Grid showing the new name, HeightMeters, and the formatted data values with commas.

1.10 Selected Standard Formats

SAS formats (also called display formats) tell SAS Enterprise Guide how to display or print data. You can apply formats in a column Properties window in a Data Grid, a task, or a query. Here are a few of the many formats that are available in SAS Enterprise Guide.

Format	Definition	Width range	Default width
Character			
$UPCASE*w*.	Converts character data to uppercase	1–32767	Length of column or 8
$*w*.	Writes standard character data—default for character data	1–32767	Length of column or 1
Date, Time, and Datetime[1]			
DATE*w*.	Writes SAS date values in the form *ddmonyy* or *ddmonyyyy*	5–11	7
DATETIME*w.d*	Writes SAS datetime values in the form *ddmmmyy:hh:mm:ss.ss*	7–40	16
DTDATE*w*.	Writes SAS datetime values in the form *ddmonyy* or *ddmonyyyy*	5–9	7
EURDFDD*w*.	Writes SAS date values in the form *dd.mm.yy* or *dd.mm.yyyy*	2–10	8
JULIAN*w*.	Writes SAS date values in the Julian date form *yyddd* or *yyyyddd*	5–7	5
MMDDYY*w*.	Writes SAS date values in the form *mm/dd/yy* or *mm/dd/yyyy*—default for dates	2–10	8
TIME*w.d*	Writes SAS time values in the form *hh:mm:ss.ss*—default for times	2–20	8
WEEKDATE*w*.	Writes SAS date values in the form *day-of-week, month-name dd, yy* or *yyyy*	3–37	29
WORDDATE*w*.	Writes SAS date values in the form *month-name dd, yyyy*	3–32	18
Numeric			
BEST*w*.	The SAS System chooses the best format—default format for numeric data	1–32	12
COMMA*w.d*	Writes numbers with commas	2–32	6
DOLLAR*w.d*	Writes numbers with a leading $ and commas separating every three digits—default for currency	2–32	6
E*w*.	Writes numbers in scientific notation	7–32	12
EUROX*w.d*	Writes numbers with a leading € and periods separating every three digits	2–32	6
PERCENT*w.d*	Writes proportions as percentages	4–32	6
w.d	Writes standard numeric data	1–32	none

[1] SAS date values are the number of days since January 1, 1960. Time values are the number of seconds past midnight, and datetime values are the number of seconds past midnight on January 1, 1960.

The examples below show unformatted data values and formatted results for each display format.

Format	Data value	Results	Data value	Results
Character				
$UPCASE10. $6.	Lassen Lassen	LASSEN Lassen	St. Helens St. Helens	ST. HELENS St. He
Date, Time, and Datetime				
DATE9.	366	01JAN1961	396	31JAN1961
DATETIME16.	37800	01JAN60:10:30	2629800	31JAN60:10:30
DTDATE9.	37800	01JAN1960	2629800	31JAN1960
EURDFDD10.	366	01.01.1961	396	31.01.1961
JULIAN7.	366	1961001	396	1961031
MMDDYY10.	366	01/01/1961	396	01/31/1961
TIME8.	37800	10:30:00	37815	10:30:15
WEEKDATE15.	366	Sun, Jan 1, 61	396	Tue, Jan 31, 61
WORDDATE12.	366	Jan 1, 1961	396	Jan 31, 1961
Numeric				
BEST10.	1000001	1000001	-12.34	-12.34
BEST6.	1000001	1E6	100001	100001
COMMA12.2	1000001	1,000,001.00	-12.34	-12.34
DOLLAR13.2	1000001	$1,000,001.00	-12.34	$-12.34
E10.	1000001	1.000E+06	-12.34	-1.234E+01
EUROX13.2	1000001	€1.000.001,00	-12.34	€-12,34
PERCENT9.2	0.05	5.00%	-1.20	(120.00%)
10.2	1000001	1000001.00	-12.34	-12.34

1.11 Documenting Projects with Notes

In many ways, projects in SAS Enterprise Guide are self-documenting. You can look at the Project Tree and Process Flow and see the parts of a project and how they fit together. However, unless your project is very simple, it is good practice to document your work. You do this with notes.

Adding a note for a process flow To add a note for an entire process flow, right-click the process flow background and select **New ▶ Note** from the pop-up menu. You can also add a note for a process flow by clicking the name of the process flow in the Project Tree, and selecting **File ▶ New ▶ Note** from the menu bar. A small text box, which looks like a sticky note, will open.

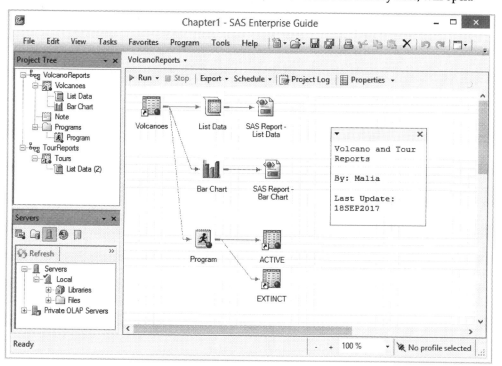

In this text box, you can type anything you want. You could type your favorite cookie recipe, but generally it makes more sense to record information about your work such as the purpose of the project and the date it was last updated. If you need more space, you can resize the text box by clicking and dragging the edges. If you click the down-arrow at the top of the text box and select **Open** from the pop-up menu, then this small text box will open in a Note window.

The Note window fills the workspace giving you more room to type. This example contains a brief description of the project.

To close the Note window, click the X in the upper-right corner. If you click the X in the upper-right corner of the small text box, it will close and a note icon 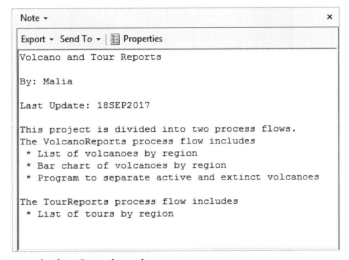 will appear in your process flow. To reopen the small text box, right-click the note icon and select **Expand** from the pop-up menu. To reopen the Note window, right-click the icon and select **Open** from the pop-up menu.

Attaching a note to an item   You can also attach notes to individual items in a process flow. To do this, click that item and select **File ▶ New ▶ Note** from the menu bar. A Note window will open. This process flow includes three notes: one for the entire process flow, one attached to a Bar Chart task, and one attached to a data table named Active. Notice that the note icon for the process flow is not linked to any other icons, but the note icons for the task and program are linked to their items.

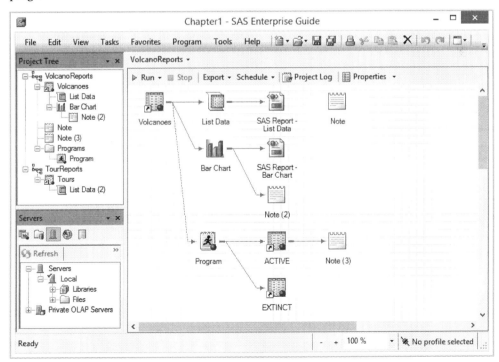

2

" There is no knowledge that is not power. "

RALPH WALDO EMERSON

From the essay "Old Age" in *The Atlantic*, 1862.

CHAPTER 2

Bringing Data into a Project

2.1 Sources of Data

Before you can analyze your data, before you can run a report, before you can do anything with your data, SAS Enterprise Guide must be able to read your data. Your data might be in a data warehouse on a mainframe, or on a piece of paper sitting on your desk. Whatever form your data take, there is a way to get your data into SAS Enterprise Guide.

 New SAS data tables If you have a small amount of data, or if you've collected the data yourself, then you may find that the easiest way to get your data into SAS Enterprise Guide is to type the data directly into a Data Grid. To do this, just open an empty Data Grid, set the properties for the columns, and enter your data. SAS Enterprise Guide makes a SAS data table (also called a SAS data set) from the data you type into a Data Grid. Sections 2.4 to 2.6 describe Data Grids in more detail.

 Existing SAS data tables You may have SAS data tables that were created in SAS or in another project in SAS Enterprise Guide. To open a SAS data table in SAS Enterprise Guide, select **File ▶ Open ▶ Data** from the menu bar. In the Open Data window, navigate to the location of the SAS data table. Once you have found the data table you want, click **Open**. SAS Enterprise Guide will immediately add the SAS data table to your project and display it in a Data Grid.

 Raw data files Raw data files are files that contain no special formatting. They are sometimes called text, ASCII, sequential, or flat files and can be viewed using a simple text editor, such as Microsoft Notepad. SAS data tables and Microsoft Excel files are not raw data files. If you open a spreadsheet or SAS data table in Microsoft Notepad, you'll see lots of strange characters that Microsoft Notepad simply can't interpret.

SAS Enterprise Guide can import just about any type of raw data file including delimited data files and fixed-column data files. In delimited data files, a delimiter separates the data values. CSV (comma-separated values) files use commas as delimiters. Other files may use a different delimiter such as a tab, semicolon, or space. Fixed-column data files are similar to delimited data files, but instead of having a delimiter separating the data values, the data values are lined up in tidy vertical columns. Importing raw data files is described in more detail in sections 2.8 and 2.9.

Other software files SAS Enterprise Guide can import files produced by many other types of software. When you install SAS Enterprise Guide, you get everything you need to import most PC data files. You do not need to install any additional software to import data in these formats:

- HTML files

- Microsoft Access files

- Microsoft Excel files

However, if you have large PC data files, you may be able to improve performance by using SAS/ACCESS software. To import files this way, you must have SAS/ACCESS (either SAS/ACCESS Interface to PC Files or SAS/ACCESS Interface to ODBC, depending on the type of data files you are reading), and it must be installed on the SAS server that SAS Enterprise Guide is using. Then you select the option **Import the data using SAS/ACCESS Interface to PC Files whenever possible** in the Advanced Options page of the Import wizard. Section 2.7 shows an example of importing a Microsoft Excel file.

 If you have SAS/ACCESS Interface to PC Files software, you can also import data in these formats:

- JMP files

- SPSS save files in Microsoft Windows format (with a .sav extension)

- Stata files in Microsoft Windows format (with a .dta extension)

To import these files, select **Tasks ▶ Data ▶ Import** *data-type* **file** from the menu bar.

SAS Enterprise Guide can read many other kinds of database files, including Oracle and DB2. To read these other database files, you must have the corresponding SAS/ACCESS product (such as SAS/ACCESS Interface to Oracle or SAS/ACCESS Interface to DB2) installed on the SAS server that SAS Enterprise Guide is using. Then you define a SAS data library on that computer using the corresponding SAS/ACCESS engine. The SAS data library tells SAS Enterprise Guide where to find the data file and how to read it.

2.2 Locations for Data

Before you can use a data file, you must tell SAS Enterprise Guide where to find it. For any particular file, there may be several ways to do this.

Servers window Most types of files can be brought into a project using the Servers window. This window appears in the Resources pane. To view the Servers window, select **View ▶ Servers** from the menu bar, or click the

Servers icon in the Resources pane.

A SAS server is any computer running SAS software. The Servers window lists all the SAS servers that are available to you, and the files and SAS data libraries on those servers. To see more detail for any part of the list (such as **Libraries** or **Files**) click the plus signs (+).

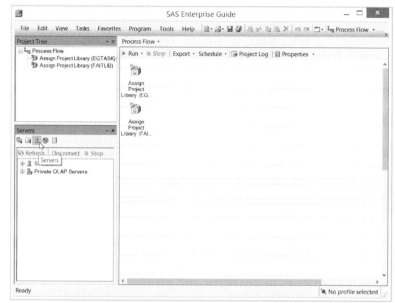

Libraries A SAS data library is a set of SAS files residing in a particular location. Instead of referring to the location by its full path, you identify it by a short name, called a libref. Here are some libraries that you are likely to see:

EGTASK is a special library. If a library with this name has been defined on your system, then SAS Enterprise Guide will use it as the default for output data tables. Data tables saved in EGTASK are permanent, which means that they will not be erased when you exit SAS Enterprise Guide.

WORK is a special library for temporary data tables. The WORK library is erased when you exit SAS Enterprise Guide. WORK is the default library for output data tables if you do not have an EGTASK library defined.

SASUSER is permanent on most systems, so your data tables in this library will not be erased by SAS Enterprise Guide. However, on z/OS and some UNIX systems, SASUSER may be temporary. In some environments, SASUSER may be read-only. If you have more than one SAS server, then you may have a SASUSER library on each server.

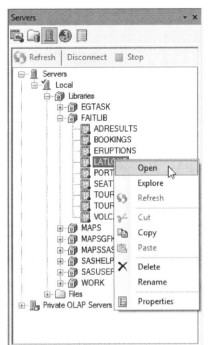

You may have other libraries that have been defined for your use. This Servers window shows that a library named FAITLIB has been defined.

If you want to define your own libraries, there are several ways to do that. These include using the Assign Project Library wizard (see the next section), and submitting a LIBNAME statement from a Program window.

To view the data tables in a SAS data library, click the plus sign (+) next to the library's name. You can add a data table to your project by clicking its name and dragging it into the Process Flow, or by right-clicking its name and selecting **Open** from the pop-up menu. In this window, the Latlong data table is being added to the project.

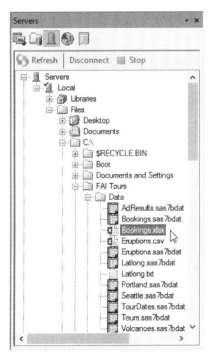

Files If you click **Files** in the Servers window, SAS Enterprise Guide will list your folders or directories on that SAS server. From there, you can navigate through the server's directory system to find the file you want. These files may be SAS data tables or other types of files such as Excel spreadsheets. The file extension for a standard SAS data table in Windows is .sas7bdat.

You can add a file to your project by clicking its name and dragging it into the Process Flow, or by right-clicking its name and selecting **Open** from the pop-up menu.

Notice that in this example, the SAS data tables in the library FAITLIB are also listed under Files. That is because the FAITLIB data library points to that Windows subdirectory.

Other ways to bring data into a project Most types of data files can be brought into a project by selecting either **File ▶ Open ▶ Data**, or **File ▶ Import Data** from the menu bar. For some types of files, opening the data produces the same result as importing it. For other types of files, importing produces a different result. See sections 2.7 to 2.9 for more information about importing Microsoft Excel and raw data files.

2.3 Assigning Project Libraries

A SAS data library is a set of SAS files stored in a particular location. You use SAS data libraries to tell SAS Enterprise Guide where to find existing data tables, and where to save new ones. This section describes how to define SAS data libraries using the Assign Project Library wizard.

Assign Project Library wizard To define a project library, select **Tools ▸ Assign Project Library** from the menu bar. The Assign Project Library wizard will open.

In the first window, type a name for your new library. The library name cannot be longer than eight characters; must start with a letter or underscore; and can contain only letters, numerals, and underscores. This name is called a libref, and it is like a nickname for the location of your library. Next select the server where your data are stored. In this example, a library named FAITLIB is being created, and it will reside on the Local server. Click **Next** when you are done.

In the second window, you specify the engine and path. The SAS data engine determines the type of data that will reside in this library. Click the down-arrow on the box labeled **Engine type** to select the general type of engine, and then click the down-arrow on the box labeled **Engine** to select the engine. Depending on the engine type you choose, other options may appear in the lower portion of the window. For ordinary SAS data tables, use an engine type of **File System**, and the **BASE** engine. In the box labeled **Path**, type the path for your library, or click the **Browse** button to navigate to the location of your data. Click **Next** when you are done.

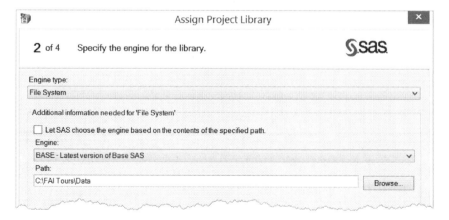

In the third window (not shown), you can specify options for your library.

In the fourth window, you can test your new library by clicking **Test Library**. Click **Finish** to close the wizard and create your library.

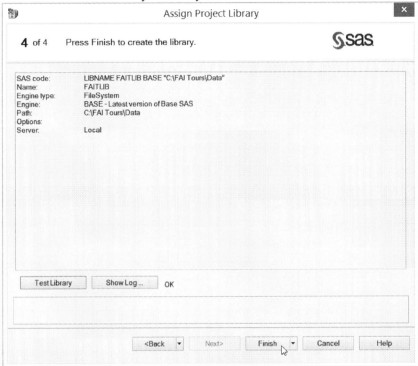

An Assign Project Library icon  will be added to your Project Tree and Process Flow window. However, the new project library may not automatically appear in the Servers window. If not, then click the server (such as Local), and click **Refresh**.

Reassigning a Project Library When you open a SAS Enterprise Guide project, project libraries defined in previous SAS Enterprise Guide sessions are not automatically reassigned. You can reassign a project library by right-clicking the Assign Project Library icon in the Project Tree or Process Flow and selecting **Run** from the pop-up menu, or by clicking its icon and selecting **Run ▶ Run Assign Project Library** on the workspace toolbar above the Process Flow. You can also rerun your entire process flow. Just be sure that your Assign Project Library icons appear before any tasks that use those libraries. Since process flows run from top left to bottom right, you may want to move any Assign Project Library icons to the upper-left corner. Alternatively, you could move your Assign Project Library icon to an Autoexec process flow. That way it will run everytime you open your project. Section 1.5 describes how to create an Autoexec process flow.

2.4 ▶ Creating New SAS Data Tables

To create an empty SAS data table, select **File ▶ New ▶ Data** from the menu bar. This opens the New Data wizard, which has two windows.

Name and location In the first window of the New Data wizard, type a name for your new data table in the **Name** box. Next choose a location where the new data table will be stored. This location must be a SAS data library. If a suitable library is not listed, then cancel the New Data wizard and define a new library (see section 2.3) before starting over. In this example, the name Seattleflights has been typed in the Name

box and the FAITLIB library has been selected. When you are satisfied, click **Next**.

Column properties In the second window of the New Data wizard, specify the properties for each column in your new data table. At first the columns are named A, B, C, and so on. To display the properties of a particular column, click its name in the list on the left under the heading **Columns**. To change a column property, click its value in the list on the right under the heading **Column Properties**. You can type a name for the column and an optional label. Then specify the data type and data group by clicking the word **Type** or **Group** and selecting from the

pull-down list. In the Seattleflights data table, the fourth column has the name FlightPrice, a label of Flight Price USD, a data type of Numeric, a data group of Currency, and a length of 8. The default length of 8 for numeric columns works for all numbers, but the length for character columns needs to be at least as long as the longest text string for the column.

To change a display format (also called a format), click its value under Column Properties. The ellipsis button will appear ⌶. Click the ellipsis button to open a Display Formats window.

The Display Formats window shown here is for the format for FlightPrice. The format is set to DOLLAR*w.d* with a width of 10 and 2 decimal places (DOLLAR10.2). See section 1.10 for a table of commonly used formats. When you are satisfied, click **OK** to return to the second window of the New Data wizard.

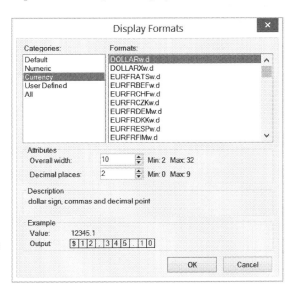

You can also open a window for the read-in format (also called an informat), and any informats you specify will be saved with the column properties. However, in SAS Enterprise Guide, Data Grids do not use informats to interpret input data. Instead, Data Grids use the data type and data group that you specify to determine how to interpret any data values you enter.

In the second window of the New Data wizard, you can add more columns by clicking **New**. You can delete columns by clicking the name of that column and then clicking the delete button ⌷. When you are satisfied with your columns and their properties, click **Finish** to close the wizard and create an empty data table.

Entering data Once you have created the data table, you can begin typing data into it. Any value you enter must fit the data type and data group you specified. You can copy and paste values. To move the cursor, click a cell, or use the tab and arrow keys. Here is the Seattleflights data table with column attributes defined, and three rows of data entered. Notice how the values for FlightPrice are typed in as plain numbers, but after entering they are displayed using the DOLLAR10.2 format.

	Origin	Destination	FlightNo	FlightPrice
1	Seattle	Catania	BA48	$1,853.00
2	Seattle	Hilo	HA21	$677.00
3	Seattle	Jakarta	AA119	1331
4				.
5				.
6				.
7				.
8				.
9				.
10				.
11				.
12				.

See Tutorial A for a more detailed example of creating a new SAS data table.

2.5 Editing SAS Data Tables in a Data Grid

Editing SAS data tables is easy—whether you need to add new rows or columns, fix errors, or update values—but there are a few points to keep in mind.

Copying a SAS data table When you edit a SAS data table in a Data Grid, any changes that you make are permanent, even if you don't save the project. Therefore, unless you are absolutely sure about the changes you make, you should make a copy of the data table before editing. To make a copy, right-click the data icon in the Project Tree or Process Flow window and select **Export ▶ Export *table-name*** from the pop-up menu. Choose a location for the new data table and give it a name. Or, open the table in a Data Grid, and select **Export ▶ Export *table-name*** from the workspace toolbar. When you export a data table, your new copy does not appear in your project, so after you export the data table, you must open it in your project.

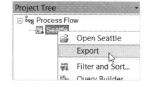

Setting the update mode Unless you are creating a new SAS data table, any data tables that you open in SAS Enterprise Guide will initially be set to read-only mode. This prevents you from accidentally changing the data. To edit SAS data tables, you must change to update mode. Open the table, then select **Edit ▶ Protect Data** from the menu bar. To switch back to read-only mode, select **Edit ▶ Protect Data** again.

Editing data values To change a value in a Data Grid, simply click the cell and start typing. You can also copy and paste values. In SAS Enterprise Guide, the Data Grid does not use informats to interpret input data. Instead, data values you enter will be interpreted based on the data type and data group for that column. After you enter a value, it will be displayed using the format for that column. If you are not sure which data type, data group, and format a column uses, you can find out by displaying the column properties. To do this, right-click the column header in the Data Grid, and select **Properties** from the pop-up menu.

Adding or removing a column To add a column to a data table, right-click a column header next to the place where you want to add a column, and select **Insert Column** from the pop-up menu. The Insert window will open.

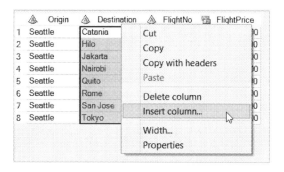

In the General page of the Insert window, indicate whether you want the new column to be inserted to the left or to the right. Then type a name and optional label for the column, and select the length, data type, and group. If you click **Formats** or **Informats** in the selection pane on the left, then you can specify display or read-in formats for the new column.

In this example, the column will be named FlightDate, and will have a label of Date of Departure. Its type will be Numeric with the default length of 8. It will be in the Date group, and will use the MMDDYY10. format which is the default for dates.

To delete a column, right-click the column you want to delete in the Data Grid and select **Delete column** from the pop-up menu.

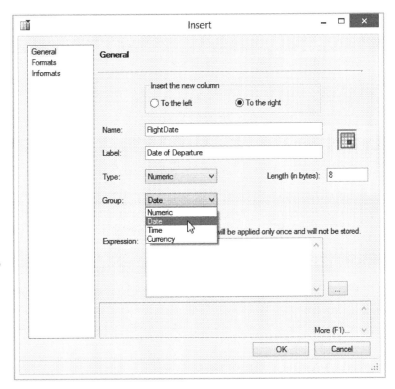

Adding or removing rows

To add rows to a data table, right-click the row number at the point where you want to add rows, and select **Insert rows** from the pop-up menu. The Insert Rows window will open (not shown). Specify the number of rows you want to insert, and whether you want them to be inserted above or below. Then click **OK**.

You can also right-click a row and select **Append a row** to add a row at the bottom of the table. To delete rows, click the row you want to delete (or use shift-click to select more than one row). Then right-click, and select **Delete rows**.

In this data table, a new row has been added for a flight to Athens, and a new column has been added for FlightDate.

2.6 Inserting Computed Columns in a Data Grid

In addition to entering and editing data, the Data Grid also allows you to compute new columns based on the value of existing columns. For example, if a teacher had scores for five exams, she could add a new column that would equal the mean of all the scores.

When you add a computed column to a data table, all the same caveats apply as when editing data tables. You'll probably want to save a copy of your table before making changes, and you must switch to update mode. For a discussion of these topics, see the previous section.

The Fire and Ice Tours company hopes to increase sales by offering a ten percent discount off the price of tours. To compute the new prices, insert a new column.

Inserting the column To add a computed column to a data table, you start the same way you would to insert an empty column. First right-click a column header next to the place where you want to add a column, and select **Insert Column** from the pop-up menu. The Insert window will open.

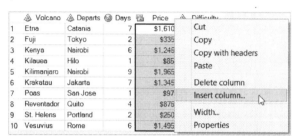

In the General page of the Insert window, indicate whether you want the new column to be inserted to the left or to the right. Then type a name and optional label for the column, and select the length, data type, and group. In this example, the new column will have the name FallPromo, label Tour Price with 10% Discount, type Numeric, group Currency, and length 8.

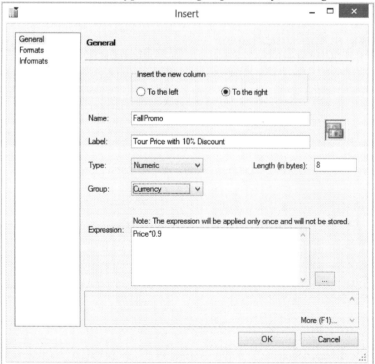

If you want to specify the display or read-in format, click **Formats** or **Informats** in the selection pane on the left. This example uses the default format and informat.

At the bottom of the Insert window is a box labeled **Expression**. You can type an expression in this box and SAS Enterprise Guide will use that expression to compute the values of the new column. In this example, you can see that the expression **Price * 0.9** has been entered so the values of the new column will equal the value of the Price column multiplied by 0.9. When you are satisfied, click **OK**, and the new column will be added to the Data Grid.

Here is the Data Grid showing the new column FallPromo.

	Volcano	Departs	Days	Price	FallPromo	Difficulty
1	Etna	Catania	7	$1,610	$1,449	m
2	Fuji	Tokyo	2	$335	$302	c
3	Kenya	Nairobi	6	$1,245	$1,121	m
4	Kilauea	Hilo	1	$85	$77	e
5	Kilimanjaro	Nairobi	9	$1,965	$1,769	c
6	Krakatau	Jakarta	7	$1,345	$1,211	e
7	Poas	San Jose	1	$97	$87	e
8	Reventador	Quito	4	$875	$788	m
9	St. Helens	Portland	2	$250	$225	e
10	Vesuvius	Rome	6	$1,495	$1,346	e

Building the expression In this example, the expression was simple so it was easy to type it in the Expression box. However, if the syntax of your expression were more complicated, you might want some help. To get help building your expression, click the ellipsis button [...] next to the box labeled **Expression** in the Insert window. The Advanced Expression Builder will open.

At the top of the Advanced Expression Builder is a box labeled **Enter an expression**. You can type in this box, or you can use the buttons and lists below to construct an expression.

The Advanced Expression Builder is similar to the expression builder that is available in the Query Builder. See Tutorial C or sections 5.3 and 5.4 for examples of building expressions.

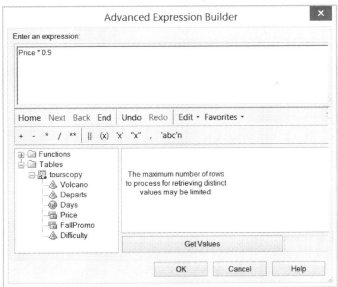

Computing columns in a Data Grid versus in a query You can add a computed column to a data table in a Data Grid or in the Query Builder, but there is an important difference. When you compute a column in a Data Grid, the expression is applied only once, and is not saved. You cannot change an expression after it has been applied. So, if you wanted to see tour prices with a 20 percent discount, you would have to insert a completely new column. On the other hand, if you compute a column in a query, then you can reopen the query, make changes, and rerun it as many times as you want.

2.7 Importing Microsoft Excel Spreadsheets

When you open or import a Microsoft Excel spreadsheet, SAS Enterprise Guide converts it to a SAS data set (also called a SAS data table).

Input data This example uses a Microsoft Excel spreadsheet named Bookings.xlsx, which contains six columns: the office that booked the tour, the customer identification number, the tour identification number, the number of travelers, the money deposited, and the date the deposit was made. Notice that the first row contains the column names.

Import Data wizard
There are several ways to open a Microsoft Excel file. You can select
File ▶ Open ▶ Data or
File ▶ Import Data from the menu bar, or drag the file from the Servers window to the Process Flow. The Import Data wizard will open.

In the first window under the heading **Output SAS data set,** appears the SAS server, SAS data library, and data set name for the data set you are creating. To change any of these, click **Browse**. When you are satisfied, click **Next**.

In the second window under the heading **Select range,** you specify either a sheet, a specific range of cells, or a named range. You can also check the option **First row of range contains field names** to use values from the first row of the spreadsheet for column names. You can check the option **Rename columns to comply with SAS naming conventions** to tell SAS Enterprise Guide to automatically rename

columns according to traditional rules for SAS names. (See section 1.7 for a discussion of column names.) For the Bookings data, import Sheet1 and use the first row as column names, and click **Next**.

In the third window, you see the column properties that SAS Enterprise Guide suggests for your data. If you find that a column is not importing correctly, you may need to change the Type or Source Informat. To make changes, highlight the column you want to change, and then click **Modify**. The Field Attributes window will open allowing you to change any column attribute. No changes are needed for this example. Click **Next**.

In the fourth window, you can choose options including **Import the data using SAS/ACCESS Interface to PC Files whenever possible**. If you have SAS/ACCESS Interface to PC Files software and you have large spreadsheets, using this option may be faster than the default.

When you are satisfied with the settings, click **Finish**.

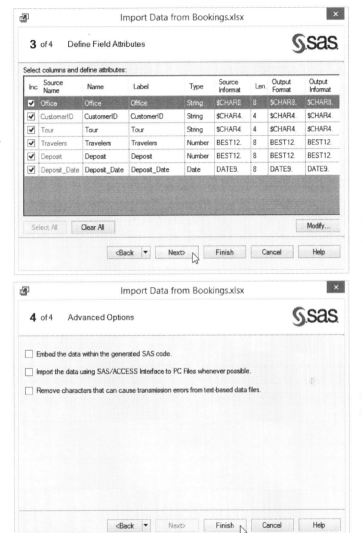

Results The new data set will appear in a Data Grid. The data set opens in read-only mode, but because the data are now in a SAS data set, you can change to update mode to edit the data. Any changes you

	Office	CustomerID	Tour	Travelers	Deposit	Deposit_Date
1	Portland	SL28	SH43	10	425	05JUL2018
2	Portland	DE27	PS27	6	75	11JUL2018
3	Portland	SL34	FJ12	4	200	19JUL2018
4	Portland	DI33	SH43	4	150	23JUL2018
5	Portland	BU12	SH43	2	75	23JUL2018
6	Portland	DE31	FJ12	3	175	25JUL2018

make will not be applied to the original Microsoft Excel spreadsheet.

2.8 Importing Delimited Raw Data

Delimited raw data files have a special character separating the data values. That character is often a comma (as in CSV or comma-separated values files), but it can also be a tab, semicolon, space, or some other character. You can open a raw data file by selecting **File ▶ Open ▶ Data** from the menu bar or by dragging it from the Servers window to the Process Flow. When you do this, SAS Enterprise Guide opens the file in a simple text editor. Using this editor, you can view the data, and you can edit the data, but you cannot use the data in any task when it is opened this way. In order to use raw data in a task, you must first convert it to a SAS data set by importing it.

Input data This example uses data from a file named Eruptions.csv. There are four variables: the volcano name, the date the eruption started, the date the eruption ended, and the Volcanic Explosivity Index (VEI). Notice that this file has commas between the data values, and the first line contains the column names.

```
Volcano, StartDate, EndDate, VEI
Barren Island, 12/20/1795, 12/21/1795, 2
Barren Island, 12/20/1994, 06/05/1995, 2
Erebus, 12/12/1912, . , 2
Erebus, 01/03/1972, . , 1
Etna, 02/06/1610, 08/15/1610, 2
Etna, 06/04/1787, 08/11/1787, 4
Etna, 01/30/1865, 06/28/1865, 2
```

Import Data wizard To import a raw data file, select **File ▶ Import Data** from the menu bar. The Open window will appear (not shown). Navigate to the file you want to import, and click **Open**. The Import Data wizard will open.

The Import Data wizard has four windows. In the first window under the heading **Output SAS data set**, appears the SAS server, SAS data library, and data set name for the data set you are creating. To change any of these, click **Browse**. When you are satisfied, click **Next**.

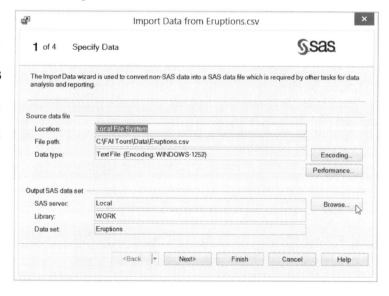

In the second window, select **Delimited fields**. To specify the delimiter for your file, click the down-arrow on the box and either select a delimiter (such as **Comma** or **Tab**) from the pull-down list, or select **Other** and type the delimiter into the box on the right. You can also check the option **File contains field names on record number**, and type a number in the corresponding box to use values in that row as column names. You can check the option **Rename columns to comply with SAS naming conventions** to tell SAS Enterprise Guide to automatically rename columns according to traditional rules for SAS names. (See section 1.7 for a discussion of column names.) For the Eruptions data, select **Comma** as the delimiter, and use the first record for column names. Click **Next**.

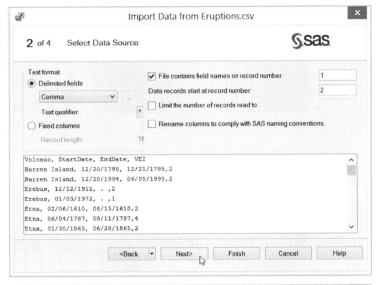

In the third window, you see the column properties that SAS Enterprise Guide suggests for your data. If you find that a column is not importing correctly, you may need to change the Type or Source Informat. To make changes, highlight the column you want to change, and then click **Modify**. The Field Attributes window will open allowing you to change any column attribute. No changes are needed for this example. Click **Next**.

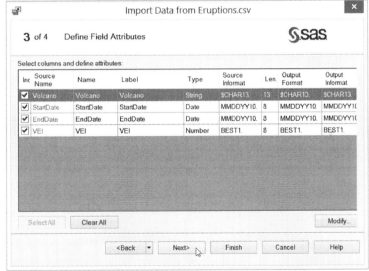

In the fourth window (not shown), you can specify advanced options for controling how the data are imported and what code is generated. When you are satisfied with the settings, click **Finish**.

Results The data set will appear in a Data Grid. The data set opens in read-only mode, but because the data are now in a SAS data set, you can change to update mode to edit the data. Any changes you make will not be applied to the original data file.

	Volcano	StartDate	EndDate	VEI
1	Barren Island	12/20/1795	12/21/1795	2
2	Barren Island	12/20/1994	06/05/1995	2
3	Erebus	12/12/1912		2
4	Erebus	01/03/1972		1
5	Etna	02/06/1610	08/15/1610	2
6	Etna	06/04/1787	08/11/1787	4
7	Etna	01/30/1865	06/28/1865	2

2.9 Importing Fixed-Column Raw Data

Fixed-column raw data files are similar to delimited raw data files, but instead of having a delimiter separating the data values, the data values are lined up in tidy vertical columns. You can open a raw data file by selecting **File ▶ Open ▶ Data** from the menu bar or by dragging it from the Servers window to the Process Flow. When you do this, SAS Enterprise Guide opens the file in a simple text editor. Using this editor, you can view the data, and you can edit the data, but you cannot use the data in any task when it is opened this way. In order to use raw data in a task, you must first convert it to a SAS data set by importing it.

Input data This example uses data from a file named LatLong.txt, which contains three variables: the name of the volcano, followed by its latitude and longitude. Notice that the column names appear in the first row, and the data values are vertically aligned.

```
Volcano            Latitude Longitude
Altar                 -1.67    -78.42
Barren Island         12.28     93.52
Elbrus                43.33     42.45
Erebus               -77.53    167.17
Etna                  37.73     15.00
Fuji                  35.35    138.73
Garibaldi             49.85   -123.00
```

Import Data wizard To import a raw data file, select **File ▶ Import Data** from the menu bar. The Open window will appear (not shown). Navigate to the file you want to import, and click **Open**. The Import Data wizard will open.

The Import Data wizard has four windows. In the first window under the heading **Output SAS data set**, appears the SAS server, SAS data library, and data set name for the data set you are creating. To change any of these, click **Browse**. When you are satisfied, click **Next**.

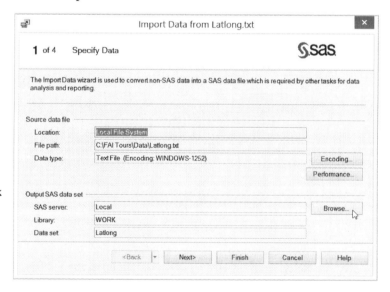

In the second window, select **Fixed columns**. At the bottom of this window is a box displaying the data file. Click the ruler above the data to insert column pointers, and drag the pointers to the columns where each variable begins. For the LatLong data, the volcano name starts at 1, latitude starts at 15, and longitude starts at 24. You can also check the option **File contains field names on record number**, and type a number in the corresponding box to use values in that row as column names. You can check the option **Rename columns to comply with SAS naming**

conventions to tell SAS Enterprise Guide to automatically rename columns according to traditional rules for SAS names. (See section 1.7 for a discussion of column names.) For the LatLong data, use the first record as column names, and click **Next**.

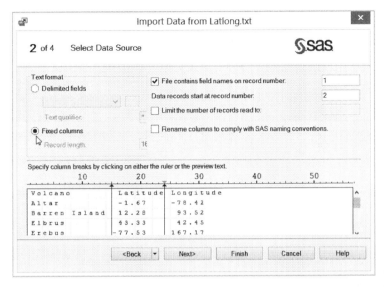

In the third window, you see the column properties that SAS Enterprise Guide suggests for your data. If you find that a column is not importing correctly, you may need to change the Type or Source Informat. To make changes, highlight the column you want to change, and then click **Modify**. The Field Attributes window will open allowing you to change any column attribute. No changes are needed for this example. Click **Next**.

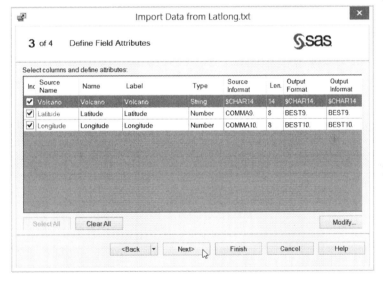

In the fourth window (not shown), you can specify advanced options for controling how the data are imported and what code is generated. When you are satisfied with the settings, click **Finish**.

Results The data set will appear in a Data Grid. The data set opens in read-only mode, but because the data are now in a SAS data set, you can change to update mode to edit the data. Any changes you make will not be applied to the original data file.

	Volcano	Latitude	Longitude
1	Altar	-1.67	-78.42
2	Barren Island	12.28	93.52
3	Elbrus	43.33	42.45
4	Erebus	-77.53	167.17
5	Etna	37.73	15
6	Fuji	35.35	138.73
7	Garibaldi	49.85	-123

2.10 Exporting Data

After you have worked with your data in SAS Enterprise Guide, you may want to access it in some other form. SAS Enterprise Guide can create several types of files including comma-separated values (CSV), Microsoft Excel, and space- and tab-delimited text files.

Here is a Data Grid showing the Tours data table, which will be exported as a Microsoft Excel file.

To export data from SAS Enterprise Guide, click **Export** on the workspace toolbar for the Data Grid and select **Export** *data-table-name* or **Export** *data-table-name* **As A Step In Project**. You can also export data by right-clicking the data icon in the Project Tree or Process Flow, and selecting **Export ▶ Export** *data-table-name* or **Export ▶ Export** *data-table-name* **As A Step In Project** from the pop-up menu.

	Volcano	Departs	Days	Price	Difficulty
1	Etna	Catania	7	$1,610	m
2	Fuji	Tokyo	2	$335	c
3	Kenya	Nairobi	6	$1,245	m
4	Kilauea	Hilo	1	$85	e
5	Kilimanjaro	Nairobi	9	$1,965	c
6	Krakatau	Jakarta	7	$1,345	e
7	Poas	San Jose	1	$97	e

Exporting If you select **Export** *data-table-name*, then a Save window will open (not shown). Navigate to the location where you want to save the new file, specify a name for the file, select the type of file you want to create, and click **Save**. When you export data in this way, no icon will appear in the Project Tree or Process Flow; and if you run your project, your results will not be automatically re-exported.

Exporting as a step in a project If you select **Export As A Step In Project**, the Export wizard will open. The number of windows in the wizard depends on the type of file that you are creating. For an Excel file, there are five windows.

In the first window, select the data table you want to export, and click **Next**.

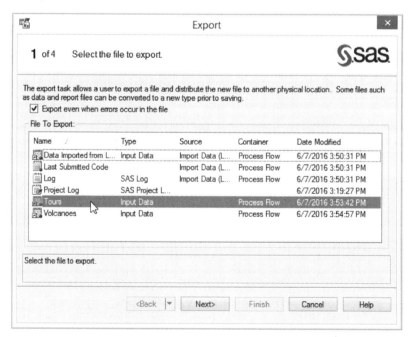

In the second window, select the type of file you want to create, and click **Next**.

In the third window (not shown), indicate whether you want to use labels for column names, and click **Next**.

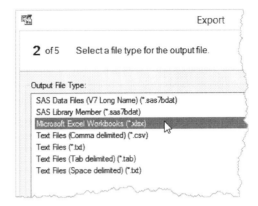

In the fourth window, choose either **Local Computer** or **SAS Servers**, and then click the **Browse** button to navigate to the location where you want the table to be saved. You can only export a SAS data table to a computer that has SAS installed on it. In this window, you can also choose whether to **Overwrite existing output**.
When you are satisfied, click **Next**.

In the fifth window (not shown), confirm your settings by clicking **Finish**.

When you export as a step in the project, an Export File icon  will be added to your project, along with an icon for the newly exported data. Every time you run your project, your data file will be automatically re-exported. Here is the Tours data table after being exported as a spreadsheet and opened in Microsoft Excel.

3

"Celui qui a de l'imagination sans érudition a des ailes, et n'a pas de pieds."

"He who has imagination without learning has wings, but no feet."

JOSEPH JOUBERT

As quoted in *The Cyclopedia of Practical Quotations: English, Latin, and Modern Foreign Languages* by Jehiel Keeler Hoyt, 1896.

CHAPTER 3

Working with Tasks

3.1 Finding and Opening Tasks

Running tasks is what SAS Enterprise Guide is all about. Tasks are point-and-click windows that generate SAS code for you. When you run them, they submit that code to your SAS server (which can be any computer with SAS installed on it that you have access to). The SAS server produces results and sends them back to SAS Enterprise Guide. Those results could be analyses, reports, graphs, or data sets. SAS Enterprise Guide offers over 90 tasks. Here are a few of the more commonly used tasks:

Category	Task Name	SAS Procedure Generated
ANOVA	One-Way ANOVA	ANOVA and GPLOT
Data	Append Table	SQL
	Create Format	FORMAT
	Filter and Sort	SQL
	Query Builder	SQL
	Sort Data	SORT
Describe	Distribution Analysis	UNIVARIATE
	List Data	PRINT
	One-Way Frequencies	FREQ
	Summary Statistics	MEANS, UNIVARIATE, and SGPLOT
	Summary Tables	TABULATE
	Table Analysis	FREQ
Graph	Bar Chart	GCHART
	Line Plot	GPLOT
	Scatter Plot	GPLOT and G3D
Multivariate	Correlations	CORR
Regression	Linear Regression	REG

Opening a task To open a task, select it from the **Tasks** menu, or click its name in the Tasks window in the Resources pane, or open a Data Grid and then select the task from the workspace toolbar.

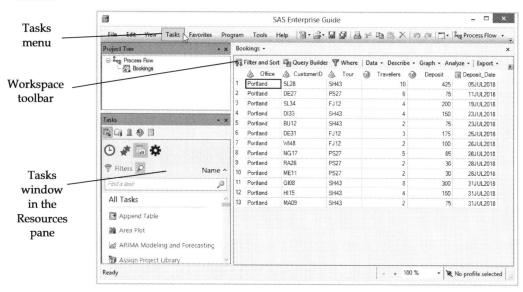

Tasks are grouped into categories. In the workspace toolbar above a Data Grid, you can find the ANOVA, Regression, and Multivariate categories (along with others) under the Analyze button.

If you select **Tasks ▶ Browse** from the menu bar, then a separate Tasks window will open. This window is similar to the Tasks window in the Resources pane, but has two tabs labeled My Tasks and Browse.

My Tasks tab In the My Tasks tab, you will see a list of recently used tasks, and a list of any tasks you have previously marked as favorites. You can open a task by clicking its name. In this example, the Summary Tables task is being selected from the list of Favorite Tasks.

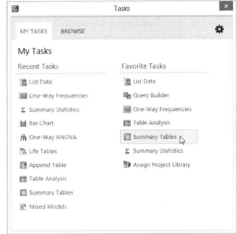

Browse tab In the Browse tab, you will see a complete list of all the tasks in SAS Enterprise Guide. On the left, you can check boxes to filter the list of tasks by category or by procedure name. Alternatively, you can type the name of a task or procedure in the search box at the top of

the window to display only tasks that match your search criteria. If you hover the cursor over the name of a task, then a box will open displaying details about that task. If you click the star ☆ in this window, then that task will be added to your list of favorites. In this example, the word tabulate has been typed in the search box to display tasks that use PROC TABULATE.

Wizards Some tasks are also available in a simplified form called a wizard. Wizards are similar to tasks, but generally offer fewer options and have windows that must be completed in a specific order. If a task is available as a wizard, then the wizard will be listed next to the task.

3.2 Selecting Data and Assigning Task Roles

Regardless of which task you run, the basic steps are the same: open the task, select the data, select options, and then run the task. This example uses the List Data task to create a simple list report with one line for each observation in the data set.

Here is a Data Grid showing the Bookings data set used in this example. To open the List Data task, select **Describe ▶ List Data** from the toolbar at the top of the Data Grid, or select **Tasks ▶ Describe ▶ List Data** from the menu bar. The List Data window will open.

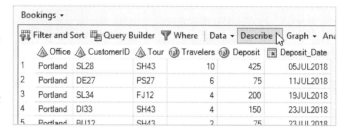

Here is the List Data window. Many other tasks use a similar window. The List Data window has four pages that are listed in the selection pane on the left: Data, Options, Titles, and Properties. The task window opens displaying the Data page where you can change the data set and assign variables to task roles.

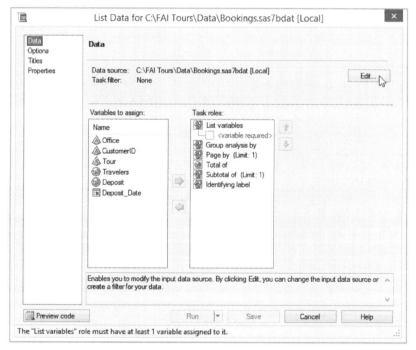

Selecting the data set When you open a task, it will use the data set that is currently active. You can make a data set active by simply clicking its icon in the Project Tree or Process Flow before you open a task. If you accidentally get the wrong data set or want to use a subset of the data, you can change that by clicking the **Edit** button in the Data page of the task window. The Edit Data and Filter window (not shown) will open where you can choose the data set and filters for the task. See section 6.1 for details about the Edit Data and Filter window.

Assigning task roles After you have opened a task and selected the right data set, the next thing to do is assign variables to task roles. You assign variables to roles by clicking the name of a variable in the section labeled **Variables to assign**, and dragging it to the section labeled **Task roles**. In the List Data task, you must assign at least one variable to the **List variables** role. In this window, the variables Office, CustomerID, Tour, Travelers, and Deposit have been assigned to serve as list variables. When you are satisfied, click **Run**.

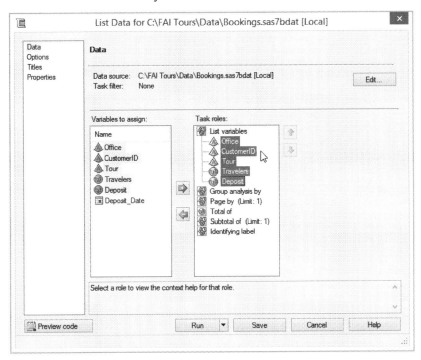

Results Here is the report listing the variables selected from the Bookings data set. This is a simple report using the default options. The rest of this chapter shows how to modify and customize your task results.

Report Listing

Row number	Office	CustomerID	Tour	Travelers	Deposit
1	Portland	SL28	SH43	10	425
2	Portland	DE27	PS27	6	75
3	Portland	SL34	FJ12	4	200
4	Portland	DI33	SH43	4	150
5	Portland	BU12	SH43	2	75
6	Portland	DE31	FJ12	3	175
7	Portland	WI48	FJ12	2	100
8	Portland	NG17	PS27	5	65
9	Portland	RA28	PS27	2	30
10	Portland	ME11	PS27	2	30
11	Portland	GI08	SH43	8	300
12	Portland	HI15	SH43	4	150
13	Portland	MA09	SH43	2	75

Generated by the SAS System ('Local', X64_8HOME) on April 27, 2016 at 11:29:17 AM

3.3 ► Reopening Tasks and Making Changes

Once you have run a task, you will probably find that you want to make some changes. There are many kinds of changes you can make including assigning variables to different task roles, and selecting options. Every task is a little different, but the way you make changes is the same. You reopen the task, make your selections, and then rerun the task. This example takes the report that was produced in the previous section and adds an option and a grouping variable.

To reopen a task, right-click the task icon in the Project Tree or Process Flow and select **Modify** *task-name* from the pop-up menu or click **Modify Task** on the toolbar at the top of the results. The task window will open showing the choices you made before.

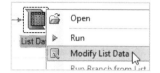

Assigning a variable to the grouping task role   Most tasks that produce reports allow you to assign one or more variables to serve as grouping variables. When you do this, SAS Enterprise Guide divides your data into groups based on the values of the grouping variables. That way, you can get a report for each salesperson, or statistics for each state, or a chart for each quarter. To do this, drag one or more variables to the **Group analysis by** role.

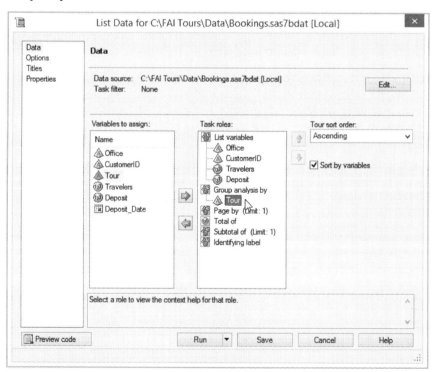

Each time you drag a variable name to the Group analysis by role, two items will appear on the right: a pull-down list for the sort order, and a check box labeled **Sort by variables**. You can use these options to tell SAS Enterprise Guide whether you want the report to be sorted by that grouping variable, and, if so, whether in ascending or descending order. In this List Data window, the variable Tour is a grouping variable, and the variables Office, CustomerID, Travelers, and Deposit are list variables.

Choosing options To customize your report further, click **Options** in the selection pane on the left. By default, the List Data task will print the row number for each line in the report. If you don't want row numbers, then uncheck **Print the row number**. You can also leave the row number, but change the heading for that particular column. In this example, the row numbers have been removed.

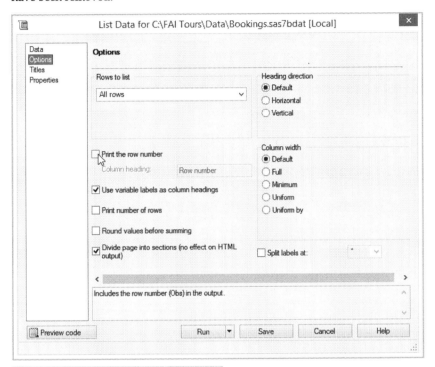

Report Listing

Tour=FJ12

Office	CustomerID	Travelers	Deposit
Portland	SL34	4	200
Portland	DE31	3	175
Portland	WI48	2	100

Tour=PS27

Office	CustomerID	Travelers	Deposit
Portland	DE27	6	75
Portland	NG17	5	65
Portland	RA28	2	30
Portland	ME11	2	30

Tour=SH43

Office	CustomerID	Travelers	Deposit
Portland	SL28	10	425
Portland	DI33	4	150
Portland	BU12	2	75
Portland	GI08	8	300
Portland	HI15	4	150
Portland	MA09	2	75

Generated by the SAS System ('Local', X64_8HOME) on June 01, 2016 at 2:08:43 PM

Rerunning tasks When you are satisfied with your changes, click **Run**. A window will open asking if you want to replace your previous results. If you click **Yes**, then only the new results will appear in your project. If you click **No**, then both the old and the new results will appear.

Results Here is the report with Tour as a grouping variable. Notice that there is now a separate section of the report for each Tour, and the row numbers have been removed. This report uses the default title and footnote. The next section shows how to customize titles and footnotes.

3.4 Customizing Titles and Footnotes

By default, reports in SAS Enterprise Guide have titles that describe the type of report, such as "Summary Statistics" or "Analysis of Variance," and footnotes that show the date and time the task was run. That's a good start, but in most cases, you will want titles and footnotes that reflect your unique report.

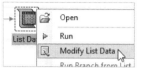

You can change the title or footnote when you first run a task, or reopen the task and modify the titles. This example takes the report that was produced in the previous section and gives it a custom title and footnote. To reopen a task, right-click the task icon in the Project Tree or Process Flow and select **Modify *task-name*** from the pop-up menu. The task window will open.

In the task window, click **Titles** in the selection pane on the left to display the Titles page.

Titles page The area labeled **Section** lists all the titles and footnotes for that particular task. For the List Data task, you can choose **Report Titles** or **Footnote**. Some tasks have additional titles that you can change.

To change a title, click its name in the area labeled **Section**. Then uncheck the **Use default text** option and type up to 10 new titles in the box below. In this example, the title "Report Listing" has been replaced with two titles: "Bookings for Portland" and "July."

To change a footnote, click **Footnote** in the area labeled **Section**. Then uncheck the **Use default text** option and type up to 10 new footnotes in the box below. In this example, the footnote has simply been deleted.

When you are satisfied with the new titles and footnotes, click **Run** in the task window.

Titles

Section:
- ✓ Report Titles
- ✓ Footnote

Checked sections will be generated based on current task settings.

Text for section: Footnote

☐ Use default text

Results Here is the report with the new titles and no footnote.

Changing default titles and footnotes

If you find yourself changing titles and footnotes a lot, you may want to change the default values. You can do this using the Options window. To open the Options window (not shown), select **Tools ▶ Options** from the menu bar. Then select **Tasks General** from the selection pane on the left. In this page you can specify new titles that will replace the default titles for all tasks. You can also set the footnote to blank, or specify new footnotes to replace the default footnote.

By default, a few tasks include the name of the procedure as a title in the results. For example, the Summary Statistics task uses the title "The MEANS Procedure." You can turn off these titles in the Options window. In the section labeled **SAS procedure settings**, uncheck **Include SAS procedure titles in results**.

Bookings for Portland

July

Tour=FJ12

Office	CustomerID	Travelers	Deposit
Portland	SL34	4	200
Portland	DE31	3	175
Portland	WI48	2	100

Tour=PS27

Office	CustomerID	Travelers	Deposit
Portland	DE27	6	75
Portland	NG17	5	65
Portland	RA28	2	30
Portland	ME11	2	30

Tour=SH43

Office	CustomerID	Travelers	Deposit
Portland	SL28	10	425
Portland	DI33	4	150
Portland	BU12	2	75
Portland	GI08	8	300
Portland	HI15	4	150
Portland	MA09	2	75

3.5 Applying Standard Formats in a Task

Every time you run a task that produces a report, SAS Enterprise Guide decides how the data should be displayed. That's good, but sometimes the way that SAS Enterprise Guide displays data may not be exactly what you want. You can change the way data are displayed by applying a format in a Data Grid or query, but then the format will be saved with the data set. If you don't want the format to be saved with the data, then you can apply the format directly in a task.

	Volcano	StartDate	EndDate	VEI
1	Barren Island	12/20/1795	12/21/1795	2
2	Barren Island	12/20/1994	06/05/1995	2
3	Erebus	12/12/1912	.	2
4	Erebus	01/03/1972	.	1
5	Etna	02/06/1610	08/15/1610	2
6	Etna	06/04/1787	08/11/1787	4
7	Etna	01/30/1865	06/28/1865	2

Here is a sample of the Eruptions data set. This example uses the List Data task to show how you can apply the format WEEKDATE*w.d* to the variable StartDate.

To open the task, click the data icon in the Project Tree or Process Flow and select **Tasks ▶ Describe ▶ List Data** from the menu bar. The List Data window will open, displaying the Data page.

Opening the Properties window To open a Properties window for a variable, right-click the name of the variable that you want to modify (in either the **Variables to assign** area or the **Task roles** area), and select **Properties** from the pop-up menu. In this example, the variables Volcano, StartDate, and VEI have been assigned to the **List variables** role, and **Properties** is being selected for StartDate.

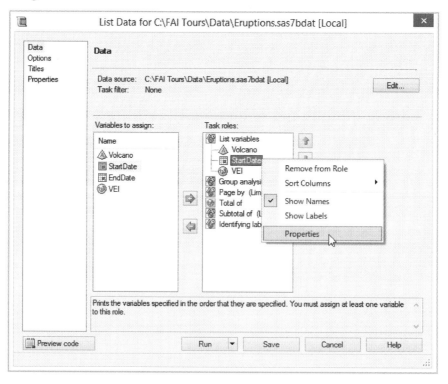

Here is the Properties window for the variable StartDate. You cannot change a variable's data type or group using the Properties window inside a task. To change those, use the Properties window inside a Data Grid, as described in section 1.9.

Click **Change** to open the Formats window.

Selecting formats In the Formats window, choose the category of formats you want to see, and then click the name of the format you want to use. In the area labeled **Attributes**, specify the overall width (the longest number of characters or digits that will be allowed for this variable). For numeric variables, you may also specify the number of decimal places. The area labeled **Example** shows a sample of how this format will look. See section 1.10 for a list of commonly used standard formats. In this Formats window, the category Date has been selected, along with the format WEEKDATE*w.d*, an overall width of 17, and no decimal places (WEEKDATE17.0).

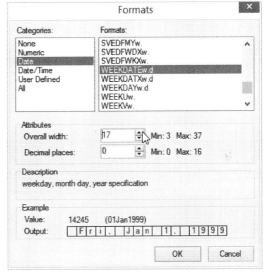

When you are satisfied with the format, click **OK**. Then click **OK** in the Properties window, and click **Run** in the task window.

Results Here is the beginning of the report using the new format for StartDate. Any formats you apply in a task are not saved in the original data set and will not be used in other tasks.

Report Listing

Row number	Volcano	StartDate	VEI
1	Barren Island	Sun, Dec 20, 1795	2
2	Barren Island	Tue, Dec 20, 1994	2
3	Erebus	Thu, Dec 12, 1912	2
4	Erebus	Mon, Jan 3, 1972	1
5	Etna	Sat, Feb 6, 1610	2
6	Etna	Mon, Jun 4, 1787	4
7	Etna	Mon, Jan 30, 1865	2

3.6 Defining Your Own Character Formats

Even with all the standard formats provided by SAS Enterprise Guide, there are times when you need something different. In those cases, you can create a user-defined format. Basically, user-defined formats allow you to specify a set of labels that will be substituted for specific values or ranges of values in your data. To do this, open the Create Format window by selecting **Tasks ▶ Data ▶ Create Format** from the menu bar. The Create Format window will open displaying the Options page.

Options page To create a format for a character variable, select a **Format type** of **Character**. Then type a name for the new format in the box labeled **Format name**. This name must be 31 characters or fewer in length; cannot start or end with a numeral; and can contain only letters, numerals, or underscores. This example shows a character format named RegionName.

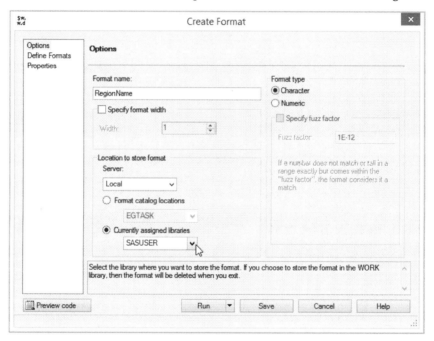

Any formats stored in the WORK library (the default) will be deleted when you exit SAS Enterprise Guide. To save your format, choose a different library. In this case, the format will be stored in the SASUSER library, which is permanent. If you have more than one SAS server, be sure to save your format on the same server where you run tasks. If you choose to leave your format in the WORK library, you can always recreate it later by rerunning the Create Format task. When you are satisfied, click **Define formats** in the selection pane on the left.

Define Formats page Defining a format is a two-step process. First, click **New** next to Label and type a label in the **Label** box. Then in the **Values** box type the data value that corresponds to that label. Repeat these steps until you have created all the labels that you want. Data values are case-sensitive, so "yes" is not the same as "Yes." In the following image, you can see that the label Africa is being applied to the data value Af.

If you want to specify a range of data values (such as A–D) rather than a discrete value, click the down-arrow under **Type** and select **Range** from the pull-down list. When you do that, a second box will appear under **Values** so that you can type in the two end points for your range

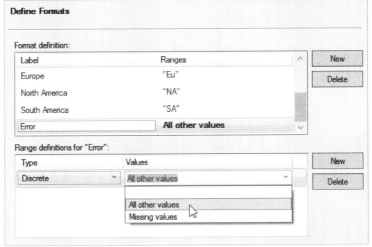

You can specify a label to be used for missing values or for all other values by clicking the down-arrow in the box labeled **Values**. In this example, you can see that the label Error will be applied to all other data values. When you are satisfied with the format labels and ranges, click **Run** to create the format.

All character format names begin with a dollar sign, and end with a period, so $RegionName. will be name of this format. A more detailed example of creating a character format appears in Tutorial B.

Using user-defined formats You can apply a user-defined format to a variable in the same ways you apply standard formats: in a Data Grid, a task, or a query. Section 3.8 shows the $RegionName. format being used in a List Data task.

3.7 Defining Your Own Numeric Formats

The previous section showed how to create a user-defined format for a character variable. Creating a user-defined format for a numeric variable is similar, but you have a few more options. Start by selecting **Tasks ▶ Data ▶ Create Format** from the menu bar to open the Create Format window. The Create Format window will open displaying the Options page.

Options page
Select a **Format type** of **Numeric**. Then type a name for the new format in the **Format name** box. This name must be 32 characters or fewer in length; cannot start or end with a numeral; and can contain only letters, numerals, or underscores. This example shows a numeric format named HeightGroup.

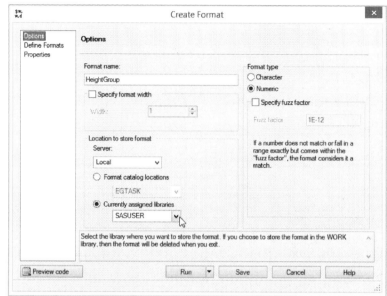

Any formats stored in the WORK library (the default) will be deleted when you exit SAS Enterprise Guide. To save your format, choose a different library. If you have more than one SAS server, be sure to save your format on the same server where you run tasks. If you choose to leave your format in the WORK library, you can always recreate it later by rerunning the Create Format task. When you are satisfied, click **Define formats** in the selection pane on the left.

Define Formats page Defining a format is a two-step process. First, click **New** next to Label and type a label in the **Label** box. Then in the **Values** box, type the data values corresponding to that label. Repeat these steps for the second label, and so on, until you have created all the labels that you want.

When you specify the data values, you have some choices. Under **Type**, click the down-arrow to open the pull-down list and select either **Discrete** (if you have a single value) or **Range**.

You can make ranges inclusive or exclusive. In this example, the label Middling maps to values from 500 up to (but excluding) 4000. If you see a red box over ranges at the top of the window, it means that your ranges are overlapping and you will probably want to make one of them exclusive.

You can specify a label to be used for special values by clicking the down-arrows in the boxes below **Values**. For discrete values, you can select **All Other Values** or **Missing Values**. For ranges, you can select **Low** (the lowest possible value) and **High** (the highest). In this window, the label Stupendous has been mapped to data values from 4000 to High. When you are satisfied with the format labels and ranges, click **Run** to create the format.

Unlike character formats, numeric formats do not begin with a dollar sign. However, they do end with a period, so HeightGroup. will be the name of this format.

Using user-defined formats

You can apply a user-defined format to a variable in the same ways you apply standard formats: in a Data Grid, a task, or a query. The next section shows the HeightGroup. format being applied in a List Data task.

3.8 Applying User-Defined Formats in a Task

You can apply user-defined formats in exactly the same ways you apply standard formats: in a Data Grid, a task, or a query. The example in this section applies two user-defined formats, $RegionName. and HeightGroup. (created in the preceding two sections) in a List Data task.

Here is a simple report from a List Data task using the Volcanoes data set. The variables Volcano, Region, and Height have been assigned to serve in the List variables role. Notice that the data values are unformatted.

Report Listing			
Row number	Volcano	Region	Height
1	Altar	SA	5321
2	Arthur's Seat	Eu	251
3	Barren Island	As	354
4	Elbrus	Eu	5633
5	Erebus	An	3794
6	Etna	Eu	3350
7	Fuii	As	3776

You can apply a format when you first run a task or you can add it later. To change an existing report, reopen the task window by right-clicking the task icon in the Project Tree or Process Flow and selecting **Modify** *task-name* from the pop-up menu.

Opening the Properties window   To apply a format in a task, right-click the name of the variable you want to change in the Data page (in either the **Variables to assign** area or the **Task roles** area), and select **Properties** from the pop-up menu. In this example, **Properties** is being selected for the variable Region.

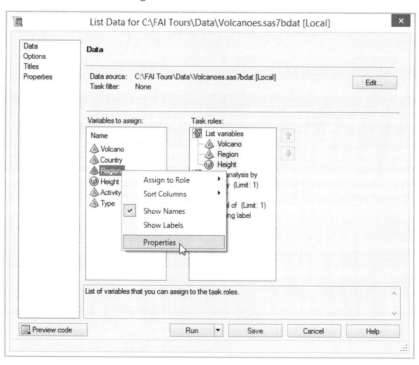

In the Properties window, click **Change** to open the Formats window for that variable.

Then in the Formats window, select the category **User Defined**. All the formats that you have created will be listed. This example shows the Formats window for the variable Region. Because Region is character, only character formats are listed. In this case, $REGIONNAME. is being selected.

Once you have selected the correct format, click **OK** in the Formats window and click **OK** in the Properties window.

After you have applied all the formats that you want, click **Run** in the task window.

Results In the new report, you can see that the values of Region are displayed using the $RegionName. format that was created in section 3.6. In addition, the values of Height are displayed using the HeightGroup. format created in section 3.7.

In this example, the user-defined formats were applied to list variables. The result was that the formats simply replaced one value with another. However, if you apply a user-defined format to a variable assigned to a task role that groups data, then it changes the structure of the report. See the next section for an example of creating a grouped report with a format.

Report Listing

Row number	Volcano	Region	Height
1	Altar	South America	Stupendous
2	Arthur's Seat	Europe	Pipsqueak
3	Barren Island	Asia	Pipsqueak
4	Elbrus	Europe	Stupendous
5	Erebus	Antarctica	Middling
6	Etna	Europe	Middling
7	Fuji	Asia	Middling

3.9 Grouping Data in Reports with Formats

Often you want to summarize your data by groups. For example, if you had a variable for age, you might want separate summary statistics for children and adults. If you already had a variable for age group, then you could assign it to the Group analysis task role. If you did not have a variable for age group, you could compute it in a Data Grid, or use the Query Builder to recode your data, but both of these methods add a new variable to your data set. If you don't want to add a new variable, then you can group your data using a format.

This example groups the Height variable from the Volcanoes data set in a One-Way Frequencies task using the HeightGroup. format created in section 3.7. The HeightGroup. format assigns volcanoes to three different groups based on the variable Height.

Here is a sample of the Volcanoes data set. To open the task, click the data icon in the Project Tree or Process Flow and select **Tasks ▸ Describe ▸ One-Way Frequencies** from the menu bar. The One-Way Frequencies window will open, displaying the Data page.

	Volcano	Country	Region	Height	Activity	Type
1	Altar	Ecuador	SA	5321	Extinct	Stratovolcano
2	Arthur's Seat	UK	Eu	251	Extinct	
3	Barren Island	India	As	354	Active	Stratovolcano
4	Elbrus	Russia	Eu	5633	Extinct	Stratovolcano
5	Erebus		An	3794	Active	Stratovolcano

Opening the Properties window To apply a format in a task, right-click the name of the variable to be grouped in the Data page (in either the **Variables to assign** area or the **Task roles** area), and select **Properties** from the pop-up menu. In this example, **Properties** is being selected for the variable Height.

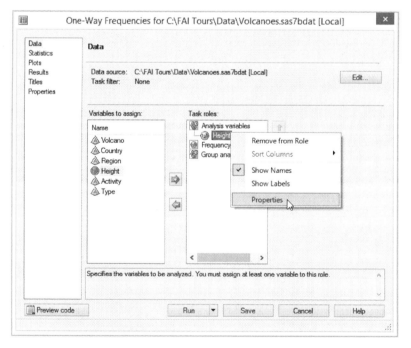

Using formats In the Properties window, click **Change** to open the Formats window for that variable.

Then in the Formats window, select the category. Since this example uses a user-define format, the category **User Defined** has been selected. All the formats in that category will be listed. Here is the Formats window for the variable Height. Because Height is numeric, only numeric formats are listed. In this example, HEIGHTGROUP. is being selected.

Once you have selected the correct format, click **OK** in the Formats window and click **OK** in the Properties window. Then click **Run** in the task window.

One-Way Frequencies

Results

The FREQ Procedure

Height	Frequency	Percent	Cumulative Frequency	Cumulative Percent
Pipsqueak	3	9.38	3	9.38
Middling	20	62.50	23	71.88
Stupendous	9	28.13	32	100.00

Results Here is the report with the data for Height grouped. Notice that the user-defined format was applied to the variable Height before it was summarized. Instead of counts for data values like 251 and 5321, the report shows counts for the formatted values: Pipsqueak, Middling, and Stupendous.

3.10 Creating Summary Data Sets

Sometimes you may want to save a summary data set so you can use it for further analysis or join it with other data. Many tasks can save summary data, including One-Way Frequencies, Table Analysis, Summary Tables, and Summary Statistics. This section shows the Summary Statistics task, but the basic steps are the same for other tasks.

Here is a sample of the Volcanoes data set. To open the task, click the data icon in the Project Tree or Process Flow and select **Tasks ▶ Describe ▶ Summary Statistics** from the menu bar. The Summary Statistics window will open, displaying the Data page.

	Volcano	Country	Region	Height	Activity	Type
1	Altar	Ecuador	SA	5321	Extinct	Stratovolcano
2	Arthur's Seat	UK	Eu	251	Extinct	
3	Barren Island	India	As	354	Active	Stratovolcano
4	Elbrus	Russia	Eu	5633	Extinct	Stratovolcano
5	Erebus		An	3794	Active	Stratovolcano
6	Etna	Italy	Eu	3350	Active	Stratovolcano

Data page For the Summary Statistics task, you must assign at least one variable to the **Analysis variables** role, and all analysis variables must be numeric. Classification variables, on the other hand, are optional and may be numeric or character.

If you assign a variable to the **Classification variables** role, then SAS Enterprise Guide

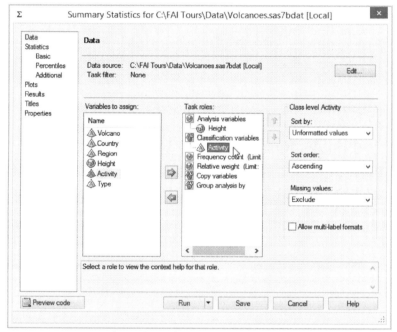

will produce separate summary statistics for each combination of the classification variables. When you drag a variable to the classification role, options will appear on the right. You can choose the sort order (Ascending or Descending) and whether to include missing values. The default is to exclude any observations with missing values for the classification variables. In this example, the variable Height has been designated as an analysis variable, and Activity as a classification variable.

Results page Click **Results** in the selection pane on the left to display the Results page. In this page, you will see options that affect both your printed report and output data set.

To save an output data set, check the **Save statistics to data set** option. SAS Enterprise Guide gives the data set a name beginning with MEAN and stores it in a default location. To specify a different name or location, click **Browse**. This opens the Save As window (not shown). Choose a library and a name for your file. When you are satisfied, click **Save** to return to the Results page. In the Results page, you will see the new data set name.

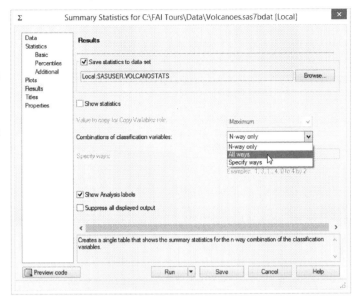

Before you run the report, you may want to make some other changes. Because you are creating an output data set, you may not care about the standard Summary Statistics report. To turn off the report, uncheck the **Show statistics** box.

You can also select the **Combinations of classification variables** to be included. **N-way only** (the default) gives you summary data by crossing all the classification variables at once. The option **All ways** gives you summary data for all combinations of the classification variables including the grand total. If you choose **Specify ways**, then you can select just the combinations you want. In this example, **All ways** is being selected. When you are satisfied, click **Run**.

Results Here is the output data set displayed in a Data Grid. The first row contains summary statistics for the grand total, while the following rows contain statistics for each level of Activity. Notice that SAS Enterprise Guide has created new variables for the summary statistics (Height_Mean, Height_StdDev, Height_Min, Height_Max, and Height_N). In addition, there are three automatic variables. _FREQ_ tells you how many observations contributed to each group, while _WAY_ and _TYPE_ reflect the type of combination. The _WAY_ and _TYPE_ are the same except that _WAY_ is a numeric variable while _TYPE_ is character.

	Activity	_WAY_	_TYPE_	_FREQ_	Height_Mean	Height_StdDev	Height_Min	Height_Max	Height_N
1		0	0	30	3035.3666667	1791.1721357	251	6458	30
2	Active	1	1	23	2852.6086957	1508.0613907	354	5976	23
3	Extinct	1	1	7	3635.8571429	2572.7681868	251	6458	7

3.11 Changing the Result Format

When you run a task that produces output, by default the result will be in a format called SAS Report. With SAS Report format, you can export results to other formats and combine multiple reports into a single report. SAS Enterprise Guide can also produce results in RTF, PDF, HTML, Excel, PowerPoint, and plain text.

Setting the default result format To set the default result format for tasks, select **Tools ▶ Options** from the menu bar. The Options window will open. Click **Results General** in the selection pane on the left to open the Results General page. The available result formats are listed under the heading **Result Formats**. You can select one or more formats by checking boxes next to the format names. When you are satisfied, click **OK**. Once you make changes, they will affect all subsequent results. In this example, because both PDF and RTF are checked, any task that you run will produce results in both formats.

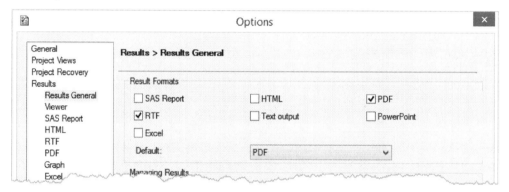

Changing the result format of an individual task If you want to change the result format for an individual task, then open the task, click **Properties** in the selection pane on the left, and click the **Edit** button. The Properties window will open. This example shows how to open the Properties window from a List Data task.

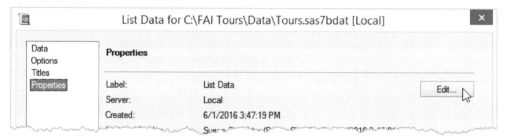

You can also open the Properties window by right-clicking the task icon in the Process Flow or Project Tree and selecting **Properties** from the pop-up menu.

In the Properties window, click **Results** in the selection pane on the left to open the Results page, and then select **Customize result formats, styles, and behavior**. Now you can choose result formats and styles for the task's results. In this example, this task will produce results only in PDF format. When you are satisfied with your settings, click **OK** to close the Properties window. Then rerun your task to see the results.

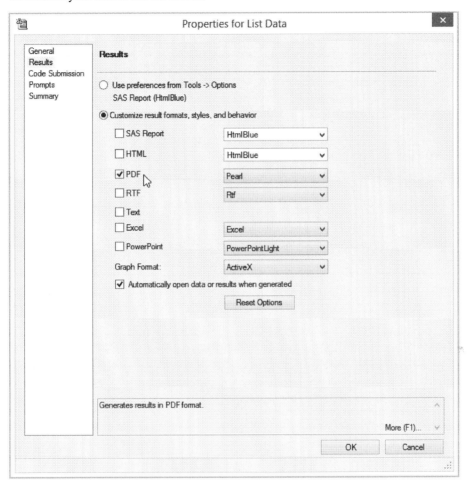

Moderate and Challenging Tours

Volcano	Departs	Days	Price	Difficulty
Etna	Catania	7	$1,610	m
Fuji	Tokyo	2	$335	c
Kenya	Nairobi	6	$1,245	m
Kilimanjaro	Nairobi	9	$1,965	c
Reventador	Quito	4	$875	m

Results When you run a task that produces results in multiple formats, you get an icon in the Process Flow, and a tab in the workspace, for each format. To open a result, click its result tab, or double-click its icon in the Process Flow. This is what the results of the List Data task look like in PDF format. Notice that, by default, results in PDF format look different than results in SAS Report format. That is because different formats may have different default styles. The next section shows how to change the result style.

3.12 Changing the Result Style

The style determines the overall look for your results. The colors, fonts, and layout of your results are all defined in the style. Text output does not have a style associated with it, but for the other result formats—HTML, RTF, PDF, Excel, PowerPoint, and SAS Report—you can choose from a number of built-in styles.

Setting the default result style You can change the default style for any result format using the Options window. Open the Options window by selecting **Tools ▶ Options** from the menu bar. Click the type of output (SAS Report, HTML, RTF, PDF, Excel or PowerPoint) in the selection pane on the left to open the page for that result format. Then select the style that you want to use for that result format from the Style drop-down list. Once you make this change, every task you run will use the style you select for that result format. In this example, the Sasweb style is being selected for SAS Report format.

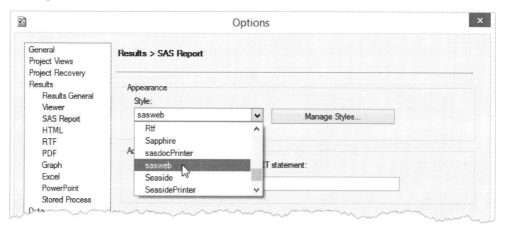

Results Here is the result of a List Data task in SAS Report format using the Sasweb style.

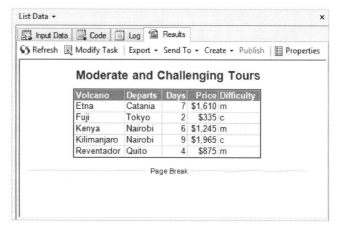

Changing the result style of an individual task If you want to change the style for the results of an individual task, then open the task, click **Properties** in the selection pane for the task, and click the **Edit** button. The Properties window will open. You can also open the Properties window by right-clicking the task icon in the Process Flow or Project Tree and selecting **Properties** from the pop-up menu.

In the Properties window, click **Results** in the selection pane on the left to open the Results page. Check the box next to **Customize result formats, styles, and behavior**, and then select the result format and a style from the drop-down list for each format. When you are satisfied with your settings, click **OK** to close the Properties window. Then rerun your task to see the results. In this example, the sasweb style is being selected for SAS Report format.

Properties for List Data

General
Results
Code Submission
Prompts
Summary

Results

○ Use preferences from Tools -> Options
  SAS Report (HtmlBlue)

● Customize result formats, styles, and behavior

☑ SAS Report   HtmlBlue
                   Sapphire
☐ HTML   sasdocPrinter
                   sasweb
☐ PDF   Seaside
                   SeasidePrinter
☐ RTF   statdoc

☐ Text

☐ Excel   Excel

☐ PowerPoint   PowerPointLight

Graph Format: ActiveX

☑ Automatically open data or results when generated

Reset Options

Select a style from the drop-down list. The style will be applied to the SAS Report results for this task.

More (F1)...

OK   Cancel

Changing the result style after running a task For results in SAS Report and HTML formats, you can also change the style after you run the task. Click the **Properties** button on the workspace toolbar for the result to open the

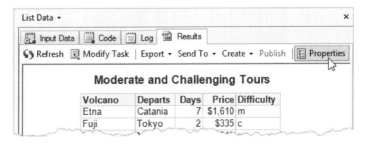

List Data ▾

📊 Input Data 📄 Code 📋 Log 📈 Results

⟳ Refresh 📝 Modify Task Export ▾ Send To ▾ Create ▾ Publish 📋 Properties

Moderate and Challenging Tours

Volcano	Departs	Days	Price	Difficulty
Etna	Catania	7	$1,610	m
Fuji	Tokyo	2	$335	c

Properties window (not shown). Then choose a style from the Style drop-down menu. Click **OK** and your result will be displayed with the selected style. You do not need to rerun the task.

3.13 Customizing Styles Using the Style Manager

Although SAS Enterprise Guide comes with many built-in styles for results, you still might want something a little different. The Style Manager allows you to modify existing styles for SAS Report and HTML results. You cannot modify styles for use with RTF, PDF, Excel, or PowerPoint result formats, and the text format does not use styles.

Opening the Style Manager   To open the Style Manager select **Tools ▶ Style Manager** from the menu bar. The Style Manager provides you with a list of available styles in a box on the left. When you click a style, you will see a preview of that style in the box on the right.

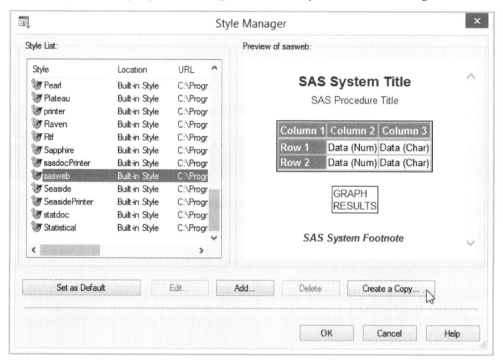

Editing an existing style   You cannot change the built-in styles, but you can make a copy of a style and edit the copy. First click a style in the Style Manager window, and then click **Create a Copy**. This opens the Save Style As window (not shown) where you can give the new style a name and choose a storage location. Now you can edit the copy of the style you just saved. Click the new style name in the Style Manager window, and click **Edit**. The Style Editor window will open.

In the Style Editor window, the preview area on the left shows the current style of various elements such as titles, headers, and data cells. To edit an element, click it in the preview area on the left, or select its name from the **Selected element** drop-down list. Then select the attributes to use for that element in the area on the right. In this example, the **SAS System Title** has been given a text style of **Bold Italic**, and a font text size of **14pt**.

In addition to changing the style of the text, you can control borders using the Borders tab, and add images to your style using the Images tab. Click **OK** when you are finished making changes to the style. Then click **OK** in the Style Manager window to save your changes.

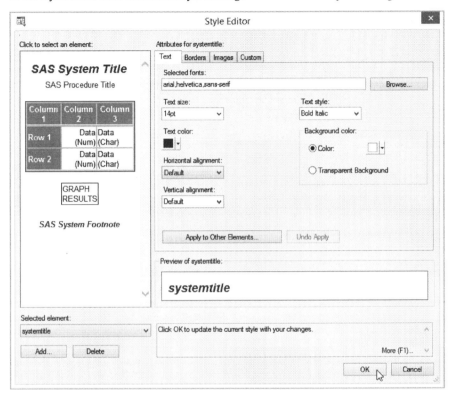

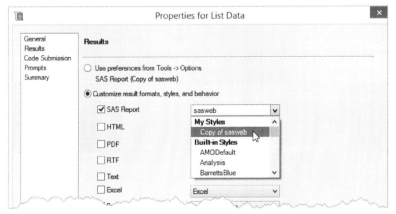

Using the new style The new style you created will appear in the **My Styles** section of the list of styles in the Results page of the Properties window. You can select it for any SAS Report or HTML results, or set it as the default style. See the preceding section

for details about changing the style for results.

3.14 Exporting Results

By default, results generated by SAS Enterprise Guide are saved inside the current project. If you want, you can export results to a file. You can export results manually or let SAS Enterprise Guide do it automatically each time you run the project.

To export results, click **Export** on the workspace toolbar above the results and select **Export** *result-format – result-name* or **Export** *result-format – result-name* **As A Step In Project**. You can access the same options by right-clicking the results icon in the Project Tree or Process Flow.

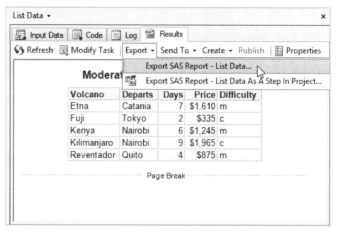

Exporting If you select **Export** *result-format – result-name*, then a Save window will open (not shown). Navigate to the location where you want to save the new file, specify a name for the file, select the type of file you want to create, and click **Save**. If your result is in SAS Report format, then you can export the file as a SAS Report, HTML, XML, or PDF file. All other result formats can only be exported in the original format. When you export results in this way, no icon will appear in the Project Tree or Process Flow; and if you run your project, your results will not be automatically re-exported.

Exporting as a step in a project If you select **Export As A Step In Project**, the Export wizard will open. In the first window, all items in the project are listed with the selected item highlighted. Click **Next**.

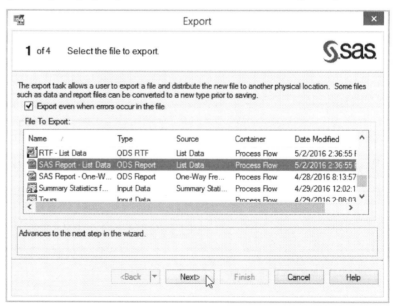

If the result that you want to export is in SAS Report format, then the second window will give you a choice for the output file type: SAS Report, HTML, or PDF. If the result format is not SAS Report, then you will not have a choice because you can only export the result in its original format, and you will not see this window. Choose the desired output file type and click **Next**.

In the next window choose either **Local Computer** or **SAS Servers**, and then click the **Browse** button to navigate to the location where you want the file to be saved. In this window, you can also choose whether to **Overwrite existing output**. Click **Next** to view a summary

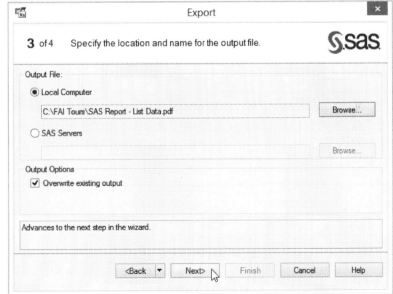

of your choices in the final window (not shown). When you are satisfied, click **Finish**.

When you export as a step in a project, an Export File task icon  will be added to your project, along with an icon for the newly exported results. Every time you run your project, your results will be automatically re-exported.

4

"Every now and then a man's mind is stretched by a new idea or sensation, and never shrinks back to its former dimensions."

OLIVER WENDELL HOLMES, SR.

From *The Autocrat of the Breakfast Table*, 1858.

CHAPTER 4

Producing Complex Reports in Summary Tables

4.1 Creating Summary Tables with Frequencies

The Summary Tables task is the most powerful and flexible of the reporting tasks in SAS Enterprise Guide. It gives you control over not only which data appear in a report, but also over how data are arranged, summarized, labeled, and even colored. There is a Summary Tables wizard that accesses basic features, but this chapter shows the task.

This example uses the Volcanoes data set to create a report showing the number of active and extinct volcanoes for each region. To open the task, click the data icon in the Project Tree or Process Flow, and select **Tasks ▸ Describe ▸ Summary Tables** from the menu bar. The Summary Tables window will open, displaying the Data page.

	Volcano	Country	Region	Height	Activity	Type
1	Altar	Ecuador	SA	5321	Extinct	Stratovolcano
2	Arthur's Seat	UK	Eu	251	Extinct	
3	Barren Island	India	As	354	Active	Stratovolcano
4	Elbrus	Russia	Eu	5633	Extinct	Stratovolcano
5	Erebus		An	3794	Active	Stratovolcano

Assigning task roles To produce a summary table showing frequencies, assign one or more variables to the **Classification variables** role. These variables may be character or numeric. SAS Enterprise Guide will divide the data into categories based on the values of the classification variables. The following window shows the Volcanoes data set with the variables Region and Activity serving as classification variables.

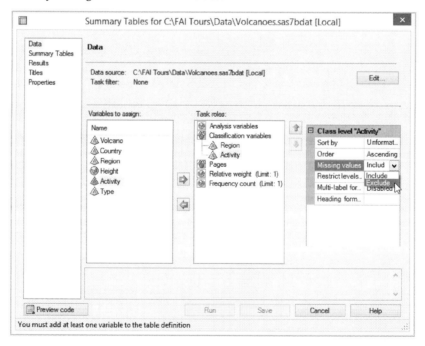

When you drag a variable to the classification role, a box appears on the right. In this box, you can select options for that variable, including how to handle missing data. By default, missing values are included as valid rows and columns, which may or may not be what you want. In this case, two volcanoes have a missing value for Activity. To avoid having an entire row devoted to missing values, click **Missing values** and select **Exclude** for the variable Activity.

Once you exclude missing values for a variable, observations with missing values will be excluded from the report even if you decide not to use that particular variable. Because of this, it's a good idea to assign variables to the classification role only if you intend to use them in the current report.

Arranging your table Before you can run a report, you must tell SAS Enterprise Guide how to arrange the report table. Start by clicking the **Summary Tables** option in the selection pane on the left. In the Summary Tables page, you will see areas labeled **Available variables** and **Preview**. To assign a variable to serve as a row or column in your report, drag the variable name from the list of available variables to the Preview area. It may take a little practice to get variables where you want them. The trick is to watch the cursor. If the cursor looks like the universal not-allowed symbol, ⊘, then you cannot drop the variable. When the cursor turns into an arrow, then you can drop the variable.

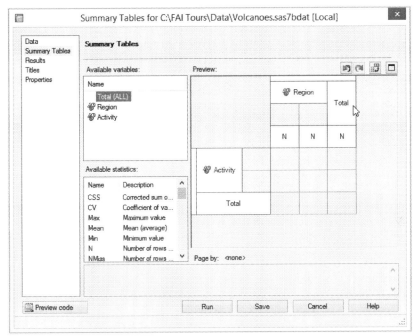

The undo and redo buttons in the upper-right corner of the Preview area can be quite useful. If you want to switch the row variables with the column variables, use the pivot button. To enlarge the Preview area, click the maximize button. You can drag the **Total(ALL)** variable to the Preview area to tell SAS Enterprise Guide where to insert totals. In this window, the values of the variable Activity form the rows, while the values of Region form the columns. When you are satisfied with the arrangement of your table, click **Run**.

Results Here is the report of Activity by Region. Notice that the value in each cell is simply the number of volcanoes in that category. N (the number of non-missing values) is the default statistic for classification variables.

Summary Tables

| | Region | | | | | | | Total (ALL) |
| | AP | Af | An | As | Eu | NA | SA | |
	N	N	N	N	N	N	N	N
Activity								
Active	3	2	1	5	4	5	3	23
Extinct	1	1	.	.	3	.	2	7
Total (ALL)	4	3	1	5	7	5	5	30

4.2 ▶ Adding Statistics to Summary Tables

The previous section showed how to produce a table containing simple counts. Sometimes that's all you need, but often you want more. You might want to know total sales by region, or the mean test score for each class. In summary tables, you can compute sums and means, plus a long list of other statistics, including maximum and minimum values, percentages, medians, quartiles, standard deviations, and variances.

This example uses the Tours data set to create a report with statistics. To open the task, click the data icon in the Project Tree or Process Flow to make it active, and select **Tasks ▶ Describe ▶ Summary Tables** from the menu bar. The Summary Tables window will open, displaying the Data page.

	Volcano	Departs	Days	Price	Difficulty
1	Etna	Catania	7	$1,610	m
2	Fuji	Tokyo	2	$335	c
3	Kenya	Nairobi	6	$1,245	m
4	Kilauea	Hilo	1	$85	e
5	Kilimanjaro	Nairobi	9	$1,965	c
6	Krakatau	Jakarta	7	$1,345	e
7	Poas	San Jose	1	$97	e
8	Reventador	Quito	4	$875	m
9	St. Helens	Portland	2	$250	e
10	Vesuvius	Rome	6	$1,495	e

Assigning task roles There are a few statistics that you can compute for classification variables. These include N and PctN (the percentage of frequency). However, most statistics can be computed only for analysis variables. Analysis variables must be numeric. (It's simply not possible to compute a mean using character values like Active and Extinct.) To produce a summary report containing sums and means, assign one or more variables to the analysis role. The following window shows the Tours data set with the variable Difficulty serving as a classification variable, and the variables Days and Price serving as analysis variables.

Arranging your table You arrange analysis variables in your table the same way you arrange classification variables. First, click the **Summary Tables** option in the selection pane on the left. In the Summary Tables page, you will see areas labeled **Available variables** and **Preview**. To assign a variable to serve as a row or column in your report, drag the variable name from the list of available variables to the Preview area. In the following window, the values of Difficulty form the rows, and the values of Days and Price form the columns.

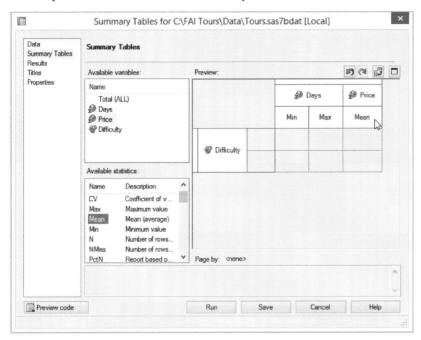

Choosing statistics The default statistic for classification variables is N (the number of non-missing values). The default statistic for analysis variables is Sum. You can choose many other statistics from the box labeled **Available statistics**. To add a statistic to your report, click the name of the statistic and drag it to the **Preview** area. Be sure to watch your cursor carefully. If the cursor looks like the universal not-allowed symbol, ⦸, then you cannot drop the statistic. When the cursor turns into an arrow, then you can drop the statistic.

In the preceding window, the statistics Min and Max have been placed under the variable Days, and the statistic Mean has been placed under the variable Price. When you are satisfied with the arrangement of your table, click **Run**.

Results Here is the report of Difficulty by Days and Price. Notice that the values in the cells are the minimum and maximum number of Days, and the mean Price.

Summary Tables

	Days		Price
	Min	Max	Mean
Difficulty			
c	2.00	9.00	1150.00
e	1.00	7.00	654.40
m	4.00	7.00	1243.33

4.3 Changing Heading Properties in Summary Tables

Once you've constructed a summary table, put each variable in its proper place, and selected statistics, you may want to change the way the table looks. In the Preview area of the Summary Tables window, you can change many properties of your report.

To modify an existing report, right-click the Summary Tables task icon in the Project Tree or Process Flow, and select **Modify Summary Tables** from the pop-up menu. The Summary Tables window will open. To display the Preview area, click the **Summary Tables** option in the selection pane on the left.

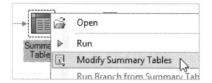

Heading Properties   To change headings that are the names of variables or statistics, use the Heading Properties window. For example, to change the heading Min to Minimum, you would right-click **Min** in the **Preview** area and select **Heading Properties** from the pop-up menu. The Heading Properties window will open.

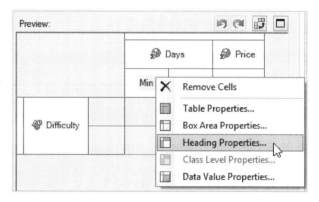

Using the **General** tab of the Heading Properties window, you can type a new label for the variable or statistic you have selected. In this window, the word Minimum has been typed in the **Label** box. Using the **Font** tab, you can change the font, font style, size, foreground color, background color, and other attributes of headings. When you are satisfied with the changes, click **OK**.

You can now change other properties. For this example, you should also change the statistic name Max to Maximum using the Heading Properties window for Max.

Box Area Properties Summary Tables reports always contain a box in the upper-left corner. By default, this box is empty. But you can put a label in that box to give your reports a nicely polished look. To do this, right-click anywhere in the **Preview** area and select **Box Area Properties** from the pop-up menu.

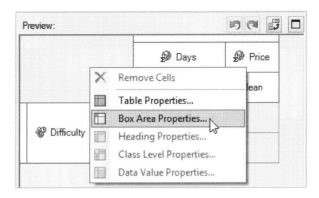

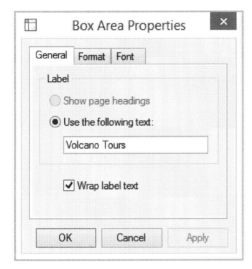

Using the **General** tab of the Box Area Properties window, you can specify the text you want printed in the box area. In this example, the words Volcano Tours have been typed in the text box. Using the **Font** tab, you can change the font, font style, size, foreground color, background color, and other attributes of the text to be printed in the box area.

When you are satisfied with the changes, click **OK**. You can then change other properties, or click **Run** to see the new results.

Results Here is the report. Notice that the labels Min and Max have been replaced with Minimum and Maximum, and the phrase Volcano Tours has been inserted in the box area.

Summary Tables			
Volcano Tours	**Days**		**Price**
	Minimum	**Maximum**	**Mean**
Difficulty			
c	2.00	9.00	1150.00
e	1.00	7.00	654.40
m	4.00	7.00	1243.33

4.4 Changing Class Level Headings and Properties in Summary Tables

The previous section showed how to change headings that are the names of variables or statistics, but data values can also serve as headings. These data values are called class level headings. When you change class level headings, you are changing the way those data values are displayed. To change the way data values are displayed, you use a format.

To modify an existing report, right-click the Summary Tables task icon in the Project Tree or Process Flow, and select **Modify Summary Tables** from the pop-up menu. The Summary Tables window will open.

Applying a format to a classification variable To change headings that are data values, you specify a format in the Data page. Click the name of the classification variable that

you want to change. A box will open on the right, listing options for that variable. Click the words **Heading format** and the ellipsis button ▫▫▫ will appear. Click the button to open a Select Column Format window for that variable. In this example, the heading format for the variable Difficulty is being selected.

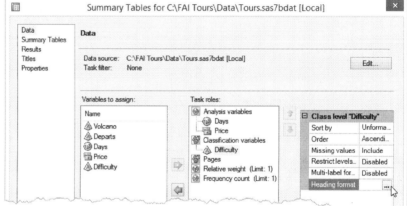

In the Select Column Format window, choose the category of formats you want to see, and then choose the name of the format you want to use. In most cases, to change a class level heading you will need a user-defined format. In this example, the user-defined format $DIFF. has been selected. The $DIFF. format was created in Tutorial B. Sections 3.6 and 3.7 also show how to create user-defined formats. Once you are satisfied, click **OK** to return to the Summary Tables window.

Class Level Properties To change other properties of class level headings, click the **Summary Tables** option in the selection pane on the left. Then right-click the name of the classification variable in the **Preview** area and select **Class Level Properties** from the pop-up menu. This example shows Class Level Properties being selected for the variable Difficulty. The Class Level Properties window will open.

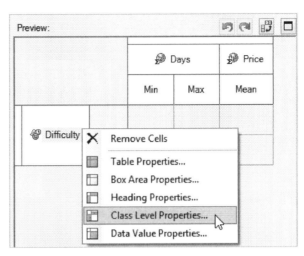

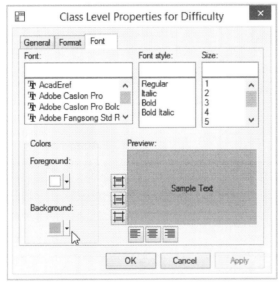

Using the **Font** tab, you can change the font, font style, size, foreground color, background color, and other attributes of headings. For this report, the background color has been changed to Gray–25%. When you are satisfied with the changes, click **OK**. Click **Run** to see the new results.

Results Here is the report. Notice that the labels c, e, and m have been replaced with Challenging, Easy, and Moderate (the values of the $DIFF. format), and have a medium gray background.

Summary Tables

Volcano Tours	Days		Price
	Minimum	Maximum	Mean
Difficulty			
Challenging	2.00	9.00	1150.00
Easy	1.00	7.00	654.40
Moderate	4.00	7.00	1243.33

4.5 Changing Table Properties in Summary Tables

In addition to changing headers and labels, you can make changes to the data cells in a table. To make a change that will apply to all the cells, use the Table Properties window.

To modify an existing report, right-click the Summary Tables task icon in the Project Tree or Process Flow, and select **Modify Summary Tables** from the pop-up menu. The Summary Tables window will open. Click the **Summary Tables** option in the selection pane on the left to display the Preview area.

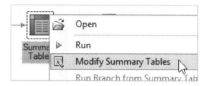

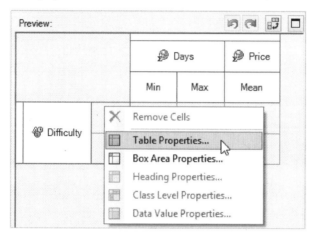

To make changes to all the data cells of a table, right-click anywhere in the **Preview** area and select **Table Properties** from the pop-up menu.

General tab Using the **General** tab of the Table Properties window, you can specify options for the treatment of missing values and class variable levels. By default, missing values are displayed as a period (.). You can specify a more meaningful label. In this example, the label none has been assigned to missing values.

Format tab Using the **Format** tab of the Table Properties window, you can choose a format for the data in the cells of the table. Here, the basic numeric format, *w.d*, has been specified with an overall width of 4 characters, and no decimal places (4.0).

Font tab Using the **Font** tab of the Table Properties window, you can change the font, font style, size, foreground color, background color, and other attributes of the data cells in your table. In this case, the font has been set to Courier New, the style to Bold, the foreground color to white, and the background color to Gray–40%.

When you are satisfied with the changes, click **OK**. You can then change other properties, or click **Run** to see the new results.

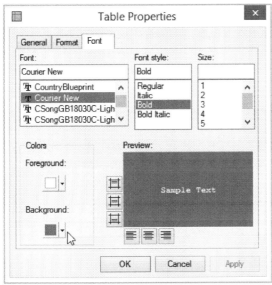

Results Here is the new report. Notice that the data cells have a dark gray background and white foreground. Also, the data are displayed in bold Courier New, and with no decimal places.

Volcano Tours	Days		Price
	Minimum	Maximum	Mean
Difficulty			
Challenging	2	9	1150
Easy	1	7	654
Moderate	4	7	1243

Summary Tables

4.6 Changing Data Value Properties in Summary Tables

Using the Table Properties window, you can make changes to all the data cells in a report, but sometimes you may want to choose different formats or fonts for different variables or statistics. To do that, use the Data Value Properties window.

To modify an existing report, right-click the Summary Tables task icon in the Project Tree or Process Flow, and select **Modify Summary Tables** from the pop-up menu. The Summary Tables window will open. Click the **Summary Tables** option in the selection pane on the left to display the Preview area.

To make changes to a particular row or column, right-click the header for that row or column in the **Preview** area and select **Data Value Properties** from the pop-up menu. In this Preview area, Data Value Properties is being selected for the column Price.

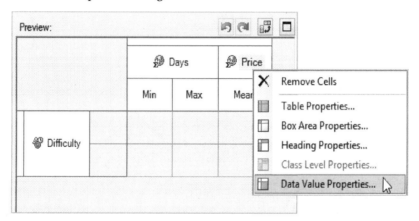

Format tab Using the **Format** tab of the Data Value Properties window, you can choose a format for the data values in the row or column. In this example, the category Currency has been selected, and SAS Enterprise Guide has listed all the available formats for currency data. The format DOLLAR*w.d* is selected, with an overall width of **9,** which includes the dollar sign, decimal point, and 2 decimal places (DOLLAR9.2).

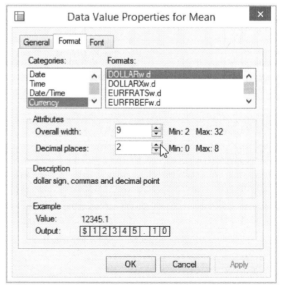

Font tab Using the **Font** tab of the Data Value Properties window, you can change the font, font style, size, foreground color, background color, and other attributes of the data cells in the row or column. In this example, the font for Price has been set to Courier New, the style to Bold, the foreground color to white, and the background color to black.

When you are satisfied with the changes, click **OK**. You can now change other properties, or click **Run** to see the new results.

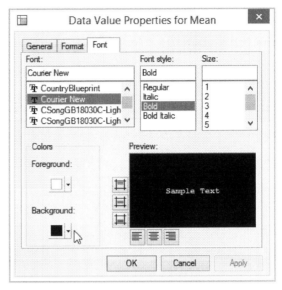

Results Here is the report. Notice that the column for Mean Price looks different from the columns for Minimum and Maximum Days. The background color is black instead of gray, and the numbers have dollar signs in front of them and two decimal places.

Summary Tables

Volcano Tours	Days		Price
	Minimum	Maximum	Mean
Difficulty			
Challenging	2	9	$1,150.00
Easy	1	7	$654.40
Moderate	4	7	$1,243.33

5

"The power to question is the basis of all human progress."

INDIRA GANDHI

Attributed to Indira Gandhi (1917-1984), prime minister of India.

CHAPTER 5

Modifying Data Using the Query Builder

5.1 Creating a Query

Sometimes the data tables available in your project may not be in the correct format for the analyses you need to perform. You may need to create new columns based on values of existing columns, summarize the data, create a subset of the data, or join data tables together. The Query Builder is a tool for doing these types of data manipulation. The Query Builder takes a table (or tables), performs some type of data manipulation, and produces either a new table or a report. Tables created by the Query Builder can be used in tasks or other queries. Reports can be viewed, or printed. The set of data manipulation instructions defined in the Query Builder is called a query.

Opening the Query Builder There are several ways to open the Query Builder. Perhaps the easiest way is to first open the data table that you want to use for your query, then click the **Query Builder** button on the workspace toolbar. You can also open the Query Builder by clicking the data icon in the Project Tree or Process Flow to make it active, and selecting **Tasks ▶ Data ▶ Query Builder** from the menu bar. Alternatively, you can right-click the data icon in the Project Tree or Process flow and select **Query Builder** from the pop-up menu.

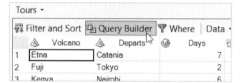

There is a lot going on in the Query Builder. The Query Builder window has three tabs for different tasks: Select Data, Filter Data, and Sort Data. In addition, there are several buttons including Add Tables, Delete, Join Tables, Computed Columns, and Prompt Manager. The name of the active data table appears in the list on the left, along with all the columns in the data table. The Query Builder opens with the Select Data tab on top and no columns selected.

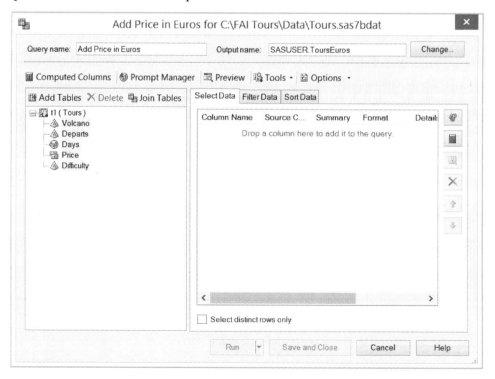

Giving the query a name Queries created in the Query Builder have names that are used to label the query icon in the Process Flow and Project Tree. By default, the first query in your project

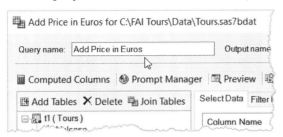

is named "Query Builder." Any additional queries will be named "Query Builder (2)," "Query Builder (3)," and so forth. To change the name, enter the new name in the box labeled **Query name** located at the top left. In this example, the query name is "Add Price in Euros."

Changing the output table name Data tables produced by the Query Builder are stored in a default location (the EGTASK library, or the SASUSER library if EGTASK is not defined) and given a name starting with the word QUERY. To change either the storage location or the table name, click the **Change** button located next to the Output name. This opens a Save File window where you can navigate to the desired storage location and give the table an appropriate name. In this example, the data table will be stored in the SASUSER library and will have the name ToursEuros.

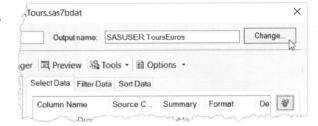

Results The result of a query can be a data table (the default), a data view, or a report. Data views do not contain data. Instead, data views contain the instructions needed to create a data table. Data tables and data views produced by the Query Builder can be used in tasks just like any other data table. Reports are for viewing or printing only and cannot be used in tasks. Changing the query result type is discussed in section 5.10.

In order to run the query, you must select the columns you want in your result (discussed in the next section), and you will probably want to perform some other data manipulations. After making the desired selections in the Query Builder and clicking **Run**, a new data table (view or report) will be added to your project.

Here is what the Process Flow looks like after running the Query Builder. In this example, the Tours data table is the input to a query named "Add Price in Euros" and the result is a data table named ToursEuros.

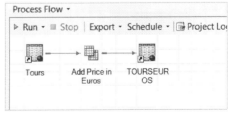

5.2 Selecting Columns in a Query

To run a query, you must tell SAS Enterprise Guide which columns to include in the result. You select columns on the **Select Data** tab of the Query Builder where you can also set properties for columns.

Open the Query Builder by clicking the data icon in the Project Tree or Process Flow to make it active, and selecting **Tasks ▶ Data ▶ Query Builder** from the menu bar. Here is a sample of the Volcanoes data table used in this example.

	Volcano	Country	Region	Height	Activity	Type
1	Altar	Ecuador	SA	5321	Extinct	Stratovolcano
2	Arthur's Seat	UK	Eu	251	Extinct	
3	Barren Island	India	As	354	Active	Stratovolcano
4	Elbrus	Russia	Eu	5633	Extinct	Stratovolcano
5	Erebus		An	3794	Active	Stratovolcano
6	Etna	Italy	Eu	3350	Active	Stratovolcano
7	Fuji	Japan	As	3776	Active	Stratovolcano
8	Garibaldi	Canada	NA	2678		Stratovolcano

Selecting the data   When you open the Query Builder window, the **Select Data** tab is on top, and no columns are selected. To select a column for the query, click the column name in the box on the left and drag it to the **Select Data** tab on the right. You can also right-click the column and choose **Select Column** from the pop-up menu. To add more than one column at a time, hold down the control (CTRL) key (or Shift if you want to select a whole group) when you click the column names. You can also add all the columns in a table to the query by clicking the table name and dragging it to the **Select Data** tab. In this example, the columns Volcano, Country, Region, and Height have been selected but not yet dragged to the Select Data tab.

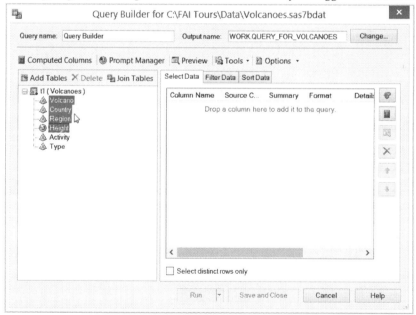

If you want to remove a column from the **Select Data** tab, click the column name on the **Select Data** tab and click the delete button [×] on the right side of the window. You can also change the order of the columns using the up and down arrow buttons [↑] [↓].

Setting properties for columns You can change the properties of a column in a query by clicking the column name on the **Select Data** tab and clicking the Properties button ⬛ located on the right side of the window.

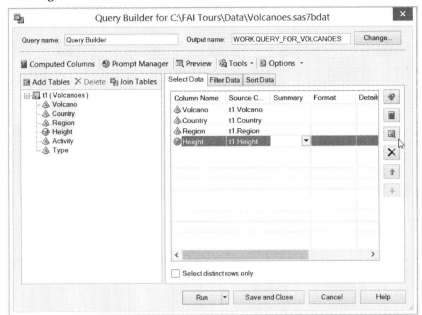

This opens the Properties window for the column. If you want the column name for the output data table to be different than the input data table, then enter the new name in the Column Name field. To change the format associated with the column, click the **Change** button to open the Formats window (not shown). You can also specify a label and length for the column. Here, the Height column is renamed Meters and given the label Height in Meters. Click **OK** to return to the Query Builder window. After selecting columns and setting properties, click **Run** in the Query Builder window.

Results Here is the data table created by the query. In this result, notice that the column that was named Height in the original table is now named Meters in the output table. Also, the Activity and Type columns from the original table are not included here.

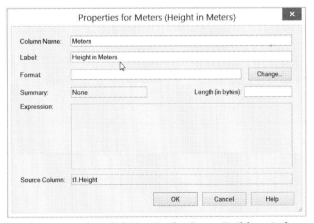

	Volcano	Country	Region	Meters
1	Altar	Ecuador	SA	5321
2	Arthur's Seat	UK	Eu	251
3	Barren Island	India	As	354
4	Elbrus	Russia	Eu	5633
5	Erebus		An	3794
6	Etna	Italy	Eu	3350
7	Fuji	Japan	As	3776
8	Garibaldi	Canada	NA	2678

5.3 Creating Columns Using Mathematical Operators

Sometimes you need to create a new column based on data values in other columns. You could do this in a Data Grid, but then if you add new rows, they will not automatically have the computed values. If you use the Query Builder, then every time you run the query it will recompute the new column for all rows including any new ones.

Here is a portion of the Eruptions data table that is used for this example. Open the Query Builder by clicking the data icon in the Project Tree or Process Flow to make it active, and selecting **Tasks ▶ Data ▶ Query Builder** from the menu bar.

	Volcano	StartDate	EndDate	VEI
1	Barren Island	12/20/1795	12/21/1795	2
2	Barren Island	12/20/1994	06/05/1995	2
3	Erebus	12/12/1912	.	2
4	Erebus	01/03/1972	.	1
5	Etna	02/06/1610	08/15/1610	2
6	Etna	06/04/1787	08/11/1787	4
7	Etna	01/30/1865	06/28/1865	2
8	Etna	12/16/2005	12/22/2005	1

The Query Builder opens with the **Select Data** tab on top. Select the columns for the query. For this example, the Volcano, StartDate, and EndDate columns are selected.

Creating a new column To create a new column, click the **Computed Columns** button located near the top of the window. This opens the Computed Columns window.

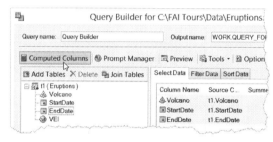

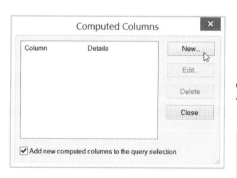

Click **New** to open the New Computed Column wizard.

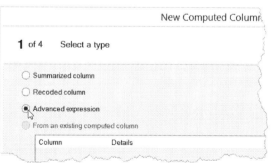

The New Computed Column wizard has up to five windows depending on which type of column you are creating. In the first window, choose **Advanced Expression**, and click **Next**.

Building the expression At the top of the second window is a box labeled **Enter an expression** where you can type your expression. If you like, you can let SAS Enterprise Guide help you build the expression. The bottom left part of the window shows nodes for **Functions, Tables,** and **Selected Columns**. To add columns to the expression, expand either the **Tables** or the **Selected Columns** node to locate the desired column. Then double-click the column and it will be added to the expression. You can use the various operator buttons that appear below the box to build your expression. In this example, the length of the eruption is computed in days.

Because the StartDate and EndDate are both SAS date values (the number of days since January 1, 1960), you can simply subtract the start date from the end date and add one. When you are finished building the expression, click **Next**.

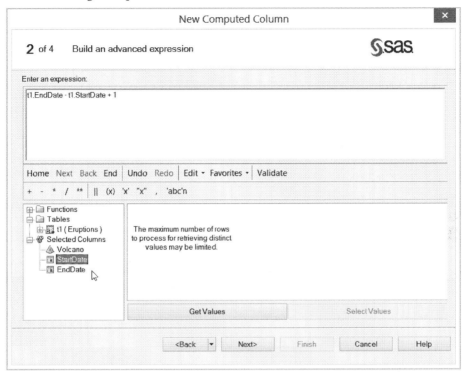

In the third window you can set the properties of the new column. In this example the column is given the name Duration. At this point, you can click **Next** to see a summary of your new column in the fourth window (not shown), or click **Finish**. Click **Close** in the Computed Columns window and then click **Run** in the Query Builder.

Results Here are the results of the query including the new column Duration. Notice that the values for Duration are missing for rows where the values for EndDate are missing. If you have missing values for columns that are part of the expression, then the results will be missing.

	Volcano	StartDa...	EndDate	Duration
1	Barren Island	12/20/1795	12/21/1795	2
2	Barren Island	12/20/1994	06/05/1995	168
3	Erebus	12/12/1912		.
4	Erebus	01/03/1972		.
5	Etna	02/06/1610	08/15/1610	191
6	Etna	06/04/1787	08/11/1787	69
7	Etna	01/30/1865	06/28/1865	150
8	Etna	12/16/2005	12/22/2005	7

A more detailed example of creating a computed column can be found in Tutorial C.

5.4 Creating Columns Using Functions

SAS Enterprise Guide has many built-in functions you can use when creating new columns. A function takes a value and turns it into another related value. For example, the MONTH function will take a date and return just the month. The LOG function will return the natural log of a number. There are many functions to choose from in over 20 different categories including character, date and time, and mathematical. Some of the commonly used functions are listed in the next section.

Here is a portion of the TourDates data table that contains data on individual tours including the departure date. To create a column that has the day of month the tour departs, you can use the DAY function. To open the Query Builder, click the data icon in the Project Tree or Process Flow to make it active, and select **Tasks ▶ Data ▶ Query Builder** from the menu bar. The Query Builder opens with the **Select Data** tab on top.

	Tour	Volcano	DepartureDate	Guide
1	PS27	Poas	08/05/2018	Carlos
2	SH40	St. Helens	06/19/2018	Casey
3	SH41	St. Helens	07/05/2018	Casey
4	SH42	St. Helens	07/23/2018	Casey
5	SH43	St. Helens	08/15/2018	Kelly
6	FJ12	Fuji	09/12/2018	Cooper
7	ET01	Etna	08/05/2018	Cooper
8	KE05	Kenya	05/31/2018	Kelly

Select the columns for the query. In this example Tour, Volcano, and DepartureDate are selected.

Creating a new column As discussed in the previous section, to create a new column, click the **Computed Columns** button in the Query Builder window. This opens the Computed Columns window (not shown). Click **New** to open the New Computed Column wizard. Then select **Advanced Expression** in the first window (not shown), and click **Next**.

Choosing a function In the second window, expand the **Functions** node located in the lower left portion of the window. The functions are listed alphabetically. To locate a function by category, expand the **Categories** node then expand the node for the desired function category. For this example, choose the **DAY** function from the **Date and Time** category. Clicking the function name will display information about the function in the lower right portion of the window. Double-clicking the function name will add it to the expression box located at the top of the window.

Defining arguments for functions Most functions take some sort of argument. When the function is inserted into the expression, a placeholder for the argument appears in the expression. You must replace the placeholder in the function with a valid argument. If the function calls for a character value, that value can be a character column or a character string enclosed in quotation marks. If the function calls for a numeric value, that value can be a numeric column or a number. The DAY function requires a SAS date value.

Collapse the Functions node to display the available tables and selected columns. After adding a function to the expression, the placeholder for the function— <datevalue> for this example— will be highlighted. Double-click the desired column name, and the placeholder will be replaced by the column you selected, in this case the DepartureDate column from the

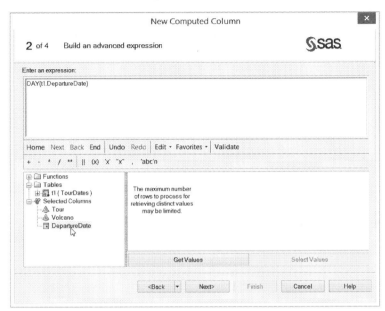

TourDates table (t1). If you want to use a constant value in the function instead of a column, you can either type the value directly in the expression box in the appropriate location, or use the **Get Values** button to list discrete values for particular columns. Note that it may take a long time to get all the values if your data table is large or if there are many possible values for the column. After listing discrete values, either double-click the value to enter it into the expression, or highlight the value and click **Select Values**.

After you define your expression, you can check it by clicking **Validate**. The Validate window (not shown) will open telling you whether your expression is valid. Close the Validate window, make any necessary changes, and click **Next.** In the third window of the wizard (not shown), you can give the new column a meaningful name and label, and also assign the column a format if desired. For this example, the new column is named Day. Click **Next** to display a summary of your new computed column in the fourth window (not shown), then click **Finish** to return to the Computed Columns window. Click **Close** in the Computed Columns window, and then click **Run** in the Query Builder.

Results Here are the query results, which now include the new column Day. Day is the day of the month the tour departs.

	Tour	Volcano	DepartureDate	Day
1	PS27	Poas	08/05/2018	5
2	SH40	St. Helens	06/19/2018	19
3	SH41	St. Helens	07/05/2018	5
4	SH42	St. Helens	07/23/2018	23
5	SH43	St. Helens	08/15/2018	15
6	FJ12	Fuji	09/12/2018	12
7	ET01	Etna	08/05/2018	5
8	KE05	Kenya	05/31/2018	31

5.5 Selected Functions

The following table lists the definition and form of commonly used functions.

Function name	Form of function	Definition
Mathematical		
LOG	LOG(*numValue*)	Natural logarithm
LOG10	LOG10(*numValue*)	Logarithm to the base 10
Descriptive Statistics		
MAX	MAX(*numValue,numValue,...*)	Largest non-missing value
MEAN	MEAN(*numValue,numValue,...*)	Arithmetic mean of non-missing values
MIN	MIN(*numValue,numValue,...*)	Smallest non-missing value
SUM	SUM(*numValue,numValue,...*)	Sum of non-missing values
Character		
CATS	CATS(*charValue, charValue,...*)	Concatenates two or more character values together stripping leading and trailing blanks
LENGTH	LENGTH(*charValue*)	Returns the position of the last non-blank character (missing values have a length of 1)
SUBSTR	SUBSTR(*charValue,position,n*)	Extracts a substring from a character value starting at 'position' for 'n' characters or until end if no 'n'
UPCASE	UPCASE(*charValue*)	Converts all letters in character value to uppercase
Date and Datetime[1]		
DATEPART	DATEPART(*SAS-datetime-value*)	Returns a SAS date value from a datetime
DAY	DAY(*SAS-date-value*)	Returns the day of the month from a SAS date value
MDY	MDY(*month,day,year*)	Returns a SAS date value from month, day, and year values
MONTH	MONTH(*SAS-date-value*)	Returns the month (1–12) from a SAS date value
QTR	QTR(*SAS-date-value*)	Returns the yearly quarter (1–4) from a SAS date value
WEEKDAY	WEEKDAY(*SAS-date-value*)	Returns the day of week (1=Sunday) from a SAS date value

[1] A SAS date value is the number of days since January 1, 1960. A SAS datetime is the number of seconds since midnight January 1, 1960.

Here are examples using the selected functions.

Function name	Example	Result	Example	Result
Mathematical				
LOG	LOG(1)	0.0	LOG(10)	2.30259
LOG10	LOG10(1)	0.0	LOG10(10)	1.0
Descriptive Statistics				
MAX	MAX(9.3,8,7.5)	9.3	MAX(–3,.,5)	5
MEAN	MEAN(1,4,7,2)	3.5	MEAN(2,.,3)	2.5
MIN	MIN(9.3,8,7.5)	7.5	MIN(–3,.,5)	–3
SUM	SUM(3,5,1)	9.0	SUM(4,7,.)	11
Character				
CATS	CATS(' Hot', ' Lava')	'HotLava'	CATS('Mt ', ' Fuji')	'MtFuji'
LENGTH	LENGTH('hot lava')	8	LENGTH('eruption')	8
SUBSTR	SUBSTR('(916)734-6281',2,3)	'916'	SUBSTR('Tour12',5)	'12'
UPCASE	UPCASE('St. Helens')	'ST. HELENS'	UPCASE('Fuji')	'FUJI'
Date and Datetime				
DATEPART	DATEPART(86400)	1	DATEPART(31536000)	365
DAY	DAY(0)	1	DAY(290)	17
MDY	MDY(1,1,1960)	0	MDY(10,17,1960)	290
MONTH	MONTH(0)	1	MONTH(290)	10
QTR	QTR(0)	1	QTR(290)	4
WEEKDAY	WEEKDAY(0)	6	WEEKDAY(290)	2

5.6 Adding a Grand Total to a Data Table

Using the Query Builder, you can create columns that contain summary statistics for existing columns. For example, you could calculate a grand total over all the rows of data and then use the grand total to compute the percent of total for each row.

Here is a sample of the AdResults data table, which contains the amounts spent on advertising by the Fire and Ice Tours company for both its Seattle and its Portland offices. This example creates a new column that has the total amount spent for both offices for the time period. To open the Query Builder, click the data icon in the Project Tree or Process Flow to make it active, and select **Tasks ▶ Data ▶ Query Builder** from the menu bar.

	City	Month	AdDollars	Bookings
9	Seattle	9	250	22
10	Seattle	10	325	20
11	Seattle	11	400	25
12	Seattle	12	500	31
13	Portland	1	325	25
14	Portland	2	290	19
15	Portland	3	250	17
16	Portland	4	300	18

Summarizing the data First select the columns for the query, in this case all the columns in the AdResults table. Initially, no summary statistics are listed for the columns. To summarize data in a column, click the column name on the **Select Data** tab, then click the down arrow in the Summary cell. Choose the summary statistic you want to use from the drop-down list. For this example, choose **SUM**.

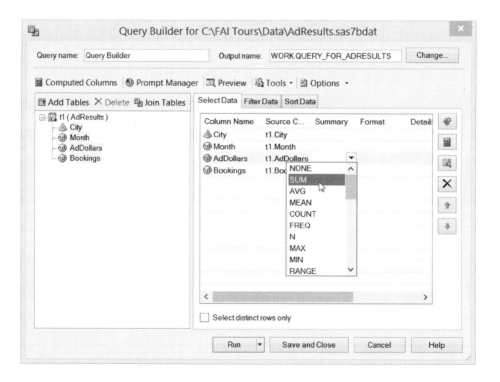

Selecting summary groups After you choose a summary statistic, the original column will be replaced by the newly summarized column. By default, all selected columns are used for the summary groups. To create a grand total, you don't want any summary groups. Uncheck **Automatically select groups** in the Summary Groups section of the Query Builder so that no groups are selected.

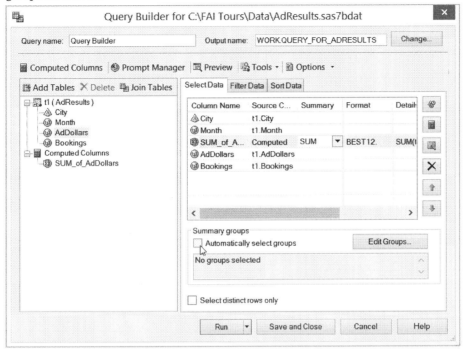

Setting properties for the new column The default name for the new column combines the summary statistic and the old column name. If you don't like the name, you can change it in the Properties window. Click the column name, then click the Properties button on the right side of the Query Builder window to open the Properties window.

Adding back the original column Because the newly computed column replaces the original column, the original column will not be in the output data table unless you add it back. If you want to keep the original column, as well as the newly computed column, then click the original column name in the box on the left and drag it to the **Select Data** tab. Use the up- or down-arrow buttons on the right side of the window to position the original column where you want. In this example, the original column, AdDollars, has been added back in the query and positioned above the Bookings column. When you are satisfied, click **Run**.

Results Here are the results of the query including the new column SUM_of_AdDollars. Notice that the new column has the same value for all rows.

	City	Month	SUM_of_AdDollars	AdDollars	Bookings
9	Seattle	9	7845	250	22
10	Seattle	10	7845	325	20
11	Seattle	11	7845	400	25
12	Seattle	12	7845	500	31
13	Portland	1	7845	325	25
14	Portland	2	7845	290	19
15	Portland	3	7845	250	17
16	Portland	4	7845	300	18

5.7 Adding Subtotals to a Data Table

The previous section showed how you can create new columns that summarize all the rows in a data table. This section shows how to summarize all the rows that belong to a group. The steps are the same as adding a grand total, with the additional step of selecting a group column.

Here is a sample of the results from the previous section where the SUM_of_AdDollars column contains the grand total of the AdDollars column. In this example, the total amount spent by each city's office will be calculated instead of the grand total. Reopen the Query Builder by clicking the **Modify Task** button on the workspace toolbar for the query result.

	City	Month	SUM_of_AdDollars	AdDollars	Bookings
9	Seattle	9	7845	250	22
10	Seattle	10	7845	325	20
11	Seattle	11	7845	400	25
12	Seattle	12	7845	500	31
13	Portland	1	7845	325	25
14	Portland	2	7845	290	19
15	Portland	3	7845	250	17
16	Portland	4	7845	300	18

Summarizing the data Here is the query from the previous section that contains all the columns from the AdResults table and the SUM_of_AdDollars column, which is the grand total for the AdDollars column. To change the SUM_of_AdDollars column to a subtotal by City, click the **Edit Groups** button. This opens the Edit Groups window.

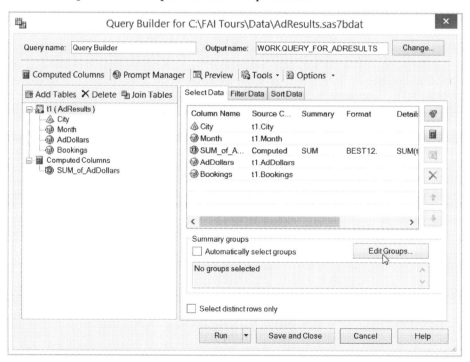

Selecting groups In the Edit Groups window, select the column or columns to use for the groups. Click the column name, City for this example, in the **Available columns** list and click the plus arrow 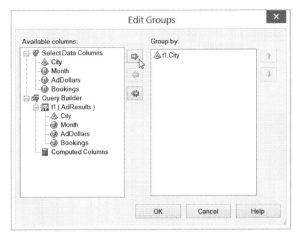 to add it to the **Group by** list. Click **OK** to return to the Query Builder window.

Notice that the name for the summarized column, in this case SUM_of_AdDollars, does not change. But now the grouping column, City from the AdResults table (t1), appears in the area labeled **Summary Groups** near the bottom of the window. Click **Run** to run the query.

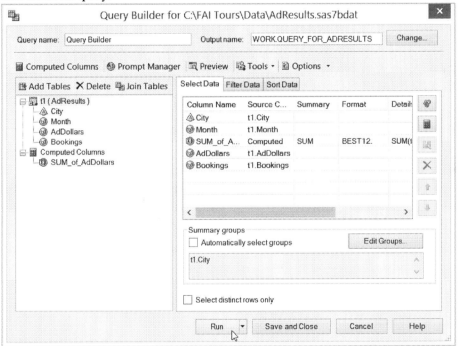

Results Here are the results of the query. Notice that the rows for Seattle have a different value for SUM_of_AdDollars than the rows for Portland. Also, the resulting data table is now sorted by the grouping column.

	City	Month	SUM_of_AdDollars	AdDollars	Bookings
9	Portland	1	3665	325	25
10	Portland	10	3665	350	24
11	Portland	12	3665	400	33
12	Portland	4	3665	300	18
13	Seattle	7	4180	150	17
14	Seattle	3	4180	525	32
15	Seattle	6	4180	325	18
16	Seattle	12	4180	500	31

5.8 Creating Summary Data Tables in a Query

The previous section showed how you can create new columns that summarize all the rows belonging to a group. The summarized values were repeated for each row that belonged to the group. But if you want only one row for each group showing just the summarized values, you can do this in a query by eliminating all columns that are not either grouped or summarized.

Here is a sample of the AdResults data table, which contains the amounts spent on advertising for the Fire and Ice Tours company for its Seattle and its Portland offices. This example creates a new table with two rows showing the total number of bookings and the amount spent by each office. To open the Query Builder, click the data icon in the Project Tree or Process Flow to make it active, and select **Tasks ▶ Data ▶ Query Builder** from the menu bar.

	City	Month	AdDollars	Bookings
9	Seattle	9	250	22
10	Seattle	10	325	20
11	Seattle	11	400	25
12	Seattle	12	500	31
13	Portland	1	325	25
14	Portland	2	290	19
15	Portland	3	250	17
16	Portland	4	300	18

Select the summary and group columns   To create a summary data table, select just the columns that will be either summarized or grouped. Choose the type of summarization from the drop-down list that appears when you click the Summary cell for the selected column on the **Select Data** tab. In this example, the AdDollars and the Bookings columns are summed. Because **Automatically select groups** is checked by default, all the columns that are not summarized are included in the group. For this example, City is the grouping column because it is the only column selected for the query that is not summarized.

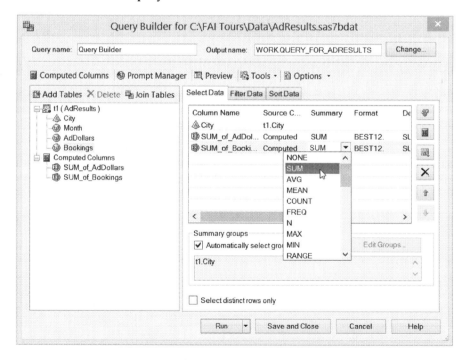

Setting properties for the new columns SAS Enterprise Guide assigns names to the summarized columns combining the summary statistic and the old column names. For example, the name for the sum of the column AdDollars would be SUM_of_AdDollars. If you don't like the name, you can change it in the Properties window for the column. Click the column name on

the **Select Data** tab of the Query Builder, then click the Properties button 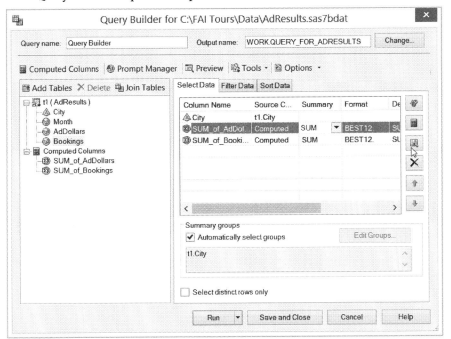 on the right side of the Query Builder to open the Properties window.

In the Properties window for the column, you can specify a new name, give the column a label, and change the format for the column. After making the desired changes to the properties, click **OK.** Then click **Run** in the Query Builder to produce the result. For this example, the name for the summarized column SUM_of_AdDollars is changed to Total_Dollars_Spent.

Results Here is the SAS data table containing the summarized data. Notice that the new table contains only one row for each value of the grouping column, City.

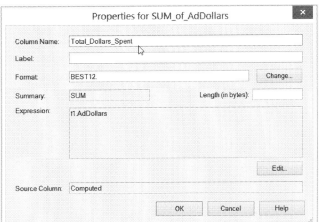

5.9 Recoding Values in a Query

If you want to group data together based on a set of values in a column, you can do this by recoding a column in the Query Builder. For example, if you have sales offices from several different cities, you may want to group them by region. If region is not already defined in the data, then you can define it using the Query Builder. Recoding a column is similar to creating and applying user-defined formats to a column. But, when you recode a column, you create a newly computed column where the data values are actually changed. When you use formats, only the way the data values are displayed is changed.

Here are a few rows from the Latlong data table, which gives the latitude and longitude of volcanoes from around the world. Using the recode feature of the Query Builder you can group the volcanoes by zone, according to the value of the column Latitude. To open the Query Builder, click the data icon in the Project Tree or Process Flow to make it active, and select **Tasks ▶ Data ▶ Query Builder** from the menu bar. This opens the Query Builder window (not shown) with the **Select Data** tab on top. Select the columns for the query. For this example, select all the columns on the table.

	Volcano	Latitude	Longitude
1	Altar	-1.67	-78.42
2	Barren Island	12.28	93.52
3	Elbrus	43.33	42.45
4	Erebus	-77.53	167.17
5	Etna	37.73	15
6	Fuji	35.35	138.73
7	Garibaldi	49.85	-123
8	Grimsvotn	64.42	-17.33

Creating the recoded column In the Query Builder window, right-click the column to recode (Latitude for this example) in the list of columns on the left and select **Recode Column**. This opens the New Computed Column wizard.

In the first window, specify the type of column to be created (either character or numeric) in the area labeled **Column Type**. For this example, choose **Character**. Then click **Add** to open the Specify a Replacement window.

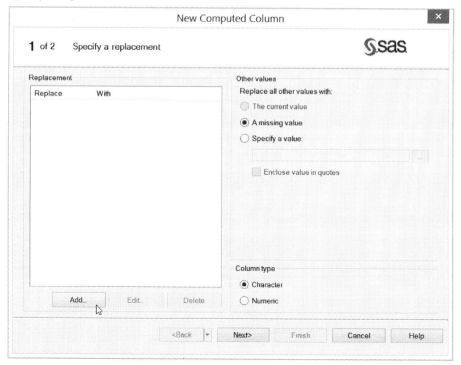

Defining the replacements In the Specify a Replacement window, there are three tabs: **Replace Values, Replace a Range**, and **Replace Condition**. Use Replace Values for one-to-one replacements. It probably makes the most sense to use the Replace a Range feature for numeric data, but it can be used for character data if you want to replace a set of values that fall into a consecutive range alphabetically. Use the Replace Condition feature when you want to use a

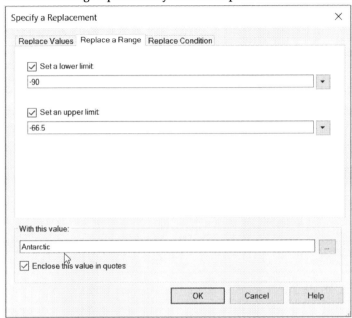

conditional operator such as "Less Than" or "In a List" to specify your replacements. For this example, click the **Replace a Range** tab. Enter the lower and upper limits of the range of values to replace in the appropriate boxes. If you want to see what the current values are, then click the down-arrow to the right of the box and a window will open (not shown) displaying all the values. In the box labeled **With this value**, type the new value that you want to replace the old range of values. When you are satisfied, click **OK**.

Replacement	
Replace	With
-23.49...23.49	'Tropical'
23.5...66.49	'N. Temperate'
-66.49...-23.5	'S. Temperate'
66.5...90	'Arctic'
-90...-66.5	'Antarctic'

The replacement logic you defined will appear in the first window of the wizard. Click **Add** again to add another replacement and repeat this procedure for all the replacements you want to make. In this example, there are five replacements. The first replacement shows that the new column will have the value 'Tropical' for all rows where the value of the column Latitude is between -23.49 and 23.49. In the first window of the wizard, you can also choose what to do with values that do not fall into the ranges you specified. For this example, replacing other values with **A missing value** is fine. When you are finished, click **Next**.

In the second window (not shown), give the new column a meaningful name and also specify the format. For this example, set the column name to Zone and the character format to $12. At this point, you can click **Next** to see a summary in the third window (not shown), or click **Finish**. Then click **Run** in the Query Builder window to run the query.

Results Here is a sample of the query result. Notice that both the Latitude column and the new column, Zone, are part of the query result.

	Volcano	Latitude	Longitude	Zone
1	Altar	-1.67	-78.42	Tropical
2	Barren Island	12.28	93.52	Tropical
3	Elbrus	43.33	42.45	N. Temperate
4	Erebus	-77.53	167.17	Antarctic
5	Etna	37.73	15	N. Temperate
6	Fuji	35.35	138.73	N. Temperate
7	Garibaldi	49.85	-123	N. Temperate
8	Grimsvotn	64.42	-17.33	N. Temperate

5.10 Changing the Result Type of Queries

When you run a query using the Query Builder, you have a choice about the type of result the
query produces. A query can produce a SAS data table, a SAS data view, or a report. A SAS data
view is similar to a SAS data table, except that it does not contain any data. Instead, SAS data
views contain the instructions required to create a new data table. Data tables and views
generated by the Query Builder can be used as a source of data for tasks. Reports are for viewing
or printing only.

Setting the default result type The default result type for queries is a data table, but you
can change the default. To do this, open the Options window by selecting **Tools ▶ Options** from
the menu bar. Click **Query** in the selection pane on the left to open the Query page. Near the
bottom of this page is a drop-down list under **Save query result set as**. Select the desired result
type. All subsequent queries you build will use this as the default result type.

Setting the result type for a query If you want to change the result type of an individual query, click the **Options** button in the Query Builder window and select **Options for This Query**. The Query Options window will open. (Note that you can also select **Defaults for All Queries** to open the Options window shown on the previous page.)

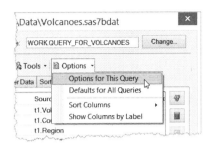

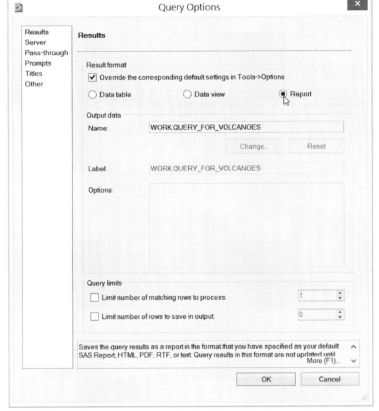

In the Results page of the Query Options window, check **Override the corresponding default settings in Tools -> Options**, and then select the type of result you want for the query. You can choose a data table, data view, or report. Changes made in the Query Options window affect only the results of the current query.

If you choose the Report type, you may also want to give your report a title or footnote. You can assign titles and footnotes in the Titles page of the Query Options window.

Query report All the query examples so far in this book have shown the result as a data table. Here is a partial view of a report generated from a query of the Volcanoes data table with the title Volcanoes Report. Note that in query reports, the column labels are used instead of the column names.

Volcanoes Report

Volcano	Country	Region	Height in Meters
Altar	Ecuador	SA	5321
Arthur's Seat	UK	Eu	251
Barren Island	India	As	354
Elbrus	Russia	Eu	5633
Erebus		An	3794
Etna	Italy	Eu	3350
Fuji	Japan	As	3776
Garibaldi	Canada	NA	2678

6

" I find that a great part of the information I have was acquired by looking up something and finding something else along the way. "

FRANKLIN P. ADAMS

Attributed to Franklin P. Adams (1881-1960), newspaper columnist, satirist, and poet.

CHAPTER 6

Sorting and Filtering Data

6.1 Filtering Data in a Task

Sometimes you don't want to use all the rows in a data table. There are several ways to subset or filter data in SAS Enterprise Guide. This section shows how you can filter the data used in a task. If your goal is simply to create a new data table that is a subset of another table, then the Filter and Sort task or the Query Builder shown later in this chapter may be more appropriate.

Here is the TourDates data table. This example uses the List Data task to demonstrate how to filter data in a task. To open the List Data task, click the data icon in the Project Tree or Process Flow to make it active. Then select **Tasks ▶ Describe ▶ List Data** from the menu bar. The List Data window will open, displaying the Data page. For this example, all the variables in the table are assigned to the List variables role.

	Tour	Volcano	DepartureDate	Guide
1	PS27	Poas	08/05/2018	Carlos
2	SH40	St. Helens	06/19/2018	Casey
3	SH41	St. Helens	07/05/2018	Casey
4	SH42	St. Helens	07/23/2018	Casey
5	SH43	St. Helens	08/15/2018	Kelly
6	FJ12	Fuji	09/12/2018	Cooper
7	ET01	Etna	08/05/2018	Cooper
8	KE05	Kenya	05/31/2018	Kelly
9	KL18	Kilauea	07/08/2018	Malia
10	KL19	Kilauea	07/15/2018	Malia
11	KL20	Kilauea	07/22/2018	Malia
12	RD02	Reventador	07/11/2018	Carlos
13	VS11	Vesuvius	07/21/2018	Cooper
14	VS12	Vesuvius	08/15/2018	Cooper
15	KJ01	Kilimanjaro	06/09/2018	Kelly
16	KK03	Krakatau	07/19/2018	Kelly

Editing the data source The Data source and Task filter are displayed at the top of the Data page in the task window. By default, no filters are applied to data in a task. To add a filter, click the **Edit** button. This opens the Edit Data and Filter window.

Creating the filter In the Edit Data and Filter window is an area labeled **Task filter** that contains four empty boxes. Click the down-arrow on the first box, and select the variable that you want to use for your filter from the drop-down list.

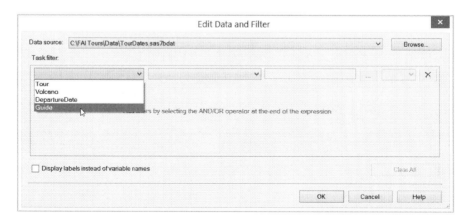

In the second box, select the operator from the drop-down list.

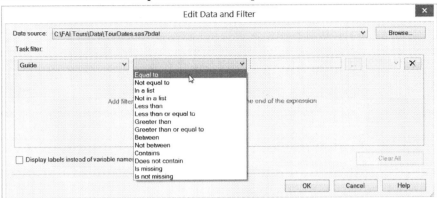

In the third box, either type in a value, or click the ellipsis button 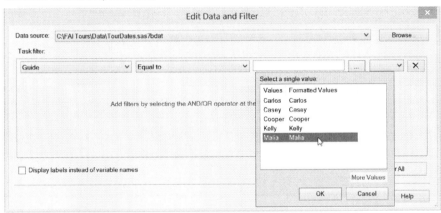 to get a list of values for the selected variable. Select the desired value and click **OK**. If you want to add another condition to the filter, select AND or OR from the drop-down list in the fourth box. A new row of boxes will appear where you can specify the additional condition. When you are finished specifying the filter conditions, click **OK.**

The filter you defined will appear in the **Task filter** area of the Data page in the task window. Click **Run** to run the task.

Results Here are the results of the List Data task showing only the rows of data that meet the filter condition where Guide is equal to "Malia."

Malia's Tours

Tour	Volcano	DepartureDate	Guide
KL18	Kilauea	07/08/2018	Malia
KL19	Kilauea	07/15/2018	Malia
KL20	Kilauea	07/22/2018	Malia

6.2 Using the Filter and Sort Task

As the name suggests, the Filter and Sort task filters and sorts data. The result of the Filter and Sort task is a data table. If you need to join tables or add any computed columns, then use the Query Builder. If you only want to sort the data, then you may choose to use the Sort Data task (covered in the next section) instead, which offers more sorting options.

Here is a sample of the Eruptions data table, which is sorted by the volcano name and start date of the eruption. To filter and sort the data, click the data icon in the Project Tree or Process Flow to make it active, and select **Tasks ▶ Data ▶ Filter and Sort** from the menu bar. If you have a Data Grid open, you can also open the Filter and Sort task by clicking **Filter and Sort** on the workspace toolbar. The Filter and Sort window will open.

	Volcano	StartDate	EndDate	VEI
1	Barren Island	12/20/1795	12/21/1795	2
2	Barren Island	12/20/1994	06/05/1995	2
3	Erebus	12/12/1912		2
4	Erebus	01/03/1972		1
5	Etna	02/06/1610	08/15/1610	2
6	Etna	06/04/1787	08/11/1787	4
7	Etna	01/30/1865	06/28/1865	2
8	Etna	12/16/2005	12/22/2005	1
9	Fuji	12/16/1707	02/24/1708	5
10	Grimsvotn	10/31/1603	11/01/1603	2

Selecting variables The Filter and Sort task has four tabs. On the **Variables** tab, choose the variables you want to keep. Move variables from the **Available** list to the **Selected** list by either dragging and dropping, or using the arrows. In this example, all variables are selected except EndDate.

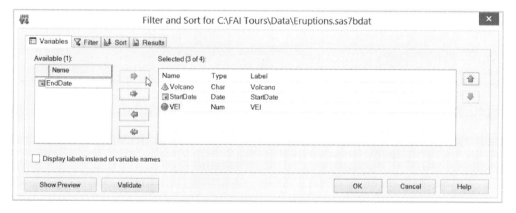

Specifying the filter Click the **Filter** tab. The area labeled **Filter description** contains four boxes. In the first box, choose the variable for the filter. In the second box, choose an operator. Then in the third box, enter the value for the filter. To get a list of all possible values for the selected variable, click the ellipsis button ⬚. If you want to add another condition to the filter, select AND or OR from the drop-down list in the fourth box. A new row of boxes will appear where you can specify the additional condition. For more complicated filters containing functions or complex logic, click the **Advanced Edit** button to open the Advanced Filter Builder window (not shown). In this example the filter selects all eruptions with a volcanic explosivity index (VEI) greater than or equal to 4.

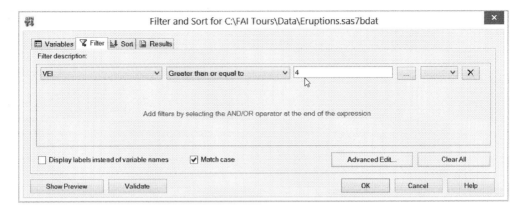

Sorting the data Click the **Sort** tab. Choose a variable from the **Sort by** drop-down list. If you want, you can choose a second variable from the **Then by** drop-down list. Each time you choose an additional variable, options will appear allowing you to choose more sorting variables. The default sort order is Ascending. Click **Descending** to reverse the order. In this example, the data will be sorted by StartDate in ascending order. When you are ready to run the task, click **OK**.

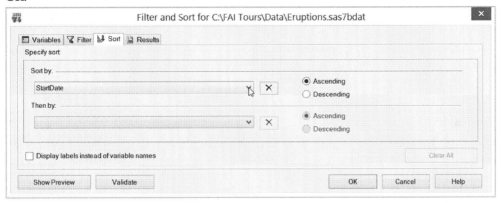

Results Here are the results, which are sorted by StartDate, and include only eruptions with VEI greater than or equal to 4. The new data table is given a name starting with the words FILTER_FOR and is stored in a default location. If you want, you can change the name and storage location of the new data table on the **Results** tab.

	Volcano	StartDate	VEI
1	Vesuvius	12/15/1631	5
2	Santorini	09/27/1650	4
3	Fuji	12/16/1707	5
4	Etna	06/04/1787	4
5	Grimsvotn	01/08/1873	4
6	Vesuvius	12/18/1875	4
7	Krakatau	05/20/1883	6
8	Kliuchevskoi	03/25/1931	4
9	St. Helens	03/27/1980	5
10	Pinatubo	04/02/1991	5
11	Reventador	11/03/2002	4

6.3 Using the Sort Data Task

There is little need for you to sort data in SAS Enterprise Guide. If a task requires data to be sorted, SAS Enterprise Guide will usually sort the data automatically. However, there may be times when you want to sort the data yourself. If you have a large data table, for example, you may want to store the data in sorted order. With the data presorted, SAS Enterprise Guide will not have to sort the data and your tasks will run more quickly. At other times, you may want to sort data to make it easier to find values in a Data Grid, or to eliminate duplicate rows.

There are three ways to sort data in SAS Enterprise Guide: the Filter and Sort task, the Sort Data task, or a query. The Sort Data task gives you the most control over how the data are sorted, while the Filter and Sort task and a query have other functions in addition to sorting. This section discusses the Sort Data task.

	⚠ Volcano	🔢 StartDate	🔢 EndDate	🔘 VEI
1	Barren Island	12/20/1795	12/21/1795	2
2	Barren Island	12/20/1994	06/05/1995	2
3	Erebus	12/12/1912		2
4	Erebus	01/03/1972		1
5	Etna	02/06/1610	08/15/1610	2
6	Etna	06/04/1787	08/11/1787	4
7	Etna	01/30/1865	06/28/1865	2
8	Etna	12/16/2005	12/22/2005	1
9	Fuji	12/16/1707	02/24/1708	5
10	Grimsvotn	10/31/1603	11/01/1603	2

Here is a portion of the Eruptions data table. To sort the data using the Sort Data task, click the data icon in the Project Tree or Process Flow to make it active, and select **Tasks ▶ Data ▶ Sort Data** from the menu bar. The Sort Data window will open.

Assigning task roles Drag the columns you want to sort by to the **Sort by** role. If there is more than one **Sort by** column, SAS Enterprise Guide will sort rows by the first column, then by the second column within values of the first column, and so on. When you assign a column to the Sort by role, a box for the sort order will appear on the right. If you click the down-arrow, you can choose to have the data sorted in ascending (the default) or descending order.

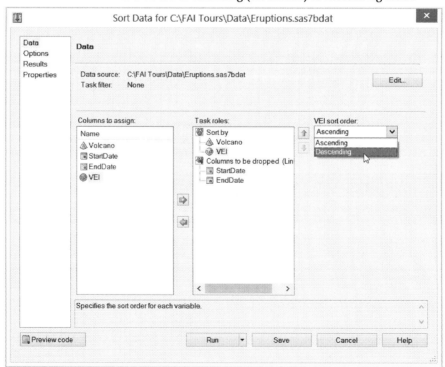

If you want to exclude columns from the output, drag those columns to the **Columns to be dropped** role. In this example, the Eruptions data table will be sorted first by Volcano in ascending order, then by VEI in descending order. The StartDate and EndDate columns will be dropped.

Sorting options To open the Options page, click **Options** in the selection pane on the left. In this page, you can select the collating sequence (such as ASCII, EBCDIC, or Server default), which determines the sort order. When SAS Enterprise Guide sorts data, missing values are always lowest in the sort order. In the ASCII collating sequence (the default for Windows computers), uppercase letters come before lowercase letters.

You can also choose options for duplicate records. You can keep all records (the default), keep only the first record for each combination of values of the Sort by columns, or delete duplicate records if they are adjacent. For this example, **Keep only the first record for each 'Sort by' group** is selected so that the result will have only one record for each Volcano and value of VEI. When you are ready to run the task, click **Run**.

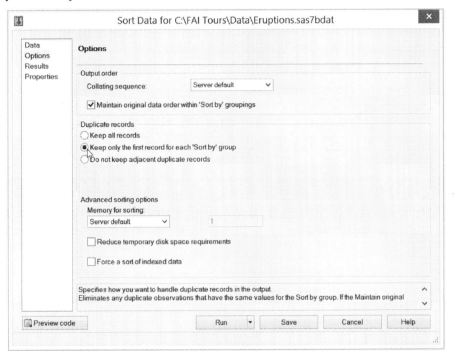

Results The Sort Data task creates a new SAS data table and displays it in a Data Grid. Notice that this table is sorted first by Volcano, and then by descending values of VEI within Volcano. The resulting data table has fewer rows than the original because it contains only one row for each combination of the two sort columns. SAS Enterprise Guide stores the table with a default name in a default location. To save the data with a different name or location, use the Results page in the Sort Data task. In the Results page, you can also choose to save, in a separate table, any duplicates that were eliminated by the sort.

	Volcano	VEI
1	Barren Island	2
2	Erebus	2
3	Erebus	1
4	Etna	4
5	Etna	2
6	Etna	1
7	Fuji	5
8	Grimsvotn	4
9	Grimsvotn	3
10	Grimsvotn	2

6.4 Sorting Data in a Query

If all you want to do is create a sorted version of a data table, then you might want to use the Sort Data, or Filter and Sort task. But with the Query Builder you can create a sorted version of your data table, and create new columns or join tables at the same time.

This example uses the Eruptions data table, which is sorted by the name of the volcano. To change the sort order using a query, click the data icon in the Project Tree or Process Flow to make it active, and select **Tasks ▶ Data ▶ Query Builder** from the menu bar. The Query Builder window will open with the **Select Data** tab on top.

Selecting the data   For all queries you need to select the columns that will be in the result. Click and drag the columns you want to the **Select Data** tab. In this example, all columns in the Eruptions table except VEI have been selected, as well as the computed column Duration. (Section 5.3 shows how to create the Duration column.)

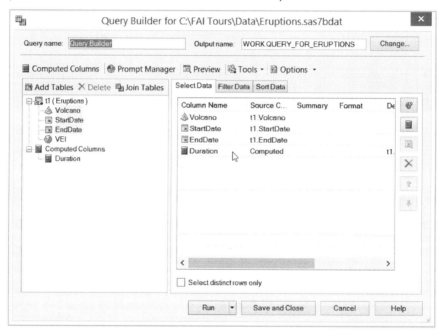

Here is a portion of the data table resulting from running the above query before any sorting. This data table contains the new computed column Duration.

	Volcano	StartDate	EndDate	Duration
1	Barren Island	12/20/1795	12/21/1795	2
2	Barren Island	12/20/1994	06/05/1995	168
3	Erebus	12/12/1912		.
4	Erebus	01/03/1972	.	.
5	Etna	02/06/1610	08/15/1610	191
6	Etna	06/04/1787	08/11/1787	69
7	Etna	01/30/1865	06/28/1865	150
8	Etna	12/16/2005	12/22/2005	7
9	Fuji	12/16/1707	02/24/1708	71
10	Grimsvotn	10/31/1603	11/01/1603	2

Sorting the data To sort the data, reopen the query by clicking **Modify Task** on the workspace toolbar for the query result, then click the **Sort Data** tab. Click the desired column in the list on the left and drag it to the **Sort Data** tab. You can sort by more than one column by dragging multiple columns to the **Sort Data** tab. Note that you can use columns for sorting even if they don't appear in the result.

If you choose more than one column for sorting, the order of the columns on the **Sort Data** tab will determine how the data are sorted. The data will be sorted by the first column in the list. Then, within unique values of the first column, the data will be sorted by the second column. You can change the sort order by clicking the column name in the **Sort Data** tab and clicking the up- or down-arrow buttons ⬆ ⬇ to move the columns. To change the sort direction, click the column name on the **Sort Data** tab. Then click the down-arrow next to the sort direction for that column, and select either Ascending or Descending from the drop-down list. In this query, the data will be sorted by the computed column Duration in ascending order, then by StartDate in descending order. Click **Run** to create a sorted data table.

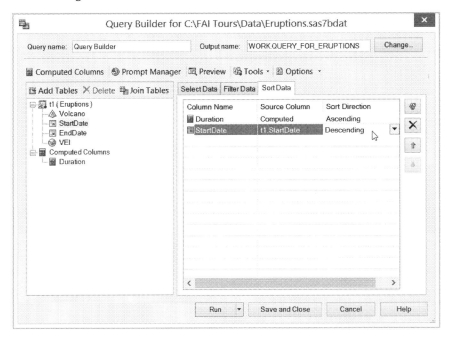

Results Here is a portion of the resulting data table sorted first by Duration in ascending order, then by StartDate in descending order. Missing values are always lowest in the sort order, so they appear first.

	⚠ Volcano	🗓 StartDate	🗓 EndDate	◉ Duration
1	Villarrica	10/26/2008	.	.
2	Erebus	01/03/1972	.	.
3	Erebus	12/12/1912	.	.
4	Poas	04/08/1996	04/08/1996	1
5	Sabancaya	05/01/1997	05/02/1997	2
6	Reventador	12/12/1856	12/13/1856	2
7	Barren Island	12/20/1795	12/21/1795	2
8	Grimsvotn	10/31/1603	11/01/1603	2
9	Kliuchevskoi	03/25/1931	03/27/1931	3
10	St. Helens	03/26/1847	03/30/1847	5

6.5 Filtering Data in a Query

If you want to create a data table that is a subset of another table, you can use the Filter and Sort task or the Query Builder. The Filter and Sort task only filters and sorts data, but the Query Builder can also create computed or summarized columns, and join tables together.

Here is a sample of the Volcanoes data table. To filter the data so that only volcanoes in North America and South America appear in the results, click the data icon in the Project Tree or Process Flow and select **Tasks ▸ Data ▸ Query Builder** from the menu bar. This opens

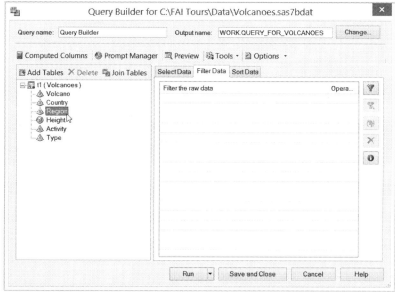

the Query Builder window, with the **Select Data** tab on top. Select the columns that you want in the query result (in this example every column except Activity and Type). Then click the **Filter Data** tab.

Select the column that you want to use for filtering purposes and drag it to the **Filter Data** tab. Notice that you can filter by columns that are not even part of the query result. In this example, drag **Region** to the filter area. When you drop the column, the New Filter wizard will open.

Building the filter   In the New Filter wizard, you can see the name of the column that you dragged to the filter area. Initially, the operator is **Equal to**. To choose a different operator, click the down-arrow in the **Operator** box. In this example, the **In a list** operator is the most useful because it allows you to specify a list of unique values for Region.

After choosing an operator, choose one or more values for your filter condition. You can type the values in the **Values** box or let SAS Enterprise Guide help you select the values. Click the down-arrow next to the **Values** box. In the window that opens, click **Get Values** and you will see a list of all possible values for the column you selected. Note that if you have large data tables, or lots of possible values, it can take a long time to retrieve the values. Highlight one or more values by holding down the control (CTRL) key as you select values. In this example, select **NA** and **SA**, and then click **OK**. The values will be inserted into the Values box of the New Filter wizard.

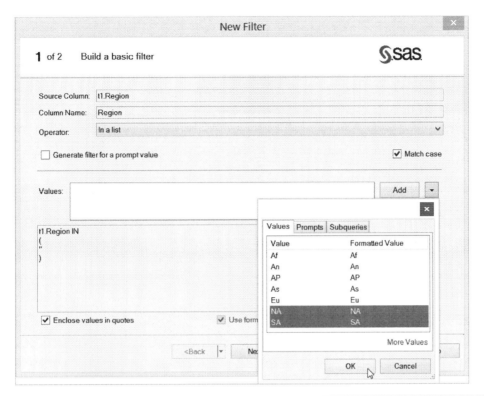

Once you have set the filter condition, click **Next** to see a summary of your filter in the second window (not shown), then click **Finish**. The filter will appear on the **Filter Data** tab of the Query Builder window. In this case, the filter selects all rows from the Volcanoes table (t1) where Region has the value of NA or SA. Click **Run** to run the query.

Results Here is the data table produced by the query. Notice that only the volcanoes from North and South America are included.

Tutorials C and D give more detailed examples of filtering data in a query.

	Volcano	Country	Region	Height
1	Altar	Ecuador	SA	5321
2	Garibaldi	Canada	NA	2678
3	Illimani	Bolivia	SA	6458
4	Lassen	USA	NA	3187
5	Poas	Costa Rica	NA	2708
6	Popocatepetl	Mexico	NA	5426
7	Reventador	Ecuador	SA	3562
8	Sabancaya	Peru	SA	5976
9	Shishaldin	USA	NA	2857
10	St. Helens	USA	NA	2549
11	Villarrica	Chile	SA	2847

6.6 Creating Compound Filters in a Query

Sometimes you want to base a filter on more than one condition. You can add conditions to a filter using the AND and OR operators. This section shows how to create a compound filter in the Query Builder, but you can create them any place you can create a filter.

In the previous section, the Volcanoes data were filtered keeping only volcanoes in North America and South America. Suppose you also want volcanoes in Japan. To modify the existing query, click **Modify Task** on the workspace toolbar for the query result. In the Query Builder window, click the **Filter Data** tab.

Adding conditions to a filter

To add a condition to an existing filter, drag the column for the new condition from the column list to the **Filter Data** tab. For this example, drag the Country column to the **Filter Data** tab. When you drop the column, the New Filter wizard will open.

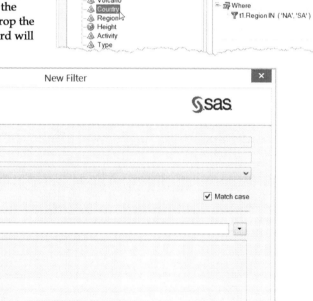

Building the Filter   The procedure for specifying the additional condition is the same as if you were creating a single condition filter. First, choose an appropriate operator for your condition, and then either type the desired value in the Value box, or click the down-arrow next to the Value box to get a list of values to choose from. In this example, the filter will choose rows where the Country column from the Volcanoes table (t1) is equal to the value **Japan**. When you are satisfied, click **Next** to see a summary of your filter, then click **Finish**.

Setting the logic After you create the additional condition, it will be added to the existing filter condition on the **Filter Data** tab. The filter now has two conditions. When you add new conditions to your filter, SAS Enterprise Guide automatically chooses the AND operator. To change to OR, click the down-arrow next to the AND operator and choose OR. For this example, set the operator to **OR**. Click **Run** to run the query.

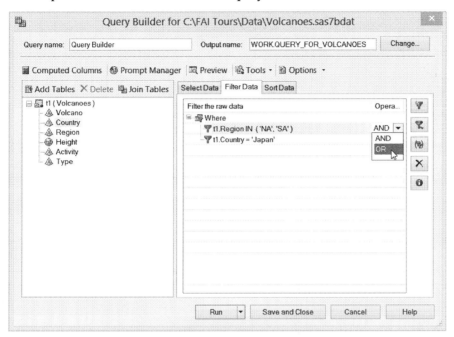

Results Here is the new data table produced after filtering the Volcanoes data table. Now, all the volcanoes from North America and South America are included, as well as all the volcanoes in Japan.

	Volcano	Country	Region	Height
1	Altar	Ecuador	SA	5321
2	Fuji	Japan	As	3776
3	Garibaldi	Canada	NA	2678
4	Illimani	Bolivia	SA	6458
5	Lassen	USA	NA	3187
6	Poas	Costa Rica	NA	2708
7	Popocatepetl	Mexico	NA	5426
8	Reventador	Ecuador	SA	3562
9	Sabancaya	Peru	SA	5976
10	Shishaldin	USA	NA	2857
11	St. Helens	USA	NA	2549
12	Villarrica	Chile	SA	2847

6.7 ▸ Creating Advanced Filters in a Query

You can accomplish a lot with basic filters, but sometimes you need filters containing arithmetic expressions, functions, or more complex logic than the basic filter provides. For these cases, you can create an advanced filter. This section shows how to create an advanced filter using the Query Builder, but you can also create advanced filters using the Filter and Sort task.

Here is a portion of the Bookings data table. This example uses the SUBSTR function in the Query Builder to select rows where the CustomerID starts with the letters "DE." To create a query,

	Office	CustomerID	Tour	Travelers	Deposit	Deposit_Date
1	Portland	SL28	SH43	10	425	05JUL2018
2	Portland	DE27	PS27	6	75	11JUL2018
3	Portland	SL34	FJ12	4	200	19JUL2018
4	Portland	DI33	SH43	4	150	23JUL2018
5	Portland	BU12	SH43	2	75	23JUL2018
6	Portland	DE31	FJ12	3	175	25JUL2018
7	Portland	WI48	FJ12	2	100	26JUL2018

click the data icon in the Project Tree or Process Flow and select **Tasks ▸ Data ▸ Query Builder** from the menu bar. This opens the Query Builder with the **Select Data** tab on top. Select the columns that you want in the query result. For this example, select all columns. Then click the **Filter Data** tab.

Opening the advanced filter window On the **Filter Data** tab of the Query Builder window, click the New Filter icon located on the right side of the window to open the New Filter wizard.

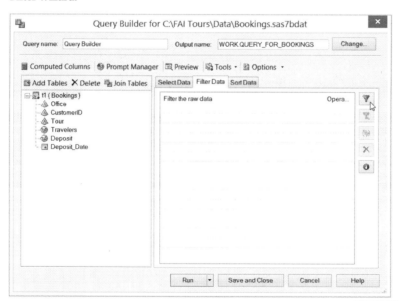

The New Filter wizard has up to four windows depending on which type of filter you select. In the first window, select **Advanced Filter** and click **Next**. (In the Filter and Sort task, click the **Advanced Edit** button on the **Filter** tab.)

Building the advanced filter In the second window, type the desired filter expression in the text box labeled **Enter a filter**. If you want to use functions in the expression, you can expand the Functions node in the box on the lower right to view all available functions. Clicking on a function will display help for that function, while double-clicking the function will add it to the filter expression. All the columns in the table, along with the selected columns for the query, are also listed in this box. In this example, the SUBSTR function is used to select all rows where the first two characters of the CustomerID column from the Bookings data table (t1) are equal to "DE." When you are finished building your filter, click **Next** to see a summary of your filter in the third window (not shown), then click **Finish** to return to the Query Builder window.

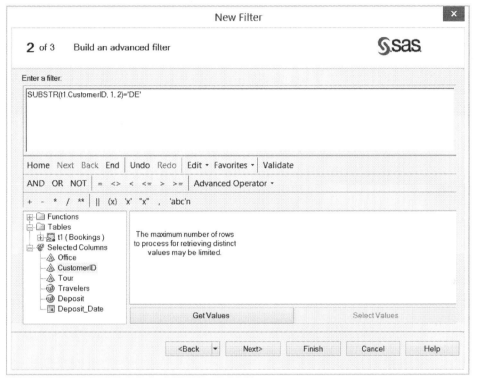

Your filter will appear on the **Filter Data** tab of the Query Builder. Click **Run** to run the query and view the results.

Results Here is the new data table produced after filtering the Bookings data table. Only the rows with a CustomerID that starts with the letters "DE" appear in the result.

	Office	CustomerID	Tour	Travelers	Deposit	Deposit_Date
1	Portland	DE27	PS27	6	75	11JUL2018
2	Portland	DE31	FJ12	3	175	25JUL2018

7

" Learning without thought is labor lost; thought without learning is perilous. "

CONFUCIUS

From *Analects* Bk. II, Ch. XV. As quoted in *The Cyclopedia of Practical Quotations: English, Latin, and Modern Foreign Languages* by Jehiel Keeler Hoyt, 1896.

CHAPTER 7

Combining Data Tables

7.1 Methods for Combining Tables

In SAS Enterprise Guide, there are two basic ways to combine data tables: appending and joining. You append when the tables contain the same (or almost the same) columns. You join when the tables contain the same (or almost the same) rows. This section describes, in general terms, what happens when you combine tables.

Appending tables Appending tables is like stacking them. It only makes sense to append tables if they have columns in common. Appending tables is done with the Append Table task, which is described in the next section.

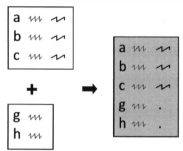

Joining tables To join tables together, the tables need to have a column (or set of columns) that can be used to match rows. You do not need to specify whether the match is one-to-one, one-to-many, or many-to-many—SAS Enterprise Guide determines this automatically. Joining tables is done in the Query Builder, which is described in section 7.3 and Tutorial D.

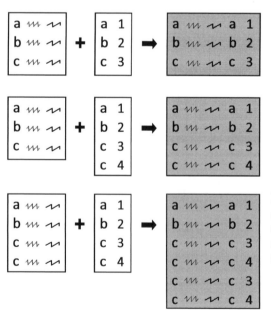

One-to-one match In a one-to-one match, one row from the first table is joined with one row from the second table. The values for the common column are unique in both tables.

One-to-many match In a one-to-many match, one row from the first table is joined with multiple rows from the second table. The values for the common column are unique in only one table.

Many-to-many match In a many-to-many match, the values for the common column are not unique in either table. Each row in the first table is joined with all the matching rows from the second table.

When you join tables together, one table may have rows that do not match any rows contained in the other table. By default, any non-matching rows are excluded from the new table. In the Query Builder, you can control which rows end up in the new table based on which table they came from. The Query Builder illustrates this with a join indicator (also known as a Venn diagram). The join indicator consists of two circles representing the two tables. The shaded areas show the parts of the tables that will be kept. You can choose different kinds of joins including inner joins, left joins, right joins, and full outer joins. Controlling the type of join is discussed in section 7.4.

The following graphics all show a one-to-one join, but the join has been modified so that different rows are included in the results.

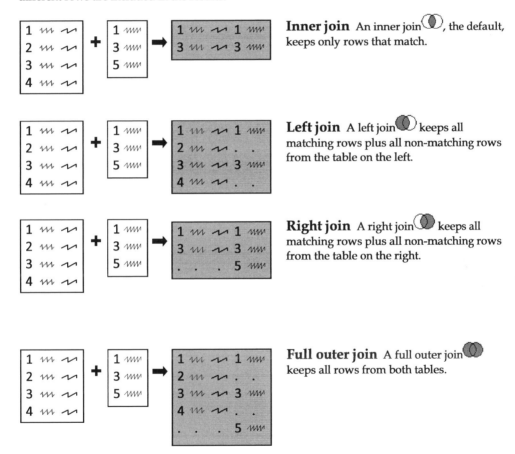

Inner join An inner join, the default, keeps only rows that match.

Left join A left join keeps all matching rows plus all non-matching rows from the table on the left.

Right join A right join keeps all matching rows plus all non-matching rows from the table on the right.

Full outer join A full outer join keeps all rows from both tables.

7.2 Appending Tables

You use the Append Table task to combine tables that contain the same (or almost the same) columns. For example, if you had sales data for January, February, and March in three separate tables, you could append the tables to create one table for the entire quarter.

In this example, a customer living in southern Washington is interested in traveling with the Fire and Ice Tours company. Because this customer lives between Seattle and Portland, she wants to see prices for flights from each city.

Here are two data tables, one showing flights from Portland and the other from Seattle. Looking at these two data tables, you can see they contain the same columns, making them good candidates for appending.

	Origin	Destination	FlightNo	FlightPrice
1	Portland	Catania	L469	$1,833.00
2	Portland	Hilo	HA25	$631.00
3	Portland	Nairobi	KLM6034	$1,229.00
4	Portland	Rome	D1576	$1,747.00
5	Portland	San Jose	CA1210	$518.00
6	Portland	Tokyo	UA383	$1,462.00

To append tables, click one data icon in the Project Tree or Process Flow to make it active, and then select **Tasks ▶ Data ▶ Append Table** from the menu bar. The Append Table window will open.

	Origin	Destination	FlightNo	FlightPrice
1	Seattle	Catania	BA48	$1,853.00
2	Seattle	Hilo	HA21	$576.00
3	Seattle	Jakarta	AA119	$1,331.00
4	Seattle	Nairobi	KLM6034	$1,396.00
5	Seattle	Quito	CA1086	$686.00
6	Seattle	Rome	USA6	$1,767.00
7	Seattle	San Jose	CA1100	$559.00
8	Seattle	Tokyo	UA875	$1,462.00

Adding tables The Append Table window opens showing the active table. To add a table, click **Add Table**, navigate to the table you want to add, and click **OK**. The table names will appear in the **Tables to append** section of the window. You can append up to 256 tables at once.

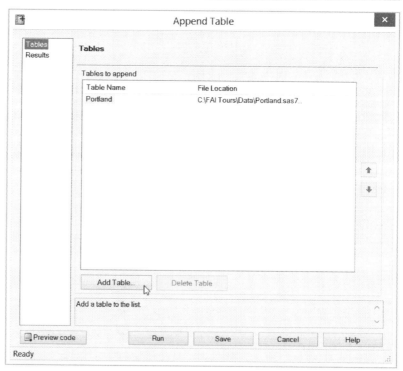

Running the task After adding all the desired tables (Portland and Seattle for this example), you can click **Run** and SAS Enterprise Guide will create the new table, store it in a default location, and give it the name **Append_Table**. (If you have more than one appended table stored in that location, SAS Enterprise Guide will add numbers to the name.) To

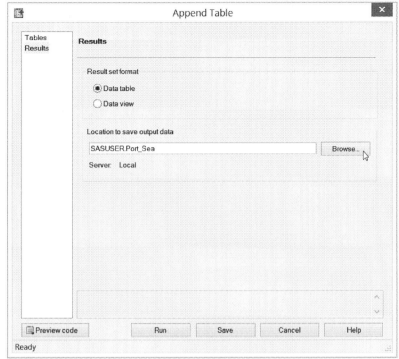

choose a different name or location, click the **Results** option in the selection pane on the left. Then click **Browse** in the Results page to open the Save File window.

In the Save File window(not shown), type a name for the new data table in the **File name** box and choose a library. To see the available libraries, click the down arrow in the **Save in** box at the top of the window. In this example, the new data table will be named Port_Sea and will be saved in the SASUSER library. Once you have specified the library and filename, click **Save**. In the Append Table window, click **Run**. SAS Enterprise Guide will display the results in a Data Grid.

Results Here is the new data table. Notice that SAS Enterprise Guide concatenated the Portland and Seattle tables by matching the columns.

In this case, the two tables contained exactly the same columns. If there had been a column that existed in one table but not the other, then that column would contain missing values for any rows from the other table.

	Origin	Destination	FlightNo	FlightPrice
1	Portland	Catania	L469	$1,833.00
2	Portland	Hilo	HA25	$631.00
3	Portland	Nairobi	KLM6034	$1,229.00
4	Portland	Rome	D1576	$1,747.00
5	Portland	San Jose	CA1210	$518.00
6	Portland	Tokyo	UA383	$1,462.00
7	Seattle	Catania	BA48	$1,853.00
8	Seattle	Hilo	HA21	$576.00
9	Seattle	Jakarta	AA119	$1,331.00
10	Seattle	Nairobi	KLM6034	$1,396.00
11	Seattle	Quito	CA1086	$686.00
12	Seattle	Rome	USA6	$1,767.00
13	Seattle	San Jose	CA1100	$559.00
14	Seattle	Tokyo	UA875	$1,462.00

7.3 Joining Tables

When you append tables, you match columns. But often, instead of matching columns, you need to match rows. For example, a teacher might record grades from homework in one table and grades from tests in another. To compute final grades she would need to match the homework and test scores for each student. This is called joining tables, and you do it with a query.

In the preceding section, two tables were appended to create one table, Port_Sea, containing all the data about flights. Now the data from the Tours table can be joined with the matching data for flights. To open the Query Builder and join the tables, hold down the control (CTRL) key as you click both data icons in the Project Tree or Process Flow, and select **Tasks ▶ Data ▶ Query Builder** from the menu bar. The data tables will appear in the Query Builder in the same order as they appear in the Project Tree or Process Flow.

	Volcano	Departs	Days	Price	Difficulty
1	Etna	Catania	7	$1,610	m
2	Fuji	Tokyo	2	$335	c
3	Kenya	Nairobi	6	$1,245	m
4	Kilauea	Hilo	1	$85	e
5	Kilimanjaro	Nairobi	9	$1,965	c
6	Krakatau	Jakarta	7	$1,345	e
7	Poas	San Jose	1	$97	e
8	Reventador	Quito	4	$875	m
9	St. Helens	Portland	2	$250	e
10	Vesuvius	Rome	6	$1,495	e

	Origin	Destination	FlightNo	FlightPrice
1	Portland	Catania	L469	$1,833.00
2	Portland	Hilo	HA25	$631.00
3	Portland	Nairobi	KLM6034	$1,229.00
4	Portland	Rome	D1576	$1,747.00
5	Portland	San Jose	CA1210	$518.00
6	Portland	Tokyo	UA383	$1,462.00
7	Seattle	Catania	BA48	$1,853.00
8	Seattle	Hilo	HA21	$576.00
9	Seattle	Jakarta	AA119	$1,331.00
10	Seattle	Nairobi	KLM6034	$1,396.00
11	Seattle	Quito	CA1086	$686.00
12	Seattle	Rome	USA6	$1,767.00
13	Seattle	San Jose	CA1100	$559.00
14	Seattle	Tokyo	UA875	$1,462.00

Specifying the join columns When you open multiple tables in the Query Builder, SAS Enterprise Guide will automatically look for columns with the same name and type. If SAS Enterprise Guide does not find any columns with the same name and type, then a warning message will appear telling you to join the columns manually. Click **OK**. The Tables and Joins window will open.

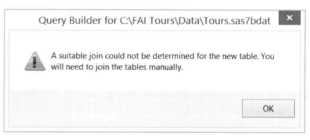

To join two tables manually, click the first table, then right-click the name of one column and select the name of the matching column from the pop-up menu. SAS Enterprise Guide will draw a line from one column to the other. To correctly match the Tours data table and the Port_Sea table, the destination of a flight must match the city from which a tour departs. To join the tables in this example, click the Tours table, and then right-click the column Departs, and select t2 and Destination from the pop-up menu. A Join Properties window will open (not shown). For this example, accept the default settings by clicking **OK**. In the Tables and Joins window, click **Close**.

You can use more than one column for matching in a join. For example, a teacher might combine homework and test scores based on both class and student ID number. To specify additional columns for matching, select them manually as described above.

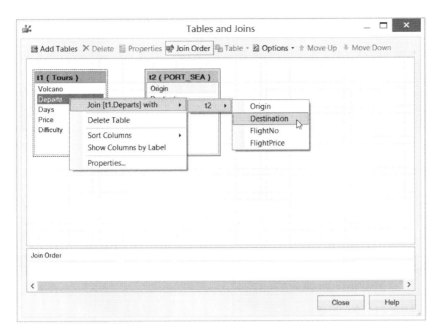

Running the query If you have not already selected the columns to be included in the results, then drag those columns to the **Select Data** tab in the Query Builder. When you are satisfied, click **Run**. SAS Enterprise Guide will display the results in a Data Grid.

Results This Data Grid shows the result of joining the two data tables. Notice that both of the columns used for matching (Departs and Destination) appear in the results. If these columns had the same name (such as City), then a number would have been automatically added to the name of the second column (resulting in City and City1). Because there are two tours departing from Nairobi, and two flights with a destination of Nairobi, this is a many-to-many join. SAS Enterprise Guide kept only the rows that matched. This is an inner join, which is the default type of join. To keep rows that don't match, modify your join as described in the next section.

	Volcano	Departs	Days	Price	Difficulty	Origin	Destination	FlightNo	FlightPrice
1	Etna	Catania	7	$1,610	m	Portland	Catania	L469	$1,833.00
2	Etna	Catania	7	$1,610	m	Seattle	Catania	BA48	$1,853.00
3	Fuji	Tokyo	2	$335	c	Portland	Tokyo	UA383	$1,462.00
4	Fuji	Tokyo	2	$335	c	Seattle	Tokyo	UA875	$1,462.00
5	Kenya	Nairobi	6	$1,245	m	Portland	Nairobi	KLM6034	$1,229.00
6	Kenya	Nairobi	6	$1,245	m	Seattle	Nairobi	KLM6034	$1,396.00
7	Kilauea	Hilo	1	$85	e	Portland	Hilo	HA25	$631.00
8	Kilauea	Hilo	1	$85	e	Seattle	Hilo	HA21	$576.00
9	Kilimanjaro	Nairobi	9	$1,965	c	Portland	Nairobi	KLM6034	$1,229.00
10	Kilimanjaro	Nairobi	9	$1,965	c	Seattle	Nairobi	KLM6034	$1,396.00
11	Krakatau	Jakarta	7	$1,345	e	Seattle	Jakarta	AA119	$1,331.00
12	Poas	San Jose	1	$97	e	Portland	San Jose	CA1210	$518.00
13	Poas	San Jose	1	$97	e	Seattle	San Jose	CA1100	$559.00
14	Reventador	Quito	4	$875	m	Seattle	Quito	CA1086	$686.00
15	Vesuvius	Rome	6	$1,495	e	Portland	Rome	D1576	$1,747.00
16	Vesuvius	Rome	6	$1,495	e	Seattle	Rome	USA6	$1,767.00

7.4 Setting the Properties of a Join

By default, when you join tables, SAS Enterprise Guide keeps only rows for which a match is found. Sometimes that may be just what you want, but at other times, you may want to keep all the rows regardless of whether they match, or all the rows from one table, but not the other. To do this, change the properties of the join.

Reopening the Query window To change a query that you have already run, right-click the query icon in the Project Tree or Process Flow and select **Modify Query Builder** from the pop-up menu. The Query Builder will open. Click the **Join Tables** button to open the Tables and Joins window.

To modify a join, right-click the join indicator between the two tables and select **Properties** from the pop-up menu. The Join Properties window will open.

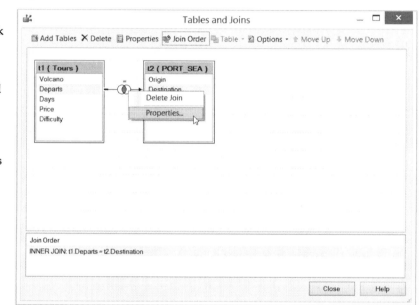

Selecting the type of join In the Join Properties window, you can choose from several types of joins. In this window, **All rows from the left table given a condition** has been selected. Tours is the table on the left, so all rows from Tours will be included regardless of whether there is a matching row in the Port_Sea table. This is called a left join. When you are satisfied with the join condition, click **OK**.

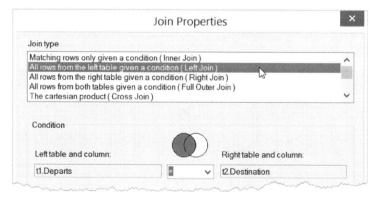

When you return to the Tables and Joins window, you will see that the join indicator between the two tables has changed. In this example, the circle on the left is filled in, indicating that all rows from the Tours data table will be included. When you are satisfied, click **Close**.

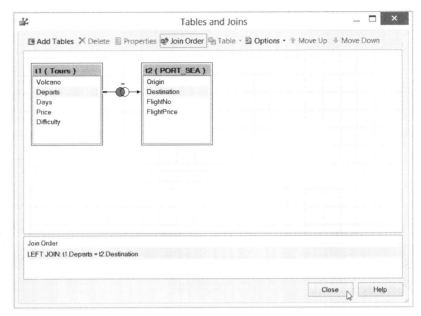

Running the query If you have not already selected the columns to be included in the results, then drag those columns to the **Select Data** tab in the Query Builder. When you are satisfied, click **Run**. SAS Enterprise Guide will display the results in a Data Grid.

Results This Data Grid shows the result of the modified join. This table contains all the tours, including the one for St. Helens. Notice that the values of columns from the Port_Sea table are missing for row 10. That is because there were no flights with a Destination of Portland. Because the customer lives near St. Helens, she doesn't need a flight to go on that tour.

	Volcano	Departs	Days	Price	Difficulty	Origin	Destination	FlightNo	FlightPrice
1	Etna	Catania	7	$1,610	m	Portland	Catania	L469	$1,833.00
2	Etna	Catania	7	$1,610	m	Seattle	Catania	BA48	$1,853.00
3	Kilauea	Hilo	1	$85	e	Portland	Hilo	HA25	$631.00
4	Kilauea	Hilo	1	$85	e	Seattle	Hilo	HA21	$576.00
5	Krakatau	Jakarta	7	$1,345	e	Seattle	Jakarta	AA119	$1,331.00
6	Kenya	Nairobi	6	$1,245	m	Seattle	Nairobi	KLM6034	$1,396.00
7	Kilimanjaro	Nairobi	9	$1,965	c	Seattle	Nairobi	KLM6034	$1,396.00
8	Kenya	Nairobi	6	$1,245	m	Portland	Nairobi	KLM6034	$1,229.00
9	Kilimanjaro	Nairobi	9	$1,965	c	Portland	Nairobi	KLM6034	$1,229.00
10	St. Helens	Portland	2	$250	e				
11	Reventador	Quito	4	$875	m	Seattle	Quito	CA1086	$686.00
12	Vesuvius	Rome	6	$1,495	e	Seattle	Rome	USA6	$1,767.00
13	Vesuvius	Rome	6	$1,495	e	Portland	Rome	D1576	$1,747.00
14	Poas	San Jose	1	$97	e	Seattle	San Jose	CA1100	$559.00
15	Poas	San Jose	1	$97	e	Portland	San Jose	CA1210	$518.00
16	Fuji	Tokyo	2	$335	c	Seattle	Tokyo	UA875	$1,462.00
17	Fuji	Tokyo	2	$335	c	Portland	Tokyo	UA383	$1,462.00

8

"The difficulty lies, not in new ideas, but in escaping from old ones."

JOHN KEYNES

From *The General Theory of Employment, Interest, and Money*, 1936.

CHAPTER 8

Working with SAS Programs

8.1 Writing and Running SAS Programs

In SAS Enterprise Guide, tasks write SAS programs for you. So, you may never need to write a SAS program. However, if you are an experienced SAS programmer, SAS Enterprise Guide can make your work easier and more efficient. If you want to learn SAS programming, SAS Enterprise Guide can help with that too.

Writing a new SAS program To create a new SAS program, select **Program ▶ New Program** from the menu bar. An empty Program window will open in the workspace. The program editor in SAS Enterprise Guide is syntax-sensitive, which means that SAS keywords are displayed in blue, comments are green, quoted strings are magenta, and so forth.

Syntax suggestion and autocompletion As you type, the editor will present a list of appropriate keywords (called syntax suggestion). To accept a suggestion (called autocompletion), double-click the keyword that you want to use, or highlight it and press the spacebar. If you do not need help, then you can just keep typing and ignore the suggestions.

Syntax suggestion ———

Integrated syntax help ———

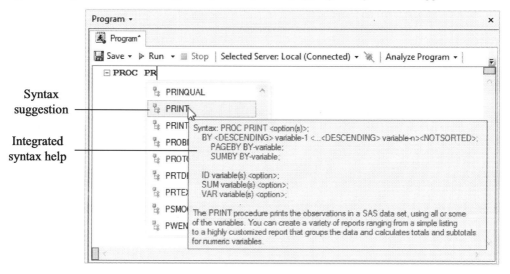

Integrated syntax help If you hover the cursor over a keyword, then the editor will display brief documentation for that keyword. This works both for keywords typed into your program and for keywords displayed in the list of syntax suggestions. In the preceding window, syntax help is being displayed for PROC PRINT.

Setting editor options You can customize almost any feature of the editor including turning off syntax suggestion and autocompletion. To change editor options, select **Program ▶ Editor Options** from the menu bar. The Enhanced Editor Options window will open (not shown).

Opening an existing SAS program If you have an existing SAS program that you want to include in your project, you can open it by selecting **Program ▶ Open Program** from the menu bar. Navigate to your SAS program and click **Open**. This opens a Program window where you can edit the program.

Formatting code A program with proper indention and line breaks is not just prettier, but easier to read and understand. If a program lacks formatting (perhaps you inherited it from the person who had your job before you), SAS Enterprise Guide can format it for you. To format a program, right-click your program and select **Format Code** from the pop-up menu. To undo the formatting,

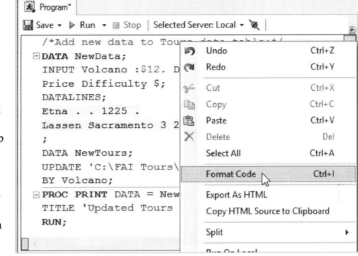

select **Undo** from the same menu. This example shows a program being formatted. The following example shows the program after formatting. In the Enhanced Editor Options window, you can customize features for formatting programs such as the number of spaces used for indenting.

Running a program
When you are ready to run your program, click **Run** on the workspace toolbar for the Program window. Your program will run on the server that has been set as your default. To choose a different server, click **Selected Server**. To run a part of a program, highlight that part. Then click **Run** on the workspace toolbar above your program and select **Run Selection** from the pull-down menu. You can also use the Program

menu on the main menu bar to run your program or selection.

8.2 Creating Process Flows from SAS Programs

Process flow diagrams make it easy to see the flow of data through your project. However, if you have SAS programs, then ordinarily each program is represented by only one program icon. A single program can include many—even hundreds—of steps. If you have a complex program, then you can use the Analyze Program feature to create a process flow visualizing your program.

Here is a program that combines the Volcanoes and Tours data sets, and runs two reports. To analyze a program, click **Analyze Program** in the toolbar above the Program window, and select **Analyze for Program Flow** from the pop-up menu. The Analyze SAS Program window will open.

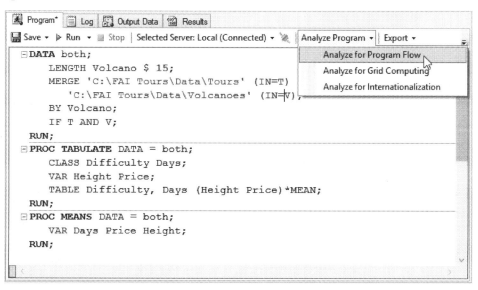

Analyze SAS Program window In the Analyze SAS Program window, click the **Begin analysis** button near the top of the window. SAS Enterprise Guide will scan your program to identify the steps, and then display them in the window.

In the box labeled **Name of process flow to create,** you can type a name for the new process flow. Then click the **Create process flow** button near the bottom of the window.

In order to analyze your program, SAS Enterprise Guide must run it. So the amount of time it takes will be similar to the time it normally takes to run your program. When SAS Enterprise Guide is done, the Analyze SAS Program window will automatically close, and your new process flow will be displayed.

Here is SAS Enterprise Guide showing the new process flow. Notice that the Project Tree also displays the new items.

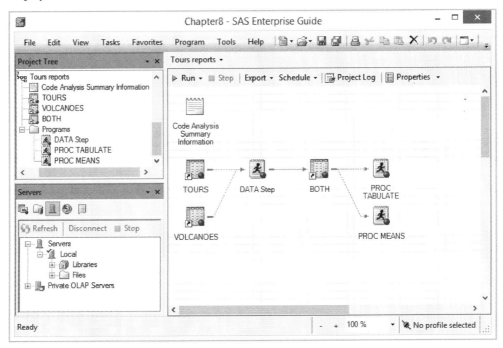

8.3 Viewing Program and Project Logs

A SAS log is a record of what SAS did. Just about everything you do in SAS Enterprise Guide generates a SAS log. Logs contain the actual code that SAS ran, plus any error messages, warnings, or notes.

Different types of logs A program log is the log that is generated when you run a SAS program. Tasks generate logs too. However, when you run tasks, you have little need to view the task log because tasks rarely produce errors. Every time you rerun a program or task, the old log is replaced with a new one.

The Project Log, on the other hand, is a single cumulative record of everything that has been run in a particular project. By default, the Project Log is turned off. Once you turn the Project Log on, nothing disappears from it unless you clear the log.

Viewing a program log After a program runs, the results are displayed in the workspace. To open the program log, click the tab labeled **Log**. If your program log is long and complex, you can use the Log Summary window to navigate it. To do this, click **Log Summary** in the toolbar above your log. The Log Summary window will open below your log.

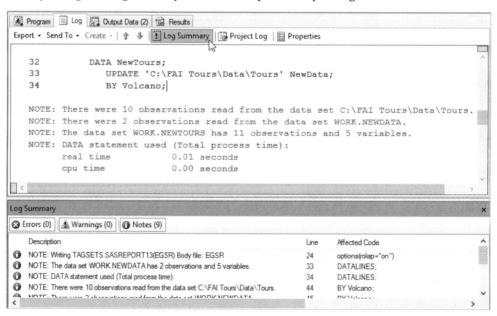

The Log Summary lists all the errors, warnings, and notes in your log. If you click a message in the Log Summary, then SAS Enterprise Guide will scroll to that point in your program log.

If your program contains any errors, its icon that appears in the Project Tree and Process Flow will include a red X ![icon]. Programs that contain warnings (but no errors) have icons with yellow triangles ![icon]. Even if there are no errors or warnings, it is a good habit to check the program log when you write your own SAS programs. Just because a program runs without errors or warnings does not mean that it produced the correct results.

Hiding wrapper code One of the first things you will notice when you look at a log is that it contains more lines of SAS code than were in your original program. That is because SAS Enterprise Guide adds housekeeping statements to the beginning and end of your program to make sure that it runs properly when it is passed to your SAS server. This is called the wrapper code. You can hide the wrapper code. To do this, select **Tools ▶ Options** from the menu bar. The Options window will open (not shown). Click **Results General** in the selection pane on the left and uncheck **Show generated wrapper code in SAS log**.

Viewing the Project Log To turn on the Project Log, first open it by clicking **Project Log** on the workspace toolbar for the Process Flow, or by selecting **View ▶ Project Log** from the menu bar. Then on the toolbar above the Project Log, click **Turn On**. Once the Project Log is turned on, it will keep a continuous history of everything that runs in that project.

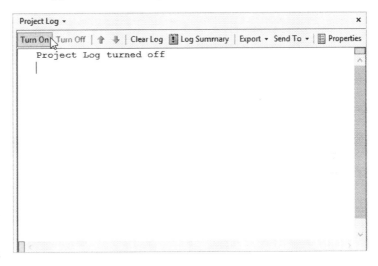

The Project Log includes the date and time when each action occurred. Click the plus sign (+) to expand a section of the log, or the minus sign (-) to collapse it.

To clear the Project Log, click **Clear Log** on the workspace toolbar above the Project Log. To turn it off, click **Turn Off**. Like the program log, the Project Log has a summary window that you can open by clicking **Log Summary** in the toolbar above the Project Log.

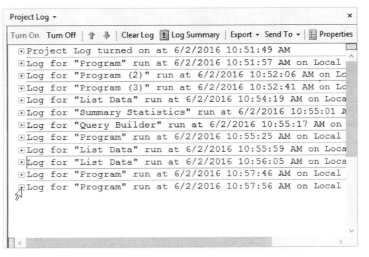

8.4 Saving SAS Programs

At first glance, saving a SAS program looks simple, but it turns out that you have an important decision to make. The basic decision is whether to save your program inside your project or in a separate file. Programs that you save inside a project are called "embedded" while programs that you save outside a project are "unembedded." Each way has advantages. If you save a program inside your project, then it will always be there; but if you save a program outside, then that program can be shared with other projects.

Saving a program inside the project By default, programs you write in SAS Enterprise Guide will be embedded inside the project. So every time you save your project, your program will be saved along with everything else in your project. Your entire project is saved in a single file with the extension .egp.

To save your entire project, including your program, select **File ▶ Save** *project-name* from the main menu bar, or right-click the program icon in the Project Tree or Process Flow and select **Save** *project-name* from the pop-up menu. You can also click **Save** on the workspace toolbar above the Program window and select **Save** *project-name* from the pull-down menu.

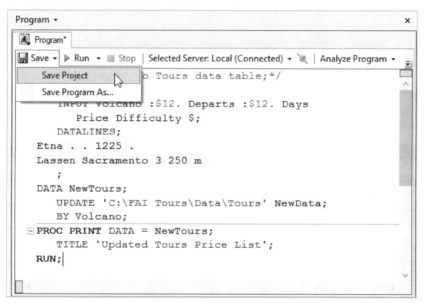

Saving a program outside the project To unembed a program and save it outside its project, click **Save** on the workspace toolbar for the Program window and select **Save Program As** from the pull-down menu, or right-click the program icon in the Project Tree or Process Flow and select **Save** *program-name* **As** from the pop-up menu.

You can also save a program from the Properties window for the program. To view the properties of a program, click **Properties** on the workspace toolbar above the Program window, or right-click the program icon in the Project Tree or Process Flow and select **Properties** from the pop-up menu. The Properties for *program-name* window will open. Then in the General page, click **Save As**.

If you save the program in a file, then it is not embedded, and any changes you make to it in SAS Enterprise Guide will be saved in the file rather than as part of your project. The icon for a program saved in a file includes a little arrow indicating that the project contains a shortcut to the program rather than the actual program. Keep in mind that once a program is saved in a separate file, if that file is

moved or deleted, then your project will no longer know where to find your program.

Embedding a program in the project When you open a SAS program that has been saved in a separate file, it is not automatically embedded in your project. If you want to embed the program in your project, then open the Properties window for the program and click **Embed**.

After you embed the program, any changes you make to it in SAS Enterprise Guide will be saved as part of your project rather than in the separate file. The icon for embedded code does not

include the shortcut arrow . Keep in mind that when you embed a program in your project, the original file will still exist outside of your project. Unless you delete the original program file, you will have two copies of your program. Changes you make to one will not automatically be made to the other.

8.5 Using Tasks to Generate SAS Programs

If you are learning SAS programming, you may be curious to see the code generated by tasks in SAS Enterprise Guide. If you are a SAS programmer, you may be tempted to make a few changes to that code. You cannot change the actual code generated by a task; but you can see the code, and you can save it in a separate program which you can then edit.

Previewing code generated by a task Many task windows have a **Preview code** button in the lower-left corner. If you click this button, SAS Enterprise Guide will open a Code Preview window displaying the code that SAS Enterprise Guide has written for that task. This example shows Preview code being selected in a List Data task.

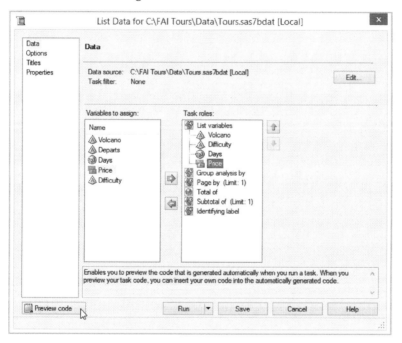

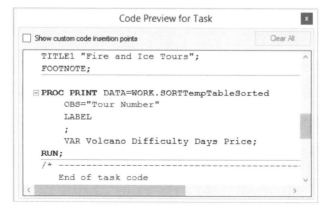

The Code Preview for Task window shows all the code generated by that task including the wrapper code at the beginning and end. If you keep the Preview window open, then you can make changes in the task window and watch in real time as SAS Enterprise Guide makes changes to the code. Here you can see the PROC PRINT generated by a List Data task.

Copying code generated by a task If you want to edit the code generated by a task (including from tasks that do not have a Preview code button), you can make a copy of the code, and then edit the copy. To do this, run the task, and then right-click the task icon in the Project Tree or Process Flow, and select **Add As Code Template**. SAS Enterprise Guide will open a Program window containing the code generated by the task.

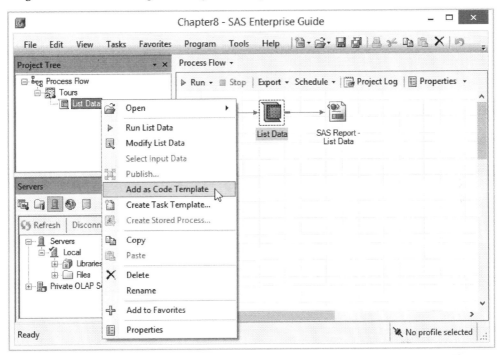

You can edit this code in any way you want. Because this code is a copy of the code generated by the task, any changes you make here will not affect the task, nor will any changes you make to the task be reflected in this code.

When you have made all the changes you want and are ready to run the program, click **Run** on the workspace toolbar above the Program window.

Programs created in this way are embedded in your project, and are not saved as separate files. For more information on saving programs, see the preceding section.

Appendix A

> "Begin at the beginning," the King said, very gravely, "and go on till you come to the end: then stop."

LEWIS CARROLL

The King speaking with the White Rabbit in *Alice's Adventures in Wonderland*, 1865.

Data Used in This Book

Reading about a topic is good, but many people learn better by doing. However, before you can do the examples in the tutorials or reference sections, you need the data. One way to get the data is to type the data shown in this appendix into a SAS Enterprise Guide Data Grid, a Microsoft Excel spreadsheet, or a text file. Another way is to download the data sets by going to

support.sas.com/authors

Select the name of one of the authors (Susan Slaughter or Lora D. Delwiche). Then find the picture of this book, click the words **Example Code and Data** underneath the picture, and follow the instructions.

Tours Data

Filename: Tours.sas7bdat
File Type: SAS data set

Column Name	Description	Possible Values
Volcano	Name of the volcano	
Departs	City from which tour departs	
Days	Length of the tour in days	
Price	Price of the tour in U.S. dollars	
Difficulty	Strenuousness of the tour	c (Challenging) m (Moderate) e (Easy)

Tours.sas7bdat

	Volcano	Departs	Days	Price	Difficulty
1	Etna	Catania	7	$1,610	m
2	Fuji	Tokyo	2	$335	c
3	Kenya	Nairobi	6	$1,245	m
4	Kilauea	Hilo	1	$85	e
5	Kilimanjaro	Nairobi	9	$1,965	c
6	Krakatau	Jakarta	7	$1,345	e
7	Poas	San Jose	1	$97	e
8	Reventador	Quito	4	$875	m
9	St. Helens	Portland	2	$250	e
10	Vesuvius	Rome	6	$1,495	e

Tour Dates Data

Filename: TourDates.sas7bdat
File Type: SAS data set

Column Name	Description
Tour	Code for tour
Volcano	Name of the volcano
DepartureDate	Date of tour departure
Guide	Name of guide for tour

TourDates.sas7bdat

	Tour	Volcano	DepartureDa...	Guide
1	PS27	Poas	08/05/2018	Carlos
2	SH40	St. Helens	06/19/2018	Casey
3	SH41	St. Helens	07/05/2018	Casey
4	SH42	St. Helens	07/23/2018	Casey
5	SH43	St. Helens	08/15/2018	Kelly
6	FJ12	Fuji	09/12/2018	Cooper
7	ET01	Etna	08/05/2018	Cooper
8	KE05	Kenya	05/31/2018	Kelly
9	KL18	Kilauea	07/08/2018	Malia
10	KL19	Kilauea	07/15/2018	Malia
11	KL20	Kilauea	07/22/2018	Malia
12	RD02	Reventador	07/11/2018	Carlos
13	VS11	Vesuvius	07/21/2018	Cooper
14	VS12	Vesuvius	08/15/2018	Cooper
15	KJ01	Kilimanjaro	06/09/2018	Kelly
16	KK03	Krakatau	07/19/2018	Kelly

Tour Bookings Data

There are two versions of the bookings data. One is a Microsoft Excel file, and the other is a SAS data set. They both contain the same columns and data values.

Filename:	Bookings.xlsx	Bookings.sas7bdat
File Type:	Microsoft Excel spreadsheet	SAS data set

Column Name	Description
Office	Office where reservation was made
CustomerID	Customer identification number
Tour	Code for tour
Travelers	Number traveling in party
Deposit	Amount of deposit
Deposit_Date	Date of deposit

Bookings.xlsx

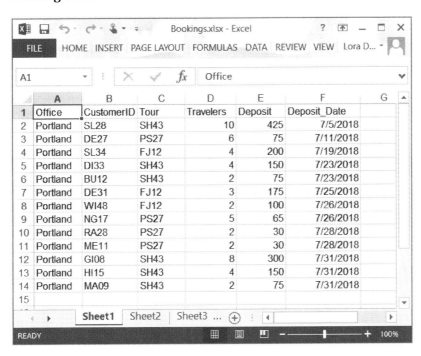

Bookings.sas7bdat

	Office	CustomerID	Tour	Travelers	Deposit	Deposit_Date
1	Portland	SL28	SH43	10	425	05JUL2018
2	Portland	DE27	PS27	6	75	11JUL2018
3	Portland	SL34	FJ12	4	200	19JUL2018
4	Portland	DI33	SH43	4	150	23JUL2018
5	Portland	BU12	SH43	2	75	23JUL2018
6	Portland	DE31	FJ12	3	175	25JUL2018
7	Portland	WI48	FJ12	2	100	26JUL2018
8	Portland	NG17	PS27	5	65	26JUL2018
9	Portland	RA28	PS27	2	30	28JUL2018
10	Portland	ME11	PS27	2	30	28JUL2018
11	Portland	GI08	SH43	8	300	31JUL2018
12	Portland	HI15	SH43	4	150	31JUL2018
13	Portland	MA09	SH43	2	75	31JUL2018

Volcanoes Data

Filename: Volcanoes.sas7bdat
File Type: SAS data set

Column Name	Description	Possible Values
Volcano	Name of the volcano	
Country	Country where the volcano is located	
Region	Region where the volcano is located	Af (Africa) An (Antarctica) AP (Australia/Pacific) As (Asia) Eu (Europe) NA (North America) SA (South America)
Height	Height of the volcano in meters	
Activity	Activity of the volcano	Active Extinct
Type	Kind of volcano	Caldera Complex Shield Stratovolcano

Volcanoes.sas7bdat

	Volcano	Country	Region	Height	Activity	Type
1	Altar	Ecuador	SA	5321	Extinct	Stratovolcano
2	Arthur's Seat	UK	Eu	251	Extinct	
3	Barren Island	India	As	354	Active	Stratovolcano
4	Elbrus	Russia	Eu	5633	Extinct	Stratovolcano
5	Erebus		An	3794	Active	Stratovolcano
6	Etna	Italy	Eu	3350	Active	Stratovolcano
7	Fuji	Japan	As	3776	Active	Stratovolcano
8	Garibaldi	Canada	NA	2678		Stratovolcano
9	Grimsvotn	Iceland	Eu	1725	Active	Caldera
10	Illimani	Bolivia	SA	6458	Extinct	Stratovolcano
11	Kenya	Kenya	Af	5199	Extinct	
12	Kilauea	USA	AP	1222	Active	Shield
13	Kilimanjaro	Tanzania	Af	5895		Stratovolcano
14	Kliuchevskoi	Russia	As	4835	Active	Stratovolcano
15	Krakatau	Indonesia	As	813	Active	Caldera
16	Lassen	USA	NA	3187	Active	Stratovolcano
17	Mauna Loa	USA	AP	4170	Active	Shield
18	Nyamuragira	DRCongo	Af	3058	Active	Shield
19	Nyiragongo	DRCongo	Af	3470	Active	Stratovolcano
20	Pinatubo	Philippines	As	1486	Active	Stratovolcano
21	Poas	Costa Rica	NA	2708	Active	Stratovolcano
22	Popocatepetl	Mexico	NA	5426	Active	Stratovolcano
23	Puy de Dome	France	Eu	1464	Extinct	Cinder Cone
24	Reventador	Ecuador	SA	3562	Active	Stratovolcano
25	Ruapehu	NZ	AP	2797	Active	Stratovolcano
26	Sabancaya	Peru	SA	5976	Active	Stratovolcano
27	Santorini	Greece	Eu	367	Active	Shield
28	Shishaldin	USA	NA	2857	Active	Stratovolcano
29	St. Helens	USA	NA	2549	Active	Stratovolcano
30	Vesuvius	Italy	Eu	1281	Active	Complex
31	Villarrica	Chile	SA	2847	Active	Stratovolcano
32	Warning	Australia	AP	1125	Extinct	Shield

Eruptions Data

There are two versions of the eruptions data. One is a text file, and the other is a SAS data set. They both contain the same columns and data values.

Filename:	Eruptions.csv	Eruptions.sas7bdat
File Type:	Text file with comma-separated values	SAS data set

Column Name	Description	Possible Values
Volcano	Name of the volcano	
StartDate	Date the eruption started in MMDDYY10. format	
EndDate	Date the eruption ended in MMDDYY10. format	
VEI	Volcanic Explosivity Index	0–8

Eruptions.csv

```
Volcano, StartDate, EndDate, VEI
Barren Island, 12/20/1795, 12/21/1795, 2
Barren Island, 12/20/1994, 06/05/1995, 2
Erebus, 12/12/1912, . , 2
Erebus, 01/03/1972, . , 1
Etna, 02/06/1610, 08/15/1610, 2
Etna, 06/04/1787, 08/11/1787, 4
Etna, 01/30/1865, 06/28/1865, 2
Etna, 12/16/2005, 12/22/2005, 1
Fuji, 12/16/1707, 02/24/1708, 5
Grimsvotn, 10/31/1603, 11/01/1603, 2
Grimsvotn, 01/08/1873, 08/01/1873, 4
Grimsvotn, 12/18/1998, 12/28/1998, 3
Kilauea, 05/30/1840, 06/25/1840, 0
Kilauea, 05/24/1969, 07/22/1974, 0
Kliuchevskoi, 09/25/1737, 11/04/1737, 2
Kliuchevskoi, 03/25/1931, 03/27/1931, 4
Kliuchevskoi, 01/20/2005, 04/07/2005, 2
Krakatau, 05/20/1883, 10/21/1883, 6
Krakatau, 07/04/1938, 07/02/1940, 3
Krakatau, 05/29/2000, 10/30/2000, 1
Lassen, 05/30/1914, 06/29/1917, 3
Mauna Loa, 06/20/1832, 07/15/1832, 0
Mauna Loa, 03/25/1984, 04/15/1984, 0
Nyamuragira, 11/07/1907, 12/05/1907, 3
Nyamuragira, 02/06/2001, 04/05/2001, 2
Nyiragongo, 06/21/1982, 10/17/1982, 1
Nyiragongo, 01/17/2002, 02/03/2002, 1
Pinatubo, 04/02/1991, 09/02/1991, 5
Poas, 12/29/1898, 12/31/1907, 1
Poas, 04/08/1996, 04/08/1996, 1
Popocatepetl, 10/13/1663, 10/19/1665, 3
Popocatepetl, 12/21/1994, 08/05/1995, 2
Reventador, 12/12/1856, 12/13/1856, 3
Reventador, 02/24/1944, 03/01/1944, 3
Reventador, 11/03/2002, 01/10/2003, 4
Ruapehu, 02/13/1861, 05/16/1861, 2
Ruapehu, 06/17/1996, 09/01/1996, 3
Sabancaya, 05/01/1997, 05/02/1997, 3
Santorini, 09/27/1650, 12/06/1650, 4
Santorini, 05/23/1707, 09/14/1711, 3
Santorini, 01/26/1866, 10/15/1870, 2
Santorini, 01/10/1950, 02/02/1950, 2
Shishaldin, 03/13/1999, 05/27/1999, 3
St. Helens, 03/26/1847, 03/30/1847, 2
St. Helens, 03/27/1980, 10/28/1986, 5
St. Helens, 10/01/2004, 01/27/2008 , 2
Vesuvius, 12/15/1631, 01/31/1632, 5
Vesuvius, 12/25/1732, 06/04/1737, 3
Vesuvius, 12/18/1875, 04/22/1906, 4
Vesuvius, 07/05/1913, 04/04/1944, 3
Villarrica, 11/07/1837, 11/21/1837, 2
Villarrica, 10/26/2008, . , 1
```

Eruptions.sas7bdat

	Volcano	StartDate	EndDate	VEI
1	Barren Island	12/20/1795	12/21/1795	2
2	Barren Island	12/20/1994	06/05/1995	2
3	Erebus	12/12/1912	.	2
4	Erebus	01/03/1972	.	1
5	Etna	02/06/1610	08/15/1610	2
6	Etna	06/04/1787	08/11/1787	4
7	Etna	01/30/1865	06/28/1865	2
8	Etna	12/16/2005	12/22/2005	1
9	Fuji	12/16/1707	02/24/1708	5
10	Grimsvotn	10/31/1603	11/01/1603	2
11	Grimsvotn	01/08/1873	08/01/1873	4
12	Grimsvotn	12/18/1998	12/28/1998	3
13	Kilauea	05/30/1840	06/25/1840	0
14	Kilauea	05/24/1969	07/22/1974	0
15	Kliuchevskoi	09/25/1737	11/04/1737	2
16	Kliuchevskoi	03/25/1931	03/27/1931	4
17	Kliuchevskoi	01/20/2005	04/07/2005	2
18	Krakatau	05/20/1883	10/21/1883	6
19	Krakatau	07/04/1938	07/02/1940	3
20	Krakatau	05/29/2000	10/30/2000	1
21	Lassen	05/30/1914	06/29/1917	3
22	Mauna Loa	06/20/1832	07/15/1832	0
23	Mauna Loa	03/25/1984	04/15/1984	0
24	Nyamuragira	11/07/1907	12/05/1907	3
25	Nyamuragira	02/06/2001	04/05/2001	2
26	Nyiragongo	06/21/1982	10/17/1982	1
27	Nyiragongo	01/17/2002	02/03/2002	1
28	Pinatubo	04/02/1991	09/02/1991	5
29	Poas	12/29/1898	12/31/1907	1
30	Poas	04/08/1996	04/08/1996	1
31	Popocatepetl	10/13/1663	10/19/1665	3
32	Popocatepetl	12/21/1994	08/05/1995	2
33	Reventador	12/12/1856	12/13/1856	3
34	Reventador	02/24/1944	03/01/1944	3
35	Reventador	11/03/2002	01/10/2003	4
36	Ruapehu	02/13/1861	05/16/1861	2
37	Ruapehu	06/17/1996	09/01/1996	3
38	Sabancaya	05/01/1997	05/02/1997	3
39	Santorini	09/27/1650	12/06/1650	4
40	Santorini	05/23/1707	09/14/1711	3
41	Santorini	01/26/1866	10/15/1870	2
42	Santorini	01/10/1950	02/02/1950	2
43	Shishaldin	03/13/1999	05/27/1999	3
44	St. Helens	03/26/1847	03/30/1847	2
45	St. Helens	03/27/1980	10/28/1986	5
46	St. Helens	10/01/2004	01/27/2008	2
47	Vesuvius	12/15/1631	01/31/1632	5
48	Vesuvius	12/25/1732	06/04/1737	3
49	Vesuvius	12/18/1875	04/22/1906	4
50	Vesuvius	07/05/1913	04/04/1944	3
51	Villarrica	11/07/1837	11/21/1837	2
52	Villarrica	10/26/2008	.	1

Latitude and Longitude Data

There are two versions of the latitude and longitude data. One is a text file, and the other is a SAS data set. They both contain the same columns and data values.

Filename:	Latlong.txt	Latlong.sas7bdat
File Type:	Fixed-width text file	SAS data set

Column Name	Description
Volcano	Name of the volcano
Latitude	Latitude
Longitude	Longitude

Latlong.txt

```
Volcano          Latitude Longitude
Altar            -1.67     -78.42
Barren Island    12.28      93.52
Elbrus           43.33      42.45
Erebus          -77.53     167.17
Etna             37.73      15.00
Fuji             35.35     138.73
Garibaldi        49.85    -123.00
Grimsvotn        64.42     -17.33
Illimani        -16.39     -67.47
Kenya            -0.09      37.18
Kilauea          19.43    -155.29
Kilimanjaro      -3.07      37.35
Kliuchevskoi     56.06     160.64
Krakatau         -6.10     105.42
Lassen           40.49    -121.51
Mauna Loa        19.48    -155.61
Nyamuragira      -1.41      29.20
Nyiragongo       -1.52      29.25
Pinatubo         15.13     120.35
Poas             10.20     -84.23
Popocatepetl     19.02     -98.62
Puy de Dome      45.50       2.75
Reventador       -0.08     -77.66
Ruapehu         -39.28     175.57
Sabancaya       -15.78     -71.85
Santorini        36.40      25.40
Shishaldin       54.76    -163.97
St. Helens       46.20    -122.18
Vesuvius         40.82      14.43
Villarrica      -39.42     -71.93
```

Latlong.sas7bdat

	Volcano	Latitude	Longitude
1	Altar	-1.67	-78.42
2	Barren Island	12.28	93.52
3	Elbrus	43.33	42.45
4	Erebus	-77.53	167.17
5	Etna	37.73	15
6	Fuji	35.35	138.73
7	Garibaldi	49.85	-123
8	Grimsvotn	64.42	-17.33
9	Illimani	-16.39	-67.47
10	Kenya	-0.09	37.18
11	Kilauea	19.43	-155.29
12	Kilimanjaro	-3.07	37.35
13	Kliuchevskoi	56.06	160.64
14	Krakatau	-6.1	105.42
15	Lassen	40.49	-121.51
16	Mauna Loa	19.48	-155.61
17	Nyamuragira	-1.41	29.2
18	Nyiragongo	-1.52	29.25
19	Pinatubo	15.13	120.35
20	Poas	10.2	-84.23
21	Popocatepetl	19.02	-98.62
22	Puy de Dome	45.5	2.75
23	Reventador	-0.08	-77.66
24	Ruapehu	-39.28	175.57
25	Sabancaya	-15.78	-71.85
26	Santorini	36.4	25.4
27	Shishaldin	54.76	-163.97
28	St. Helens	46.2	-122.18
29	Vesuvius	40.82	14.43
30	Villarrica	-39.42	-71.93

Portland Flights Data

Filename: Portland.sas7bdat
File Type: SAS data set

Column Name	Description
Origin	City from which flight departs
Destination	City in which flight arrives
FlightNo	Flight number
FlightPrice	Price of flight in U.S. dollars

Portland.sas7bdat

	Origin	Destination	FlightNo	FlightPrice
1	Portland	Catania	L469	$1,833.00
2	Portland	Hilo	HA25	$631.00
3	Portland	Nairobi	KLM6034	$1,229.00
4	Portland	Rome	D1576	$1,747.00
5	Portland	San Jose	CA1210	$518.00
6	Portland	Tokyo	UA383	$1,462.00

Seattle Flights Data

Filename: Seattle.sas7bdat
File Type: SAS data set

Column Name	Description
Origin	City from which flight departs
Destination	City in which flight arrives
FlightNo	Flight number
FlightPrice	Price of flight in U.S. dollars

Seattle.sas7bdat

	Origin	Destination	FlightNo	FlightPrice
1	Seattle	Catania	BA48	$1,853.00
2	Seattle	Hilo	HA21	$576.00
3	Seattle	Jakarta	AA119	$1,331.00
4	Seattle	Nairobi	KLM6034	$1,396.00
5	Seattle	Quito	CA1086	$686.00
6	Seattle	Rome	USA6	$1,767.00
7	Seattle	San Jose	CA1100	$559.00
8	Seattle	Tokyo	UA875	$1,462.00

Advertising Results Data

Filename: AdResults.sas7bdat
File Type: SAS data set

Column Name	Description	Possible Values
City	City	
Month	Month	1–12
AdDollars	Money spent on advertising in U.S. dollars	
Bookings	Number of tours booked for that month	

AdResults.sas7bdat

	City	Month	AdDollars	Bookings
1	Seattle	1	350	30
2	Seattle	2	330	19
3	Seattle	3	525	32
4	Seattle	4	400	18
5	Seattle	5	375	21
6	Seattle	6	325	18
7	Seattle	7	150	17
8	Seattle	8	250	17
9	Seattle	9	250	22
10	Seattle	10	325	20
11	Seattle	11	400	25
12	Seattle	12	500	31
13	Portland	1	325	25
14	Portland	2	290	19
15	Portland	3	250	17
16	Portland	4	300	18
17	Portland	5	300	21
18	Portland	6	275	19
19	Portland	7	200	13
20	Portland	8	225	15
21	Portland	9	325	23
22	Portland	10	350	24
23	Portland	11	425	27
24	Portland	12	400	33

Index

Ready to take your SAS® and JMP® skills up a notch?

Be among the first to know about new books,
special events, and exclusive discounts.
support.sas.com/newbooks

Share your expertise. Write a book with SAS.
support.sas.com/publish

sas.com/books
for additional books and resources.

THE POWER TO KNOW.

Made in the USA
Middletown, DE
30 May 2018